W9-BGA-057

THE CODE BOOK

ALSO BY SIMON SINGH

Fermat's Enigma

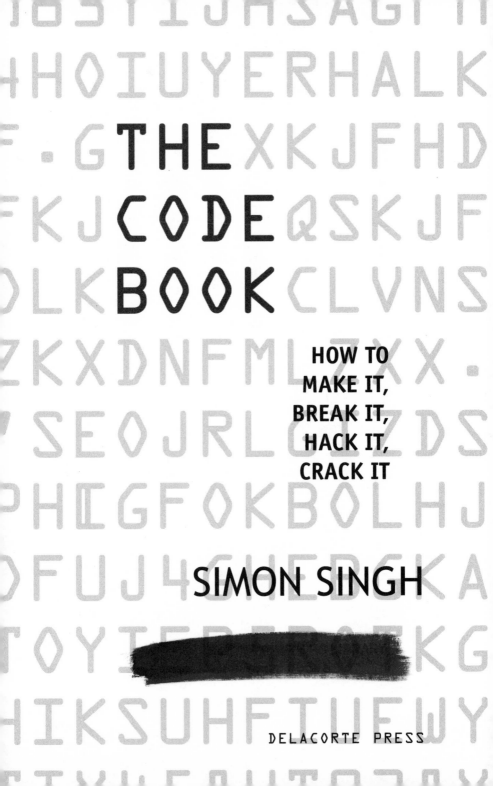

THE CODE BOOK

HOW TO MAKE IT, BREAK IT, HACK IT, CRACK IT

SIMON SINGH

DELACORTE PRESS

Published by
Delacorte Press
an imprint of
Random House Children's Books
a division of Random House, Inc.
1540 Broadway
New York, New York 10036

Visit us on the Web! www.randomhouse.com/teens

Educators and librarians, for a variety of teaching tools,
visit us at www.randomhouse.com/teachers

Library of Congress Cataloging-in-Publication Data
Singh, Simon.
The code book : how to make it, break it, hack it, crack it /
Simon Singh.
p.   cm.
Includes bibliographical references and index.
ISBN 0-385-72913-8 — ISBN 0-385-90032-5
1. Coding theory. 2. Cryptography. I. Title.
TK5102.92.S56   2002
652'.8—dc21
2001042131

The text of this book is set in 12-point Adobe Caslon Regular.

Book design by Ericka O'Rourke

Manufactured in the United States of America

March 2002

10 9 8 7 6 5 4 3 2

BVG

To the Teachers and Mortals
who took the time to inspire me
XICYIQKMHR, VOIR RFH LKRQT

The urge to discover secrets is deeply ingrained in human nature; even the least curious mind is roused by the promise of sharing knowledge withheld from others. Some are fortunate enough to find a job which consists in the solution of mysteries, but most of us are driven to sublimate this urge by the solving of artificial puzzles devised for our entertainment. Detective stories or crossword puzzles cater for the majority; the solution of secret codes may be the pursuit of a few.

John Chadwick
The Decipherment of Linear B

CONTENTS

INTRODUCTION

For centuries, kings, queens and generals have relied on efficient communication in order to govern their countries and command their armies. At the same time, they have all been aware of the consequences of their messages falling into the wrong hands, revealing precious secrets to rival nations and betraying vital information to opposing forces. It was the threat of enemy interception that motivated the development of codes and ciphers: techniques for disguising a message so that only the intended recipient can read it.

The desire for secrecy has meant that nations have operated codemaking departments, which were responsible for ensuring the security of communications by inventing and implementing the best possible codes. At the same time, enemy codebreakers have attempted to break these codes and steal secrets. Codebreakers are linguistic alchemists, a mystical tribe attempting to conjure sensible words out of meaningless symbols. The history of codes and ciphers is the story of the centuries-old battle between codemakers and codebreakers, an intellectual arms race that has had a dramatic impact on the course of history.

In writing *The Code Book*, I have had two main objectives. The first is to chart the evolution of codes. *Evolution* is a wholly appropriate term, because the development of codes can be viewed as an evolutionary struggle. A code is constantly under attack from codebreakers. When the codebreakers have developed a new weapon that reveals a code's weakness, then the code is no longer useful. It either becomes extinct or it evolves into a new, stronger code. In turn, this new code thrives only until the codebreakers identify its weakness, and so on. This is similar to the situation facing, for example, a strain of infectious bacteria. The bacteria live, thrive and survive until doctors discover an antibiotic that exposes a weakness in the bacteria and kills them. The bacteria are forced to evolve and outwit the antibiotic, and if successful, they will thrive once again and reestablish themselves.

History is punctuated with codes. They have decided the outcomes of battles and led to the deaths of kings and queens. I have therefore been able to call upon stories of political intrigue and tales of life and death to illustrate the key turning points in the evolutionary development of codes. The history of codes is so inordinately rich that I have been forced to leave out many fascinating stories, which in turn means that my account is not definitive. If you would like to find out more about your favorite tale or your favorite codebreaker, then I would refer you to the list of further reading.

Having discussed the evolution of codes and their impact on history, the book's second objective is to demonstrate how the subject is more relevant today than ever before. As information becomes an increasingly valuable commodity, and as the communications revolution changes society, so the process of encoding messages, known as encryption, will play an increasing role in everyday life. Nowadays our phone calls bounce off satellites and our e-mails pass through various computers, and both forms of communication can be intercepted with ease, so jeopardizing our privacy. Similarly, as more and more business is conducted over the Internet, safeguards must be put in place to protect companies and their clients. Encryption is the only way to protect our privacy and guarantee the success of the digital marketplace. The art of secret communication, otherwise known as cryptography, will provide the locks and keys of the Information Age.

However, the public's growing demand for cryptography conflicts with the needs of law enforcement and national security. For decades, the police and the intelligence services have used wiretaps to gather evidence against terrorists and organized crime syndicates, but the recent development of ultrastrong codes threatens to undermine the value of wiretaps. The forces of law and order are lobbying governments to restrict the use of cryptography, while civil libertarians and businesses are arguing for the widespread use of encryption to protect privacy. Who wins the argument depends on which we value more, our privacy or an effective police force. Or is there a compromise?

Before concluding this introduction, I must mention a problem that faces any author who tackles the subject of cryptography: The science of secrecy is largely a secret science. Many of the heroes in this book never gained recognition for their work during their lifetimes because their contribution could not be publicly acknowledged while their invention was still of diplomatic or military value. This culture of secrecy continues today, and organizations such as the U.S. National Security Agency still conduct classified research into cryptography. It is clear that there is a great deal more going on of which neither I nor any other science writer is aware.

Figure 1 Mary Queen of Scots.

1

The Cipher of Mary Queen of Scots

The birth of cryptography, the substitution cipher and the invention of codebreaking by frequency analysis

On the morning of Saturday, October 15, 1586, Queen Mary entered the crowded courtroom at Fotheringhay Castle. Years of imprisonment and the onset of rheumatism had taken their toll, yet she remained dignified, composed and indisputably regal. Assisted by her physician, she made her way past the judges, officials and spectators, and approached the throne that stood halfway along the long, narrow chamber. Mary had assumed that the throne was a gesture of respect toward her, but she was mistaken. The throne symbolized the absent Queen Elizabeth, Mary's enemy and prosecutor. Mary was gently guided away from the throne and toward the opposite side of the room, to the defendant's seat, a crimson velvet chair.

Mary Queen of Scots was on trial for treason. She had been accused of plotting to assassinate Queen Elizabeth in order to take the English crown for herself. Sir Francis Walsingham, Elizabeth's principal secretary, had already arrested the other conspirators, extracted confessions and executed them. Now he planned to prove that Mary was at the heart of the plot, and was therefore equally to blame and equally deserving of death.

Walsingham knew that before he could have Mary executed, he would have to convince Queen Elizabeth of her guilt. Although Elizabeth despised Mary, she had several reasons for being reluctant to see her put to death. First, Mary was a Scottish queen, and many questioned whether an English court had the authority to execute a foreign head of state. Second, executing Mary might establish an awkward precedent—if the state is allowed to kill one queen, then perhaps rebels might have fewer reservations about killing another, namely Elizabeth. Third, Elizabeth and Mary were cousins, and their blood tie made Elizabeth all the more squeamish about ordering the execution. In short, Elizabeth would sanction Mary's execution only if Walsingham could prove beyond any hint of doubt that she had been part of the assassination plot.

The conspirators were a group of young English Catholic noblemen intent on removing Elizabeth, a Protestant, and replacing her with Mary, a fellow Catholic. It was apparent to the court that Mary was a figurehead for the conspirators, but it was not clear that she had given her blessing to the conspiracy. In fact, Mary had authorized the plot. The challenge for Walsingham was to demonstrate a clear link between Mary and the plotters.

On the morning of her trial, Mary sat alone in the dock, dressed in sorrowful black velvet. In cases of treason, the accused was forbidden counsel and was not permitted to call witnesses. Mary was not even allowed secretaries to help her prepare her case. However, her plight was not hopeless, because she had been careful to ensure that all her correspondence with the conspirators had been written in cipher. The cipher turned her words into a meaningless series of symbols, and Mary believed that even if Walsingham had captured the letters, he could have no idea of the meaning of the words within them. If their contents were a mystery, then the letters could not be used as evidence against her. However, this all depended on the assumption that her cipher had not been broken.

Unfortunately for Mary, Walsingham was not merely principal secretary, but also England's spymaster. He had intercepted Mary's letters to the plotters, and he knew exactly who might be capable of deciphering them. Thomas Phelippes was the nation's foremost expert on breaking codes, and for years he had been deciphering the messages of those who plotted against Queen Elizabeth, thereby providing the evidence needed to condemn them. If he could decipher the incriminating letters between Mary and the conspirators, then her death would be inevitable. On the other hand, if Mary's cipher was strong enough to conceal her secrets, then there was a chance that she might survive. Not for the first time, a life hung on the strength of a cipher.

THE EVOLUTION OF SECRET WRITING

Some of the earliest accounts of secret writing date back to Herodotus—"the father of history," according to the Roman philosopher and statesman Cicero. In *The Histories*, Herodotus chronicled the conflicts between Greece and Persia in the fifth century B.C., which he viewed as a confrontation between freedom and slavery, between the independent Greek states and the oppressive Persians. According to Herodotus, it was the art of secret writing that saved Greece from being conquered by Xerxes, the despotic leader of the Persians.

The long-running feud between Greece and Persia reached a crisis soon after Xerxes began constructing a city at Persepolis, the new capital for his kingdom. Tributes and gifts arrived from all over the empire and neighboring states, with the notable exceptions of Athens and Sparta. Determined to avenge this insolence, Xerxes began mobilizing a force, declaring that "we shall extend the empire of Persia such that its boundaries will be God's own sky, so the sun will not look down upon any land beyond the boundaries of what is our own." He spent the next five years secretly assembling the greatest fighting force in history, and then, in 480 B.C., he was ready to launch a surprise attack.

However, the Persian military buildup had been witnessed by Demaratus, a Greek who had been expelled from his homeland and who lived in the Persian city of Susa. Despite being exiled, he still felt some loyalty to Greece, so he decided to send a message to warn the Spartans of Xerxes' invasion plan. The challenge was how to dispatch the message without it being intercepted by the Persian guards. Herodotus wrote:

> As the danger of discovery was great, there was only one way in which he could contrive to get the message through: this was by scraping the wax off a pair of wooden folding tablets, writing on the wood underneath what Xerxes intended to do, and then covering the message over with wax again. In this way the tablets, being apparently blank, would cause no trouble with the guards along the road. When the message reached its destination, no one was able to guess the secret, until, as I understand, Cleomenes' daughter Gorgo, who was the wife of Leonidas, divined and told the others that if they scraped the wax off, they would find something written on the wood underneath. This was done; the message was revealed and read, and afterward passed on to the other Greeks.

As a result of this warning, the hitherto defenseless Greeks began to arm themselves. Profits from the state-owned silver mines, which were usually shared among the citizens, were instead diverted to the navy for the construction of two hundred warships.

Xerxes had lost the vital element of surprise, and on September 23, 480 B.C., when the Persian fleet approached the Bay of Salamis near Athens, the Greeks were prepared. Although Xerxes believed he had trapped the Greek navy, the Greeks were deliberately enticing the Persian ships to enter the bay. The Greeks knew that their ships, smaller and fewer in number, would have been destroyed in the open sea, but they realized that within the confines of the bay they might outmaneuver the Persians. As the wind changed direction the Persians found themselves being blown into the bay, forced into an engagement on Greek terms. The Persian princess Artemisia became surrounded on three sides and attempted to head back out to sea, only to ram one of her own ships. Panic ensued, more Persian ships collided and the Greeks launched a full-blooded onslaught. Within a day, the formidable forces of Persia had been humbled.

Demaratus' strategy for secret communication relied on simply hiding the message. Herodotus also recounted another incident in which concealment was sufficient to secure the safe passage of a message. He chronicled the story of Histaiaeus, who wanted to encourage Aristagoras of Miletus to revolt against the Persian king. To convey his instructions securely, Histaiaeus shaved the head of his messenger, wrote the message on his scalp, and then waited for the hair to regrow. This was clearly not an urgent message. The messenger, apparently carrying nothing contentious, could travel without being harassed. Upon arriving at his destination, he then shaved his head and pointed it at the intended recipient.

Secret communication achieved by hiding the existence of a message is known as *steganography*, derived from the Greek words *steganos*, meaning "covered," and *graphein*, meaning "to write." In the two thousand years since Herodotus, various forms of steganography have been used throughout the world.

For example, the ancient Chinese wrote messages on fine silk, which was scrunched into a tiny ball and covered in wax. The messenger would then swallow the ball of wax. Steganography also includes the practice of writing in invisible ink. As far back as the first century A.D., Pliny the Elder explained how the "milk" of the tithymalus plant could be used as an invisible ink. Although the ink is transparent after drying, gentle heating chars it and turns it brown. Many organic fluids behave in a similar way, because they are rich in carbon and therefore char easily. Indeed, it is not unknown for modern spies who have run out of standard-issue invisible ink to improvise by using their own urine.

The longevity of steganography illustrates that it certainly offers some degree of security, but it suffers from a fundamental weakness: If the messenger is searched and the message is discovered, then the contents of the secret communication are revealed at once. Interception of the message immediately compromises all security. A thorough guard might routinely search any person crossing a border, scraping any wax tablets, heating blank sheets of paper, shaving people's heads, and so on, and inevitably there will be occasions when a message is uncovered.

Hence, along with the development of steganography, there was the evolution of *cryptography* (the word is derived from the Greek *kryptos,* meaning "hidden"). The aim of cryptography is not to hide the existence of a message, but rather to hide its meaning, a process known as *encryption.* To render a message unintelligible, it is scrambled according to a particular protocol, which is agreed beforehand between the sender and the intended recipient. Thus the recipient can reverse the scrambling protocol and make the message comprehensible. The advantage of cryptography is that if the enemy intercepts an encrypted message, the message is unreadable. Without knowing the scrambling protocol, the enemy should find it difficult, if not impossible, to re-create the original message from the encrypted text.

Cryptography itself can be divided into two branches, known as *transposition* and *substitution*. In transposition, the letters of the message are simply rearranged, effectively generating an anagram. For very short messages, such as a single word, this method is relatively insecure because there are only a limited number of ways of rearranging a handful of letters. For example, three letters can be arranged in only six different ways, e.g., **cow, cwo, ocw, owc, wco, woc**. However, as the number of letters gradually increases, the number of possible arrangements rapidly explodes, making it impossible to get back to the original message unless the exact scrambling process is known. **For example, consider this short sentence.** It contains just thirty-five letters, and yet there are more than 50,000,000,000,000,000,000,000,000,000,000 distinct arrangements of them. If one person could check one arrangement per second, and if all the people in the world worked night and day, it would still take more than a thousand times the lifetime of the universe to check all the arrangements.

A random transposition of letters seems to offer a very high level of security, because it would be impractical for an enemy interceptor to unscramble even a short sentence. But there is a drawback. Transposition effectively generates an incredibly difficult anagram, and if the letters are randomly jumbled, with neither rhyme nor reason, then unscrambling the anagram is impossible for the intended recipient, as well as for an enemy interceptor. In order for transposition to be effective, the rearrangement of letters needs to follow a straightforward system, one that has been previously agreed by sender and receiver but kept secret from the enemy. For example, it is possible to send messages using the "rail fence" transposition, in which the message is written with alternating letters on separate upper and lower lines. The sequence of letters on the lower line is then tagged on at the end of the sequence on the upper line to create the final encrypted message. For example:

THY SECRET IS THY PRISONER; IF THOU LET IT GO, THOU ART A PRISONER TO IT

↓

T Y E R T S H P I O E I T O L T T O H U R A R S N R O T
H S C E I T Y R S N R F H U E I G T O A T P I O E T I

↓

TYERTSHPIOEITOLTTOHURARSNROTHSCEITYRSNRFHUEIGTOATPIOETI

Another form of transposition is embodied in the first-ever military cryptographic device, the Spartan *scytale*, dating back to the fifth century B.C. The scytale is a wooden staff around which a strip of leather or parchment is wound, as shown in Figure 2. The sender writes the message along the length of the scytale and then unwinds the strip, which now appears to carry a list of meaningless letters. The message has been scrambled. The messenger would take the leather strip, and, as a steganographic twist, he would sometimes disguise it as a belt with the letters hidden on the inside. To recover the message, the receiver simply wraps the leather strip around a scytale of the same diameter as the one used by the sender. In 404 B.C.

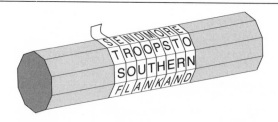

Figure 2 When it is unwound from the sender's scytale (wooden staff), the leather strip appears to carry a list of random letters: **S, T, S, F,** . . . Only by rewinding the strip around another scytale of the correct diameter will the message reappear.

Lysander of Sparta was confronted by a messenger, bloody and battered, the only one of five to have survived the difficult journey from Persia. The messenger handed his belt to Lysander, who wound it around his scytale to learn that Pharnabazus of Persia was planning to attack him. Thanks to the scytale, Lysander was prepared for the attack and successfully resisted it.

The alternative to transposition is substitution. One of the earliest descriptions of encryption by substitution appears in the *Kāma-sūtra*, a text written in the fourth century A.D. by the Brahmin scholar Vātsyāyana, but based on manuscripts dating back to the fourth century B.C. The *Kāma-sūtra* recommends that women should study sixty-four arts, such as cooking, dressing, massage and the preparation of perfumes. The list also includes some less obvious arts, including conjuring, chess, bookbinding and carpentry. Number forty-five on the list is *mlecchita-vikalpā*, the art of secret writing, recommended in order to help women conceal the details of their liaisons. One of the recommended techniques is to pair letters of the alphabet at random, and then substitute each letter in the original message with its partner. If we apply the principle to the English alphabet, we could pair letters as follows:

A	D	H	I	K	M	O	R	S	U	W	Y	Z
↕	↕	↕	↕	↕	↕	↕	↕	↕	↕	↕	↕	↕
V	X	B	G	J	C	Q	L	N	E	F	P	T

Then, instead of **meet at midnight**, the sender would write **CUUZ VZ CGXSGIBZ**. This form of secret writing is called a *substitution cipher* because each letter in the *plaintext* (the message before encryption) is substituted for a different letter to produce the *ciphertext* (the message after encryption), thus acting in a complementary way to the transposition cipher. In transposition each letter retains its identity but changes its position, whereas in substitution each letter changes its identity but retains its position.

The first documented use of a substitution cipher for military purposes appears in Julius Caesar's *Gallic Wars*. Caesar describes how he sent a message to Cicero, who was besieged and on the verge of surrendering. The substitution replaced Roman letters with Greek letters, making the message unintelligible to the enemy. Caesar described the dramatic delivery of the message:

> The messenger was instructed, if he could not approach, to hurl a spear, with the letter fastened to the thong, inside the entrenchment of the camp. Fearing danger, the Gaul discharged the spear, as he had been instructed. By chance it stuck fast in the tower, and for two days was not sighted by our troops; on the third day it was sighted by a soldier, taken down, and delivered to Cicero. He read it through and then recited it at a parade of the troops, bringing the greatest rejoicing to all.

Caesar used secret writing so frequently that Valerius Probus wrote an entire treatise on his ciphers, which unfortunately has not survived. However, thanks to Suetonius' *Lives of the Caesars LVI*, written in the second century A.D., we do have a detailed description of one of the types of substitution cipher used by Julius Caesar. He simply replaced each letter in the message with the letter that is three places further down the alphabet. Cryptographers often think in terms of the *plain alphabet*, the alphabet used to write the original message, and the *cipher alphabet*, the letters that are substituted in place of the plain letters. When the plain alphabet is placed above the cipher alphabet, as shown in Figure 3, it is clear that the cipher alphabet has been shifted by three places, and hence this form of substitution is often called the *Caesar shift cipher*, or simply the Caesar cipher. *Cipher* is the name given to any form of cryptographic substitution in which each letter is replaced by another letter or symbol.

Although Suetonius mentions only a Caesar shift of three places, it is clear that by using any shift between one and twenty-five places, it is possible to generate twenty-five distinct ciphers. In fact, if we do not restrict ourselves to shifting the alphabet and permit the cipher alphabet to be any rearrangement of the plain alphabet, then we can generate an even greater number of distinct ciphers. There are over 400,000,000,000,000,000,000,000,000 such rearrangements, and therefore the same number of distinct ciphers.

Each distinct cipher can be considered in terms of a general encrypting method, known as the *algorithm,* and a *key,* which specifies the exact details of a particular encryption. In this case, the algorithm involves substituting each letter in the plain alphabet with a letter from a cipher alphabet, and the cipher alphabet is allowed to consist of any rearrangement of the plain alphabet. The key defines the exact cipher alphabet to be used for a particular encryption. The relationship between the algorithm and the key is illustrated in Figure 4.

An enemy studying an intercepted scrambled message may have a strong suspicion of the algorithm but would not know

Plain alphabet	a b c d e f g h i j k l m n o p q r s t u v w x y z
Cipher alphabet	D E F G H I J K L M N O P Q R S T U V W X Y Z A B C

Plaintext	i came, i saw, i conquered
Ciphertext	L FDPH, L VDZ, L FRQTXHUHG

Figure 3 The Caesar cipher applied to a short message. The Caesar cipher is based on a cipher alphabet that is shifted a certain number of places (in this case three) relative to the plain alphabet. The convention in cryptography is to write the plain alphabet in lower-case letters, and the cipher alphabet in capitals. Similarly, the original message, the plaintext, is written in lower case, and the encrypted message, the ciphertext, is written in capitals.

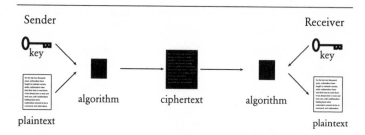

Sender   Receiver

key   key

algorithm   ciphertext   algorithm

plaintext   plaintext

Figure 4 To encrypt a plaintext message, the sender passes it through an encryption algorithm. The algorithm is a general system for encryption, and needs to be specified exactly by selecting a key. Applying the key and algorithm together to a plaintext generates the encrypted message, or ciphertext. The ciphertext may be intercepted by an enemy while it is being transmitted to the receiver, but the enemy should not be able to decipher the message. However, the receiver, who knows both the key and the algorithm used by the sender, is able to turn the ciphertext back into the plaintext message.

the exact key. For example, they may well suspect that each letter in the plaintext has been replaced by a different letter according to a particular cipher alphabet, but they are unlikely to know which cipher alphabet has been used. If the cipher alphabet, the key, is kept a closely guarded secret between the sender and the receiver, then the enemy cannot decipher the intercepted message. The significance of the key, as opposed to the algorithm, is an enduring principle of cryptography. It was definitively stated in 1883 by the Dutch linguist Auguste Kerckhoffs von Nieuwenhof in his book *La Cryptographie militaire:* "Kerckhoffs' Principle: The security of a cryptosystem must not depend on keeping secret the crypto-algorithm. The security depends only on keeping secret the key."

In addition to keeping the key secret, a secure cipher system must also have a wide range of potential keys. For example, if the sender uses the Caesar shift cipher to encrypt a message, then encryption is relatively weak because there are only twenty-five potential keys. From the enemy's point of view, if they intercept the message and suspect that the algorithm being used is the Caesar shift, then they merely have to check the twenty-five possible keys. However, if the sender uses the more general substitution algorithm, which permits the cipher alphabet to be any rearrangement of the plain alphabet, then there are 400,000,000,000,000,000,000,000,000 possible keys from which to choose. One such is shown in Figure 5. From the enemy's point of view, even if the message is intercepted and the algorithm is known, there is still the horrendous task of checking all possible keys. If an enemy agent were able to check one of the 400,000,000,000,000,000,000,000,000 possible keys every second, it would take roughly a billion times the lifetime of the universe to check all of them and decipher the message.

The beauty of this type of cipher is that it is easy to implement but provides a high level of security. It is easy for the sender to define the key, which consists merely of stating the order of the 26 letters in the rearranged cipher alphabet, and yet it is effectively impossible for the enemy to check all possible keys by the so-called brute-force attack. The simplicity of the key is important, because the sender and receiver have to share knowledge of the key, and the simpler the key, the less the chance of a misunderstanding.

In fact, an even simpler key is possible if the sender is prepared to accept a slight reduction in the number of potential keys. Instead of randomly rearranging the plain alphabet to

Plain alphabet	a b c d e f g h i j k l m n o p q r s t u v w x y z
Cipher alphabet	J L P A W I Q B C T R Z Y D S K E G F X H U O N V M

Plaintext	b e w a r e t h e i d e s o f m a r c h
Ciphertext	L W O J G W X B W C A W F S I Y J G P B

Figure 5 An example of the general substitution algorithm, in which each letter in the plaintext is substituted with another letter according to a key. The key is defined by the cipher alphabet, which can be any rearrangement of the plain alphabet.

achieve the cipher alphabet, the sender chooses a *keyword* or *keyphrase*. For example, to use **JULIUS CAESAR** as a keyphrase, begin by removing any spaces and repeated letters (**JULISCAER**), and then use this as the beginning of the jumbled cipher alphabet. The remainder of the cipher alphabet is merely the remaining letters of the alphabet, in their correct order, starting where the keyphrase ends. Hence, the cipher alphabet would read as follows.

Plain alphabet	a b c d e f g h i j k l m n o p q r s t u v w x y z
Cipher alphabet	J U L I S C A E R T V W X Y Z B D F G H K M N O P Q

The advantage of building a cipher alphabet in this way is that it is easy to memorize the keyword or keyphrase, and hence the cipher alphabet. This is important, because if the sender has to keep the cipher alphabet on a piece of paper, the enemy can capture the paper, discover the key and read any communications that have been encrypted with it. However, if the key can be committed to memory, it is less likely to fall into enemy hands.

This simplicity and strength meant that the substitution cipher dominated the art of secret writing throughout the first millennium A.D. Codemakers had evolved a system for guaranteeing secure communication, so there was no need for further development—without necessity, there was no need for invention. The onus had fallen upon the codebreakers, those who were attempting to crack the substitution cipher. Was there any way for an enemy interceptor to unravel an encrypted message? Many ancient scholars considered that the substitution cipher was unbreakable, thanks to the gigantic number of possible keys, and for centuries this seemed to be true. However, codebreakers would eventually find a shortcut to the process of exhaustively searching through all the keys. Instead of taking billions of years to crack a cipher, the shortcut could reveal the message in a matter of minutes. The breakthrough occurred in the East and required a brilliant combination of linguistics, statistics and religious devotion.

THE ARAB CRYPTANALYSTS

At the age of about forty, Muhammad began regularly visiting an isolated cave on Mount Hira just outside Mecca. This was a retreat, a place for prayer, meditation and contemplation. It was during a period of deep reflection, around A.D. 610, that he was visited by the archangel Gabriel, who proclaimed that Muhammad was to be the messenger of God. This was the first of a series of revelations that continued until Muhammad died some twenty years later. The revelations were recorded by various scribes during the Prophet's life, but only as fragments, and it was left to Abū Bakr, the first caliph of Islam, to gather them together into a single text. The work was continued by Umar, the second caliph, and his daughter Hafsa, and was eventually completed by Uthmān, the third caliph. Each revelation became one of the 114 chapters of the Koran.

The ruling caliph was responsible for carrying on the work of the Prophet, upholding his teachings and spreading his word. Between the appointment of Abū Bakr in 632 and the death of the fourth caliph, Alī, in 661, Islam spread until half of the known world was under Muslim rule. Then in 750, after a century of consolidation, the start of the Abbasid caliphate (or dynasty) heralded the golden age of Islamic civilization. The arts and sciences flourished in equal measure. Islamic craftsmen bequeathed us magnificent paintings, ornate carvings, and the most elaborate textiles in history, while the legacy of Islamic scientists is evident from the number of Arabic words that pepper the language of modern science, such as *algebra, alkali* and *zenith.*

The richness of Islamic culture was in large part the result of a wealthy and peaceful society. The Abbasid caliphs were less interested than their predecessors in conquest, and instead concentrated on establishing an organized and affluent society. Lower taxes encouraged businesses to grow and gave rise to greater commerce and industry, while strict laws reduced corruption and protected the citizens. All of this relied on an effective system of administration, and in turn the administrators relied on secure communication achieved through the use of encryption. As well as encrypting sensitive affairs of state, it is documented that officials protected tax records, demonstrating a widespread and routine use of cryptography. Further evidence comes from the many administrative manuals, such as the tenth-century *Adab al-Kuttāb* (The Secretaries' Manual), that include sections devoted to cryptography.

The administrators usually employed a cipher alphabet that was simply a rearrangement of the plain alphabet, as described earlier, but they also used cipher alphabets that contained other types of symbols. For example, **a** in the plain alphabet might be replaced by **#** in the cipher alphabet, **b** might be replaced by **+**, and so on. The *monoalphabetic substitution cipher* is the general name given to any substitution cipher in which the cipher alphabet consists of letters, symbols or a mix of both. All the substitution ciphers that we have met so far come within this general category.

Had the Arabs merely been familiar with the use of the monoalphabetic substitution cipher, they would not warrant a significant mention in any history of cryptography. However, in addition to employing ciphers, the Arab scholars were also capable of destroying ciphers. They in fact invented *cryptanalysis,* the science of unscrambling a message without knowledge of the key. While the cryptographer develops new methods of secret writing, it is the cryptanalyst who struggles to find weaknesses in these methods in order to break into secret messages. Arabian cryptanalysts succeeded in finding a method for breaking the monoalphabetic substitution cipher, a cipher that had remained unbreakable for several centuries.

Cryptanalysis could not be invented until a civilization had reached a sufficiently sophisticated level of education in several disciplines, including mathematics, statistics and linguistics. The Muslim civilization provided an ideal birthplace for cryptanalysis, because Islam demands justice in all spheres of human activity, and achieving this requires knowledge, or *ilm*. Every Muslim is obliged to pursue knowledge in all its forms, and the economic success of the Abbasid caliphate meant that scholars had the time, money and materials required to fulfill their duty. They endeavored to acquire the knowledge of previous civilizations by obtaining Egyptian, Babylonian, Indian, Chinese, Farsi, Syriac, Armenian, Hebrew and Roman texts and translating them into Arabic. In 815, the Caliph al-Ma'mūn established in Baghdad the Bait al-Hikmah (House of Wisdom), a library and center for translation.

In addition to a greater understanding of secular subjects, the invention of cryptanalysis also depended on the growth of religious education. Major theological schools were established in Basra, Kufa and Baghdad, where theologians studied the revelations of Muhammad as contained in the Koran. The theologians were interested in establishing the chronology of the revelations, which they did by counting the frequencies of words contained in each revelation. The theory was that certain words had evolved relatively recently, and hence if a revelation contained a high number of these newer words, this would indicate that it came later in the chronology. Theologians also studied the

Hadīth, which consists of the Prophet's daily utterances. They tried to demonstrate that each statement was indeed attributable to Muhammad. This was done by studying the etymology of words and the structure of sentences, to test whether particular texts were consistent with the linguistic patterns of the Prophet.

Significantly, the religious scholars did not stop their investigation at the level of words. They also analyzed individual letters, and in particular they discovered that some letters are more common than others. The letters a and l are the most common in Arabic, partly because of the definite article al-, whereas the letter j appears only a tenth as frequently. This apparently minor observation would lead to the first great breakthrough in cryptanalysis.

The earliest known description of the technique is by the ninth-century scientist Abū Yūsuf Ya'qūb ibn Is-hāq ibn as-Sabbāh ibn 'omrān ibn Ismaīl al-Kindī. Known as "the philosopher of the Arabs," al-Kindī was the author of 290 books on medicine, astronomy, mathematics, linguistics and music. His greatest treatise, which was rediscovered only in 1987 in the Sulaimaniyyah Ottoman Archive in Istanbul, is entitled *A Manuscript on Deciphering Cryptographic Messages.* Although it contains detailed discussions on statistics, Arabic phonetics and Arabic syntax, al-Kindī's revolutionary system of cryptanalysis is summarized in two short paragraphs:

> One way to solve an encrypted message, if we know its language, is to find a different plaintext of the same language long enough to fill one sheet or so, and then we count the occurrences of each letter. We call the most frequently occurring letter the "first," the next most occurring letter the "second," the following most occurring letter the "third," and so on, until we account for all the different letters in the plaintext sample.
>
> Then we look at the ciphertext we want to solve and we also classify its symbols. We find the most occurring symbol and

change it to the form of the "first" letter of the plaintext sample, the next most common symbol is changed to the form-of the "second" letter, and the third most common symbol is changed to the form of the "third" letter, and so on, until we account for all symbols of the cryptogram we want to solve.

Al-Kindī's explanation is easier to explain in terms of the English alphabet. First of all, it is necessary to study a lengthy piece of normal English text, perhaps several, in order to establish the frequency of each letter of the alphabet. In English, **e** is the most common letter, followed by **t**, then **a**, and so on, as given in Table 1. Next, examine the ciphertext in question, and work out the frequency of each letter. If the most common letter in the ciphertext is, for example, **J**, then it would seem likely that this is a substitute for **e**. And if the second most common letter in the ciphertext is **P**, then this is probably a substitute for **t**, and so on. Al-Kindī's technique, known as *frequency analysis,*

Table 1 This table of relative frequencies is based on passages taken from newspapers and novels, and the total sample was 100,362 alphabetic characters. The table was compiled by H. Beker and F. Piper, and originally published in *Cipher Systems: The Protection of Communication.*

Letter	Percentage	Letter	Percentage
a	8.2	n	6.7
b	1.5	o	7.5
c	2.8	p	1.9
d	4.3	q	0.1
e	12.7	r	6.0
f	2.2	s	6.3
g	2.0	t	9.1
h	6.1	u	2.8
i	7.0	v	1.0
j	0.2	w	2.4
k	0.8	x	0.2
l	4.0	y	2.0
m	2.4	z	0.1

shows that it is unnecessary to check each of the billions of potential keys. Instead, it is possible to reveal the contents of a scrambled message simply by analyzing the frequency of the characters in the ciphertext.

However, it is not possible to apply al-Kindī's recipe for cryptanalysis unconditionally, because the standard list of frequencies in Table 1 is only an average, and it will not correspond exactly to the frequencies of every text. For example, a brief message discussing the effect of the atmosphere on the movement of striped quadrupeds in Africa ("From Zanzibar to Zambia and Zaire, ozone zones make zebras run zany zigzags") would not, if encrypted, yield to straightforward frequency analysis. In general, short texts are likely to deviate significantly from the standard frequencies, and if there are fewer than a hundred letters, then decipherment will be very difficult. On the other hand, longer texts are more likely to follow the standard frequencies, although this is not always the case. In 1969, the French author Georges Perec wrote *La Disparition*, a two-hundred-page novel that did not use words that contain the letter **e**. Doubly remarkable is the fact that the English novelist and critic Gilbert Adair succeeded in translating *La Disparition* into English while still following Perec's avoidance of the letter **e**. Entitled *A Void*, Adair's translation is surprisingly readable (see Appendix A). If the entire book were encrypted via a monoalphabetic substitution cipher, then a naive attempt to decipher it might be prevented by the complete lack of the most frequently occurring letter in the English alphabet.

Having described the first tool of cryptanalysis, I shall continue by giving an example of how frequency analysis is used to decipher a ciphertext. I have avoided littering the whole book with examples of cryptanalysis, but with frequency analysis I make an exception. This is partly because frequency analysis is not as difficult as it sounds, and partly because it is the primary cryptanalytic tool. Furthermore, the example that follows provides insight into the method of the cryptanalyst. Although frequency analysis requires logical thinking, you will see that it also demands cunning, intuition, flexibility and guesswork.

CRYPTANALYZING A CIPHERTEXT

PCQ VMJYPD LBYK LYSO KBXBJXWXV BXV ZCJPO EYPD KBXBJYUXJ LBJOO KCPK. CP LBO LBCMKXPV XPV IYJKL PYDBL, QBOP KBO BXV OPVOV LBO LXRO CI SX'XJMI, KBO JCKO XPV EYKKOV LBO DJCMPV ZOICJO BYS, KXUYPD: "DJOXL EYPD, ICJ X LBCMKXPV XPV CPO PYDBLK Y BXNO ZOOP JOACMPLYPD LC UCM LBO IXZROK CI FXKL XDOK XPV LBO RODOPVK CI XPAYOPL EYPDK. SXU Y SXEO KC ZCRV XK LC AJXNO X IXNCMJ CI UCMJ SXGOKLU?"

OFYRCDMO, LXROK IJCS LBO LBCMKXPV XPV CPO PYDBLK

Imagine that we have intercepted this scrambled message. The challenge is to decipher it. We know that the text is in English, and that it has been scrambled according to a monoalphabetic substitution cipher, but we have no idea of the key. Searching all possible keys is impractical, so we must apply frequency analysis. What follows is a step-by-step guide to cryptanalyzing the ciphertext, but if you feel confident, then you might prefer to ignore this and attempt your own independent cryptanalysis.

The immediate reaction of any cryptanalyst upon seeing such a ciphertext is to analyze the frequency of all the letters, which results in Table 2. Not surprisingly, the letters vary in their frequency. The question is, can we identify what any of them represent, based on their frequencies? The ciphertext is relatively short, so we cannot rely wholly on frequency analysis. It would be naive to assume that the commonest letter in the ciphertext, **O**, represents the commonest letter in English, **e**, or that the eighth most frequent letter in the ciphertext, **Y**, represents the eighth most frequent letter in English, **h**. An

Table 2 Frequency analysis of enciphered message.

Letter	Frequency		Letter	Frequency	
	Occurrences	Percentage		Occurrences	Percentage
A	3	0.9	N	3	0.9
B	25	7.4	O	38	11.2
C	27	8.0	P	31	9.2
D	14	4.1	Q	2	0.6
E	5	1.5	R	6	1.8
F	2	0.6	S	7	2.1
G	1	0.3	T	0	0.0
H	0	0.0	U	6	1.8
I	11	3.3	V	18	5.3
J	18	5.3	W	1	0.3
K	26	7.7	X	34	10.1
L	25	7.4	Y	19	5.6
M	11	3.3	Z	5	1.5

unquestioning application of frequency analysis would lead to gibberish. For example, the first word, **PCQ**, would be deciphered as **aov**.

However, we can begin by focusing attention on the only three letters that appear more than thirty times in the ciphertext, namely **O**, **X** and **P**. Let us assume that the commonest letters in the ciphertext probably represent the commonest letters in the English alphabet, but not necessarily in the right order. In other words, we cannot be sure that **O = e**, **X = t** and **P = a**, but we can make the tentative assumption that

O = e, t or **a,   X = e, t** or **a,   P = e, t** or **a**

In order to proceed with confidence and pin down the identity of the three most common letters, **O**, **X** and **P**, we need a more subtle form of frequency analysis. Instead of simply counting the frequency of the three letters, we can focus on how often they appear next to all the other letters. For example, does the letter **O** appear before or after several other letters, or does it tend to neighbor just a few special letters? Answering this question will be a good indication of whether **O** represents a vowel or a consonant. If **O** represents a vowel, it should appear before and after most of the other letters, whereas if it represents a consonant, it will tend to avoid many of the other letters. For example, the vowel **e** can appear before and after virtually every other letter, but the consonant **t** is rarely seen before or after **b, d, g, j, k, m, q** or **v**.

The table below takes the three most common letters in the ciphertext, **O, X** and **P**, and lists how frequently each appears before or after every letter. For example, **O** appears before **A** on one occasion but never appears immediately after it, giving a total of one in the first box. The letter **O** neighbors the majority of letters, and there are only seven that it avoids completely, represented by the seven zeroes in the **O** row. The letter **X** is equally sociable, because it too neighbors most of the letters and avoids only eight of them. However, the letter **P** is much less friendly. It tends to lurk around just a few letters and avoids fifteen of them. This evidence suggests that **O** and **X** represent vowels, while **P** represents a consonant.

	A	B	C	D	E	F	G	H	I	J	K	L	M	N	O	P	Q	R	S	T	U	V	W	X	Y	Z
O	1	9	0	3	1	1	1	0	1	4	6	0	1	2	2	8	0	4	1	0	0	3	0	1	1	2
X	0	7	0	1	1	1	1	0	2	4	6	3	0	3	1	9	0	2	4	0	3	3	2	0	0	1
P	1	0	5	6	0	0	0	0	0	1	1	2	2	0	8	0	0	0	0	0	0	11	0	9	9	0

Now we must ask ourselves which vowels are represented by **O** and **X**. They are probably **e** and **a**, the two most popular vowels in the English language, but does **O = e** and **X = a**, or does **O = a** and **X = e**? An interesting feature in the ciphertext is that the combination **OO** appears twice, whereas **XX** does not appear at all. Since the letters **ee** appear far more often than **aa** in plaintext English, it is likely that **O = e** and **X = a**.

At this point, we have confidently identified two of the letters in the ciphertext. Our conclusion that X = a is supported by the fact that X appears on its own in the ciphertext, and a is one of only two English words that consist of a single letter. The only other letter that appears on its own in the ciphertext is Y, and it seems highly likely that this represents the only other one-letter English word, which is i. Focusing on words with only one letter is a standard cryptanalytic trick, and I have included it among a list of cryptanalytic tips in Appendix B. This particular trick works only because this ciphertext still has spaces between the words. Often, a cryptographer will remove all the spaces to make it harder for an enemy interceptor to unscramble the message.

Although we have spaces between words, the following trick would also work where the ciphertext has been merged into a single string of characters. The trick allows us to spot the letter h once we have already identified the letter e. In the English language, the letter h frequently goes before the letter e (as in **the, then, they,** etc.), but rarely after e. The table below shows how frequently the O, which we think represents e, goes before and after all the other letters in the ciphertext. The table suggests that B represents h, because it appears before O on nine occasions but never goes after it. No other letter in the table has such an asymmetric relationship with O.

	A	B	C	D	E	F	G	H	I	J	K	L	M	N	O	P	Q	R	S	T	U	V	W	X	Y	Z
After O	1	0	0	1	0	1	0	0	1	0	4	0	0	0	2	5	0	0	0	0	2	0	1	0	0	0
Before O	0	9	0	2	1	0	1	0	0	4	2	0	1	2	2	3	0	4	1	0	0	1	0	0	1	2

Each letter in the English language has its own unique personality, which includes its frequency and its relation to other letters. It is this personality that allows us to establish the true identity of a letter, even when it has been disguised by monoalphabetic substitution.

We have now confidently established four letters, O = e, X = a,

Y = i and **B = h,** and we can begin to replace some of the letters in the ciphertext with their plaintext equivalents. I shall stick to the convention of keeping ciphertext letters in uppercase, while putting plaintext letters in lowercase. This will help to distinguish between those letters we still have to identify and those that have already been established.

PCQ VMJiPD LhiK LiSe KhahJaWaV haV ZCJPe EiPD
KhahJiUaJ LhJee KCPK. CP Lhe LhCMKaPV aPV liJKL PiDhL,
QheP Khe haV ePVeV Lhe LaRe CI Sa'aJMI, Khe JCKe aPV
EiKKev Lhe DJCMPV ZeICJe hiS, KaUiPD: "DJeaL EiPD, ICJ a
LhCMKaPV aPV CPe PiDhLK i haNe ZeeP JeACMPLiPD LC UCM
Lhe IaZReK CI FaKL aDeK aPV Lhe ReDePVK CI aPAiePL EiPDK.
SaU i SaEe KC ZCRV aK LC AJaNe a IaNCMJ CI UCMJ SaGeKLU?"

efiRCDMe, LaReK IJCS Lhe LhCMKaPV aPV CPe PiDhLK

This simple step helps us to identify several other letters, because we can guess some of the words in the ciphertext. For example, the most common three-letter words in English are **the** and **and,** and these are relatively easy to spot—**Lhe,** which appears six times, and **aPV,** which appears five times. Hence, **L** probably represents **t**, **P** probably represents **n** and **V** probably represents **d**. We can now replace these letters in the ciphertext with their true values:

nCQ dMJinD thiK tiSe KhahJaWad had ZCJne EinD
KhahJiUaJ thJee KCnK. Cn the thCMKand and liJKt niDht,
Qhen Khe had ended the taRe CI Sa'aJMI, Khe JCKe and
EiKKed the DJCMnd ZeICJe hiS, KaUinD: "DJeat EinD, ICJ a
thCMKand and Cne niDhtK i haNe Zeen JeACMntinD tC UCM
the IaZReK CI FaKt aDeK and the ReDendK CI anAient EinDK.
SaU i SaEe KC ZCRd aK tC AJaNe a IaNCMJ CI UCMJ SaGeKtU?"

efiRCDMe, taReK IJCS the thCMKand and Cne niDhtK

Once a few letters have been established, cryptanalysis progresses very rapidly. For example, the word at the beginning of the second sentence is **Cn**. Every word has a vowel in it, so **C** must be a vowel. There are only two vowels that remain to be identified, **u** and **o**; **u** does not fit, so **C** must represent **o**. We also have the word **Khe**, which implies that **K** represents either **t** or **s**. But we already know that **L = t**, so it becomes clear that **K = s**. Having identified these two letters, we insert them into the ciphertext, and there appears the phrase **thoMsand and one niDhts**. A sensible guess for this would be **thousand and one nights**, and it seems likely that the final line is telling us that this is a passage from *Tales from the Thousand and One Nights*. This implies that **M = u, I = f, J = r, D = g, R = l** and **S = m**.

We could continue trying to establish other letters by guessing other words, but instead let us have a look at what we know about the plain alphabet and cipher alphabet. These two alphabets form the key, and they were used by the cryptographer to perform the substitution that scrambled the message. Already, by identifying the true values of letters in the ciphertext, we have effectively been working out the details of the cipher alphabet. A summary of our achievements, so far, is given in the plain and cipher alphabets below.

Plain alphabet	a b c d e f g h i j k l m n o p q r s t u v w x y z
Cipher alphabet	X - - V O I D B Y - - R S P C - - J K L M - - - - -

By examining the partial cipher alphabet, we can complete the cryptanalysis. The sequence **VOIDBY** in the cipher alphabet suggests that the cryptographer has chosen a keyphrase as the basis for the key. Some guesswork is enough to suggest the keyphrase might be **A VOID BY GEORGES PEREC**, which is reduced to **AVOIDBYGERSPC** after removing spaces and repetitions. Thereafter, the letters continue in alphabetical order, omitting any that have already appeared in the keyphrase. In this particular case, the cryptographer took the unusual step of not starting the keyphrase at the beginning of the cipher alphabet, but rather starting it three letters in. This is possibly because the keyphrase begins with the letter A, and the cryptographer wanted to avoid encrypting a as A. At last, having established the complete cipher alphabet, we can unscramble the entire ciphertext, and the cryptanalysis is complete.

Plain alphabet	a b c d e f g h i j k l m n o p q r s t u v w x y z
Cipher alphabet	X Z A V O I D B Y G E R S P C F H J K L M N Q T UW

Now during this time Shahrazad had borne King Shahriyar three sons. On the thousand and first night, when she had ended the tale of Ma'aruf, she rose and kissed the ground before him, saying: "Great King, for a thousand and one nights I have been recounting to you the fables of past ages and the legends of ancient kings. May I make so bold as to crave a favour of your majesty?"

Epilogue, *Tales from the Thousand and One Nights*

RENAISSANCE IN THE WEST

Between A.D. 800 and 1200 Arab scholars enjoyed a vigorous period of intellectual achievement. At the same time, Europe was firmly stuck in the Dark Ages. While al-Kindī was describing the invention of cryptanalysis, Europeans were still struggling with the basics of cryptography. The only European institutions to encourage the study of secret writing were the monasteries, where monks would study the Bible in search of hidden meanings, a fascination that has persisted through to modern times (see Appendix C).

By the fifteenth century, however, European cryptography was a growing industry. The revival in the arts, sciences and scholarship during the Renaissance nurtured the capacity for cryptography, while an explosion in political intrigue offered ample motivation for secret communication. Italy, in particular, provided the ideal environment for cryptography. As well as being at the heart of the Renaissance, it consisted of independent city-states, each trying to outsmart the others. Diplomacy flourished, and each state would send ambassadors to the courts of the others. Each ambassador received messages from his respective head of state, describing details of the foreign policy he was to implement. In response, each ambassador would send back any information that he had gathered. Clearly there was a great incentive to encrypt communications in both directions, so each state established a cipher office, and each ambassador had a cipher secretary.

At the same time that cryptography was becoming a routine diplomatic tool, the science of cryptanalysis was beginning to emerge in the West. Diplomats had only just familiarized themselves with the skills required to establish secure communications, and already there were individuals attempting to destroy this security. It is quite probable that cryptanalysis was independently discovered in Europe, but there is also the possibility that it was introduced from the Arab world. Islamic discoveries in science and mathematics strongly influenced the rebirth of science in Europe, and cryptanalysis might have been among the imported knowledge.

Arguably the first great European cryptanalyst was Giovanni Soro, appointed as Venetian cipher secretary in 1506. Soro's reputation was known throughout Italy, and friendly states would send intercepted messages to Venice for cryptanalysis. Even the Vatican, probably the second most active center of cryptanalysis, would send Soro seemingly impenetrable messages that had fallen into its hands.

This was a period of transition, with cryptographers still relying on the monoalphabetic substitution cipher, while cryptanalysts were beginning to use frequency analysis to break it. Those yet to discover the power of frequency analysis continued to trust monoalphabetic substitution, ignorant of the extent to which cryptanalysts such as Soro were able to read their messages.

Meanwhile, countries that were alert to the weakness of the straightforward monoalphabetic substitution cipher were anxious to develop a better cipher, something that would protect their own nation's messages from being unscrambled by enemy cryptanalysts. One of the simplest improvements to the security of the monoalphabetic substitution cipher was the introduction of *nulls*, symbols or letters that were not substitutes for actual letters, merely blanks that represented nothing. For example, one could substitute each plain letter with a number between 1 and 99, which would leave 73 numbers that represent nothing, and these could be randomly sprinkled throughout the ciphertext with varying frequencies. The nulls would pose no problem to the intended recipient, who would know that they were to be ignored. However, the nulls would baffle an enemy interceptor because they would confuse an attack by frequency analysis.

Another attempt to strengthen the monoalphabetic substitution cipher involved the introduction of codewords. The term *code* has a very broad meaning in everyday language, and it is often used to describe any method for communicating in secret. However, it actually has a very specific meaning, and applies only to a certain form of substitution. So far we have concentrated on the idea of a substitution cipher, whereby each letter is replaced by a different letter, number or symbol. However, it is also possible to have substitution at a much higher level, whereby each word is represented by another word or symbol—this would be a code. For example,

assassinate	= D	general	= Σ	immediately	= 08
blackmail	= P	king	= Ω	today	= 73
capture	= J	minister	= Ψ	tonight	= 28

Using this very limited set of coded words, we can encode a simple message as follows:

Plain message   = **assassinate the king tonight**

Encoded message = **D-Ω-28**

Technically, a *code* is defined as substitution at the level of words or phrases, whereas a *cipher* is defined as substitution at the level of letters. Hence the term *encipher* means to scramble a message using a cipher, while *encode* means to scramble a message using a code. Similarly, the term *decipher* applies to unscrambling an enciphered message, and *decode* to unscrambling an encoded message. The terms *encrypt* and *decrypt* are more general, and cover scrambling and unscrambling with respect to both codes and ciphers. Figure 6 presents a brief summary of these definitions. In general, I shall keep to these definitions, but when the sense is clear, I might use a term such as *codebreaking* to describe a process that is really cipher breaking—the latter phrase might be technically accurate, but the former phrase is widely accepted.

At first sight, codes seem to offer more security than ciphers, because words are much less vulnerable to frequency analysis than letters. To decipher a monoalphabetic cipher you need only identify the true value of each of the twenty-six characters, whereas to decipher a code you need to identify the true value of hundreds or even thousands of codewords. However, if we examine codes in more detail, we see that they suffer from two major practical failings when compared with ciphers. First, once the sender and receiver have agreed upon the twenty-six letters in the cipher alphabet (the key), they can encipher any message, but to achieve the same level of flexibility using a code they would need to go through the painstaking task of defining a codeword for every one of the thousands of possible plaintext words. The codebook would consist of hundreds of pages, and would look something like a dictionary. In other words, compiling a codebook is a major task, and carrying it around is a major inconvenience.

Second, the consequences of having a codebook captured by the enemy are devastating. Immediately, all the encoded communications would become transparent to the enemy. The senders and receivers would have to go through the process of having to compile an entirely new codebook, and then this hefty new book would have to be distributed to everyone in the communications network, which might mean securely transporting it to every ambassador in every state. In comparison, if the enemy succeeds in capturing a cipher key, then it is relatively easy to compile a new cipher alphabet of twenty-six letters, which can be memorized and easily distributed.

Even in the sixteenth century, cryptographers appreciated the inherent weaknesses of codes and instead relied largely on ciphers, or sometimes *nomenclators*. A nomenclator is a system of encryption that relies on a cipher alphabet, which is used to encrypt the majority of a message, and a limited list of codewords. For example, a nomenclator book might consist of a front page containing the cipher alphabet, and then a second page containing a list of codewords. Despite the addition of codewords, a nomenclator is not much more secure than a straightforward cipher, because the bulk of a message can be

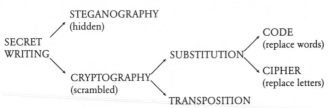

Figure 6 The science of secret writing and its main branches.

deciphered using frequency analysis, and the remaining encoded words can be guessed from the context.

As well as coping with the introduction of the nomenclator, the best cryptanalysts were also capable of dealing with the presence of nulls. In short, they were able to break the majority of encrypted messages. Their skills provided a steady flow of uncovered secrets, which influenced the decisions of their masters and mistresses, thereby affecting Europe's history at critical moments.

Nowhere is the impact of cryptanalysis more dramatically illustrated than in the case of Mary Queen of Scots. The outcome of her trial depended wholly on the battle between her codemakers and Queen Elizabeth's codebreakers. Mary was one of the most significant figures of the sixteenth century—queen of Scotland, queen of France, pretender to the English throne—yet her fate would be decided by a slip of paper, the message it bore, and whether or not that message could be deciphered.

THE BABINGTON PLOT

On November 24, 1542, the English forces of Henry VIII demolished the Scottish army at the Battle of Solway Moss. It appeared that Henry was on the verge of conquering Scotland and stealing the crown of King James V. After the battle, the distraught Scottish king suffered a complete mental and physical breakdown, and withdrew to the palace at Falkland. Even the birth of a daughter, Mary, just two weeks later could not revive the ailing king. It was as if he had been waiting for news of an heir so that he could die in peace, safe in the knowledge that he had done his duty. Just a week after Mary's birth, King James V, still only thirty years old, died. The baby princess had become Mary Queen of Scots.

Mary was born prematurely, and initially there was considerable concern that she would not survive. Rumors in England suggested that the baby had died, but this was merely wishful thinking at the English court, which was anxious to learn of anything that might destabilize Scotland. In fact, Mary soon grew strong and healthy, and at the age of nine months, on September 9, 1543, she was crowned in the chapel of Stirling Castle, surrounded by three earls, bearing on her behalf the royal crown, scepter and sword.

The fact that Queen Mary was so young offered Scotland a break from English attacks. It would have been considered unchivalrous had Henry VIII attempted to invade the country of a recently dead king, now under the rule of an infant queen. Instead, the English king decided on a policy of wooing Mary in the hope of arranging a marriage between her and his son Edward, thereby uniting the two nations under a Tudor ruler. He began his maneuvering by releasing the Scottish nobles captured at Solway Moss, on the condition that they campaign in favor of a union with England.

However, after considering Henry's offer, the Scottish court rejected it in favor of a marriage to Francis, the dauphin of France. Scotland was choosing to ally itself with a fellow Roman Catholic nation, a decision that pleased Mary's mother, Mary of Guise, whose own marriage with James V had been intended to cement the relationship between Scotland and France. Mary and Francis were still children, but the plan for the future was that they would eventually marry, and Francis would ascend the throne of France with Mary as his queen, thereby uniting Scotland and France. In the meantime, France would defend Scotland against any English onslaught.

The promise of protection was reassuring, particularly as Henry VIII had switched from diplomacy to intimidation in order to persuade the Scots that his own son was a more worthy groom for Mary Queen of Scots. His forces committed acts of piracy, destroyed crops, burned villages and attacked towns and cities along the border. The "rough wooing," as it is known, continued even after Henry's death in 1547. On the orders of his son, King Edward VI (the would-be suitor), the attacks culminated in the Battle of Pinkie Cleugh, in which the Scottish army was crushed. As a result of this slaughter, it was decided that, for her own safety, Mary should leave for France, beyond the reach of the English threat, where she could prepare for her marriage to Francis. On August 7, 1548, at the age of six, she set sail for the port of Roscoff.

Mary's first few years in the French court would be the most idyllic time of her life. She was surrounded by luxury and protected from harm, and she grew to love her future husband, the dauphin. At the age of sixteen they married, and the following year Francis and Mary became king and queen of France. Everything seemed set for her triumphant return to Scotland, until her husband, who had always suffered from poor health, fell gravely ill. An ear infection that he had nursed since he was a child had worsened, the inflammation spread toward his brain and an abscess began to develop. In 1560, within a year of being crowned, Francis was dead and Mary was widowed.

From this point onward, Mary's life would be repeatedly struck by tragedy. She returned to Scotland in 1561, where she discovered a transformed nation. During her long absence Mary had confirmed her Catholic faith, while her Scottish subjects had increasingly moved toward the Protestant church. Mary tolerated the wishes of the majority and at first reigned with relative success, but in 1565 she married her cousin, Henry Stewart, the Earl of Darnley, an act that led to a spiral of decline. Darnley was a vicious and brutal man whose ruthless greed for power lost Mary the loyalty of the Scottish nobles. The following year Mary witnessed for herself the full horror of her husband's barbaric nature when he murdered David Riccio, her secretary, in front of her. It became clear to everyone that for the sake of Scotland it was necessary to get rid of Darnley. Historians debate whether it was Mary or the Scottish nobles who instigated the plot, but on the night of February 9, 1567, Darnley's house was blown up, and as he attempted to escape, he was strangled. The only good to come from the marriage was a son and heir, James.

Mary's next marriage, to James Hepburn, the fourth Earl of Bothwell, was hardly more successful. By the summer of 1567, the Protestant Scottish nobles had become completely disillusioned with their Catholic queen, and they exiled Bothwell and imprisoned Mary, forcing her to give up the throne in favor of her fourteen-month-old son, James VI, while her half-brother, the Earl of Moray, acted as regent, ruling until the young king came of age. The next year, Mary escaped from her prison, gathered an army of six thousand royalists and made a final attempt to regain her crown. Her soldiers confronted the regent's army at the small village of Langside, near Glasgow, and Mary witnessed the battle from a nearby hilltop. Although her troops were greater in number, they lacked discipline, and Mary watched as they were torn apart. When defeat was inevitable, she fled. Ideally she would have headed east to the coast and then on to France, but this would have meant crossing territory loyal to her half-brother, so instead she headed south to England, where she hoped that her cousin Queen Elizabeth I would provide refuge.

Mary had made a terrible misjudgment. Elizabeth offered Mary nothing more than another prison. The official reason for her arrest was in connection with the murder of Darnley, but the true reason was that Mary posed a threat to Elizabeth, because English Catholics considered Mary to be the true queen of England. Through her grandmother, Margaret Tudor, the elder sister of Henry VIII, Mary did indeed have a claim to the throne, but Henry's last surviving offspring, Elizabeth I, would seem to have had a prior claim. However, according to Catholics, Elizabeth was illegitimate because she was the daughter of Anne Boleyn, Henry's second wife after he had divorced Catherine of Aragon in defiance of the Pope. English Catholics did not recognize Henry VIII's divorce, they did not acknowledge his next marriage, to Anne Boleyn, and they certainly did not accept the resulting daughter, Elizabeth, as queen. Catholics saw Elizabeth as a "bastard usurper."

Mary was imprisoned in a series of castles and manors. Although Elizabeth thought of her as one of the most dangerous figures in England, many Englishmen admitted that they admired her gracious manner, her obvious intelligence and her great beauty. William Cecil, Elizabeth's Great Minister, commented on "her cunning and sugared entertainment of all men," and Nicholas White, Cecil's emissary, made a similar observation: "She hath withal an alluring grace, a pretty Scotch accent, and a searching wit, clouded with mildness." But as each year passed, her appearance waned, her health deteriorated and she began to lose hope. Her jailer, Sir Amyas Paulet, a Puritan, was immune to her charms, and treated her with increasing harshness.

By 1586, after eighteen years of imprisonment, she had lost all her privileges. She was confined to Chartley Hall in Staffordshire and was no longer allowed to take the waters at Buxton, which had previously helped to alleviate her frequent illnesses. On her last visit to Buxton she used a diamond to inscribe a message on a windowpane: "Buxton, whose warm waters have made thy name famous, perchance I shall visit thee no more—Farewell." It appears that she suspected that she was about to lose what little freedom she had. Mary's growing sorrow was worsened by the actions of her nineteen-year-old son, King James VI of Scotland. She had always hoped that one day she would escape and return to Scotland to share power with her son, whom she had not seen since he was one year old. However, James felt no such affection for his mother. He had been brought up by Mary's enemies, who had taught James that his mother had murdered his father in order to marry her lover. James despised her and feared that if she returned, then she might seize his crown. His hatred toward Mary was demonstrated by the fact that he had no qualms in seeking a marriage with Elizabeth I, the woman responsible for his mother's imprisonment (and who was also thirty years his senior). Elizabeth declined the offer.

Mary wrote to her son in an attempt to win him over, but her letters never reached the Scottish border. By this stage, Mary was more isolated then ever before: All her outgoing letters were confiscated, and any incoming correspondence was kept by her jailer. Mary's morale was at its lowest, and it seemed that all hope was lost. It was under these severe and desperate circumstances that, on January 6, 1586, she received an astonishing package of letters.

The letters were from Mary's supporters on the Continent, and they had been smuggled into her prison by Gilbert Gifford, a Catholic who had left England in 1577 and trained as a priest at the English College in Rome. Upon returning to England in 1585, apparently eager to serve Mary, he immediately approached the French embassy in London, where a pile of correspondence had accumulated. The embassy had known that if they forwarded the letters by the formal route, Mary would never see them. However, Gifford claimed that he could smuggle the letters into Chartley Hall, and sure enough, he lived up to his word. This delivery was the first of many, and

Gifford began a career as a courier, not only passing messages to Mary but also collecting her replies. He had a rather cunning way of sneaking letters into Chartley Hall. He took the messages to a local brewer, who wrapped them in a leather packet, which was then hidden inside a hollow bung used to seal a barrel of beer. The brewer would deliver the barrel to Chartley Hall, whereupon one of Mary's maids would open the bung and take the contents to her mistress. The process worked equally well for getting messages out of Chartley Hall.

Meanwhile, unknown to Mary, a plan to rescue her was being hatched in the taverns of London. At the center of the plot was Anthony Babington, only twenty-four years old but already well known in the city as a handsome, charming and witty man about town. What his many admirers and close friends failed to appreciate was that Babington deeply resented the government, which had persecuted him, his family and his faith. The state's anti-Catholic policies had reached new heights of horror, with priests being accused of treason, and anybody caught harboring them punished by the rack, mutilation and disemboweling while still alive. The Catholic mass was officially banned, and families who remained loyal to the Pope were forced to pay extremely high taxes. Babington's resentment was fueled by the death of Lord Darcy, his great-grandfather, who was beheaded for his involvement in the Pilgrimage of Grace, a Catholic uprising against Henry VIII.

The conspiracy began one evening in March 1586, when Babington and six confidants gathered in The Plough, an inn outside Temple Bar. As the historian Philip Caraman observed, "He drew to himself by the force of his exceptional charm and personality many young Catholic gentlemen of his own standing, gallant, adventurous and daring in defence of the Catholic faith in its day of stress; and ready for any arduous enterprise whatsoever that might advance the common Catholic cause." Over the next few months an ambitious plan emerged to free Mary Queen of Scots, assassinate Queen Elizabeth and incite a rebellion supported by an invasion from abroad.

The conspirators were agreed that the Babington Plot, as it became known, could not proceed without the blessing of Mary, but there was no apparent way to communicate with her. Then, on July 6, 1586, Gifford arrived on Babington's doorstep. He delivered a letter from Mary, explaining that she had heard about Babington via her supporters in Paris and looked forward to hearing from him. In reply, Babington compiled a detailed letter in which he outlined his scheme, including a reference to the excommunication of Elizabeth by Pope Pius V in 1570, which he believed legitimized her assassination.

> Myself with ten gentlemen and a hundred of our followers will undertake the delivery of your royal person from the hands of your enemies. For the dispatch of the usurper, from the obedience of whom we are by the excommunication of her made free, there be six noble gentlemen, all my private friends, who for the zeal they bear to the Catholic cause and your Majesty's service will undertake that tragical execution.

As before, Gifford used his trick of putting the message in the bung of a beer barrel in order to sneak it past Mary's guards. This can be considered a form of steganography, because the letter was being hidden. As an extra precaution, Babington enciphered his letter so that even if it was intercepted by Mary's jailer, it would be indecipherable and the plot would not be uncovered. He used a cipher that was not a simple monoalphabetic substitution, but rather a nomenclator, as shown in Figure 7. It consisted of twenty-three symbols that were to be substituted for the letters of the alphabet (excluding **j, v** and **w**), along with thirty-five symbols representing words or phrases. In addition, there were four nulls (*ff*, *⌐*, *⌐*, *ꝺ*) and a symbol (*σ*) signifying that the next symbol represents a double letter ("dowbleth").

Gifford was still a youth, even younger than Babington, and yet he conducted his deliveries with confidence and cleverness. His aliases, such as Mr. Colerdin, Pietro and Cornelys, enabled him to travel the country without suspicion, and his contacts within the Catholic community provided him with a series of safe houses between London and Chartley Hall. However, each time Gifford traveled to or from Chartley Hall, he would make a detour. Although Gifford was apparently acting as an agent for Mary, he was actually a double agent. Back in 1585, before his return to England, Gifford had written to Sir Francis Walsingham, principal secretary to Queen Elizabeth, offering his services. Gifford realized that his Catholic background would act as a perfect mask for infiltrating plots against Queen Elizabeth. In the letter to Walsingham, he wrote, "I have heard of the

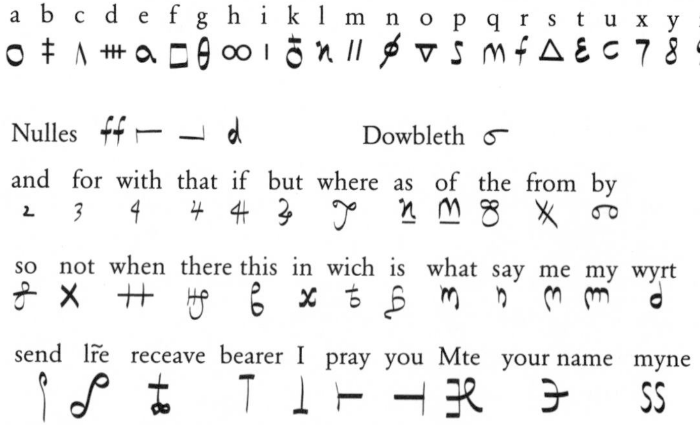

Figure 7 The nomenclator of Mary Queen of Scots, consisting of a cipher alphabet and codewords.

work you do and I want to serve you. I have no scruples and no fear of danger. Whatever you order me to do I will accomplish."

Walsingham was Elizabeth's most ruthless minister, a spymaster who was responsible for the security of the monarch. He had inherited a small network of spies, which he rapidly expanded into the Continent, where many of the plots against Elizabeth were being hatched. After his death it was discovered that he had been receiving regular reports from twelve locations in France, nine in Germany, four in Italy and four in Spain, as well as having informants in Constantinople, Algiers and Tripoli.

Walsingham recruited Gifford as a spy, and in fact it was Walsingham who ordered Gifford to approach the French embassy and offer himself as a courier. Each time Gifford collected a message to or from Mary, he would first take it to Walsingham. The vigilant spymaster would then pass it to his counterfeiters, who would break the seal on each letter, make a copy, and reseal the original letter with an identical stamp before handing it back to Gifford. The apparently untouched letter could then be delivered to Mary or her correspondents, who remained oblivious to what was going on.

When Gifford handed Walsingham a letter from Babington to Mary, the first objective was to decipher it. Walsingham employed Thomas Phelippes as his cipher secretary, a man "of low stature, slender every way, dark yellow haired on the head, and clear yellow bearded, eaten in the face with smallpox, of short sight, thirty years of age by appearance." Phelippes was a linguist who could speak French, Italian, Spanish, Latin and German, and, more importantly, he was one of Europe's finest cryptanalysts.

Upon receiving any message to or from Mary, Phelippes devoured it. He was a master of frequency analysis, and it would be merely a matter of time before he found a solution. He established the frequency of each character, and tentatively proposed values for those that appeared most often. When a particular approach hinted at absurdity, he would backtrack and try alternative substitutions. Gradually he would identify the nulls, the cryptographic red herrings, and put them to one side. Eventually all that remained were the handful of codewords, whose meaning could be guessed from the context.

When Phelippes deciphered Babington's message to Mary, which clearly proposed the assassination of Elizabeth, he immediately forwarded the damning text to his master. At this point Walsingham could have pounced on Babington, but he wanted more than the execution of a handful of rebels. He bided his time in the hope that Mary would reply and authorize the plot, thereby incriminating herself. Walsingham had long wished for the death of Mary Queen of Scots, but he was aware of Elizabeth's reluctance to execute her cousin. However, if he could prove that Mary was endorsing an attempt on the life of Elizabeth, then surely his queen would permit the execution of her Catholic rival. Walsingham's hopes were soon fulfilled.

On July 17, Mary replied to Babington, effectively signing her own death warrant. She explicitly wrote about the "design," showing particular concern that she should be released simultaneously with, or before, Elizabeth's assassination, otherwise news might reach her jailer, who might then murder her. Before reaching Babington, the letter made the usual detour to Phelippes. Having cryptanalyzed the earlier message, he deciphered this one with ease, read its contents and marked it with a Π—the sign of the gallows.

Walsingham had all the evidence he needed to arrest Mary and Babington, but still he was not satisfied. In order to destroy the conspiracy completely, he needed the names of all those involved. He asked Phelippes to forge a postscript to Mary's letter, which would entice Babington to name names. One of

Phelippes's additional talents was forgery, and it was said that he had the ability "to write any man's hand, if he had once seen it, as if the man himself had writ it." Figure 8 shows the postscript that was added at the end of Mary's letter to Babington. It can be deciphered using Mary's nomenclator, as shown in Figure 7, to reveal the following plaintext:

> I would be glad to know the names and qualities of the six gentlemen which are to accomplish the designment; for it may be that I shall be able, upon knowledge of the parties, to give you some further advice necessary to be followed therein, as also from time to time particularly how you proceed: and as soon as you may, for the same purpose, who be already, and how far everyone is privy hereunto.

Soon after receiving the message and its postscript, Babington needed to go abroad to organize the invasion, and had to register at Walsingham's department in order to acquire a passport. This would have been an ideal time to capture the traitor, but the bureaucrat who was manning the office, John Scudamore, was not expecting the most wanted traitor in England to turn up at his door. Scudamore, with no support to hand, took the

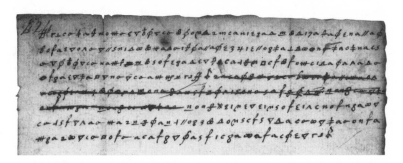

Figure 8 The forged postscript added by Thomas Phelippes to Mary's message. It can be deciphered by referring to Mary's nomenclator (Figure 7).

unsuspecting Babington to a nearby tavern, stalling for time while his assistant organized a group of soldiers. A short while later a note arrived at the tavern, informing Scudamore that it was time for the arrest. Babington, however, caught sight of it. He casually said that he would pay for the beer and meal and rose to his feet, leaving his sword and coat at the table, implying that he would return in an instant. Instead, he slipped out the back door and escaped, first to St. John's Wood and then on to Harrow. He attempted to disguise himself, cutting his hair short and staining his skin with walnut juice to mask his aristocratic background. He managed to elude capture for ten days, but by August 15, Babington and his six colleagues were captured and brought to London. Church bells across the city rang out in triumph. Their executions were horrid in the extreme. In the words of the Elizabethan historian William Camden, "they were all cut down, their privities were cut off, bowelled alive and seeing, and quartered!"

Meanwhile, on August 11, Mary Queen of Scots and her entourage had been allowed the exceptional privilege of riding in the grounds of Chartley Hall. As Mary crossed the moors she spied some horsemen approaching, and immediately thought that these must be Babington's men coming to rescue her. It soon became clear that these men had come to arrest her, not release her. Mary had been implicated in the Babington Plot and was charged under the Act of Association, an Act of Parliament passed in 1584 specifically designed to convict anybody involved in a conspiracy against Elizabeth.

The trial was held in Fotheringhay Castle, a bleak, miserable place in the middle of the featureless fens of East Anglia. It began on Wednesday, October 15, in front of two chief justices, four other judges, the lord chancellor, the lord treasurer, Walsingham, and various earls, knights and barons. At the back of the courtroom there was space for spectators, such as local villagers and the servants of the commissioners, all eager to see the humiliated Scottish queen beg forgiveness and plead for her life. However, Mary remained dignified and composed throughout the trial. Mary's main defense was to deny any connection with Babington. "Can I be responsible for the criminal projects of a few desperate men," she proclaimed, "which they planned without my knowledge or participation?" Her statement had little impact in the face of the deciphered letters.

The trial went into a second day, and Mary continued to deny any knowledge of the Babington Plot. When the trial finished, she left the judges to decide her fate, pardoning them in advance for the inevitable decision. Ten days later, the Star Chamber met in Westminster and concluded that Mary had been guilty of "compassing and imagining since June 1st matters tending to the death and destruction of the Queen of England." They recommended the death penalty, and Elizabeth signed the death warrant.

On February 8, 1587, in the Great Hall of Fotheringhay Castle, an audience of three hundred gathered to watch the beheading. Walsingham was determined to minimize Mary's influence as a martyr, and he ordered that the block, Mary's clothing and everything else relating to the execution be burned afterward in order to avoid the creation of any holy relics. He also planned a lavish funeral procession for his son-in-law, Sir Philip Sidney, to take place the following week. Sidney, a popular and heroic figure, had died fighting Catholics in the Netherlands, and Walsingham believed that a magnificent parade in his honor would dampen sympathy for Mary. However, Mary was equally determined that her final appearance should be a defiant gesture, an opportunity to reaffirm her Catholic faith and inspire her followers.

While the dean of Peterborough led the prayers, Mary spoke aloud her own prayers for the salvation of the English

Catholic Church, for her son and for Elizabeth. With her family motto, "In my end is my beginning," in her mind, she composed herself and approached the block. The executioners requested her forgiveness, and she replied, "I forgive you with all my heart, for now I hope you shall make an end of all my troubles." Richard Wingfield, in his *Narration of the Last Days of the Queen of Scots,* describes her final moments:

> Then she laide herself upon the blocke most quietlie, & stretching out her armes & legges cryed out In manus tuas domine three or foure times, & at the laste while one of the executioners held her slightlie with one of his handes, the other gave two strokes with an axe before he cutt of her head, & yet lefte a little gristle behinde at which time she made verie small noyse & stirred not any parte of herself from the place where she laye. . . . Her lipps stirred up & downe almost a quarter of an hower after her head was cutt of. Then one of her executioners plucking of her garters espied her little dogge which was crept under her clothes which could not be gotten forth but with force & afterwardes could not depart from her dead corpse, but came and laye betweene her head & shoulders a thing dilligently noted.

Figure 9 The execution of Mary Queen of Scots.

2

The Anonymous Codebreaker

The Vigenère cipher,
why cryptographers seldom get
credit for their breakthroughs
and a tale of buried treasure

For centuries, the simple monoalphabetic substitution cipher had been sufficient to ensure secrecy. The subsequent development of frequency analysis, first in the Arab world and then in Europe, destroyed its security. The tragic execution of Mary Queen of Scots was a dramatic illustration of the weaknesses of monoalphabetic substitution, and in the battle between cryptographers and cryptanalysts it was clear that the cryptanalysts had gained the upper hand. Anybody sending an encrypted message had to accept that an expert enemy codebreaker might intercept and decipher their most precious secrets.

The burden was clearly on the cryptographers to concoct a new, stronger cipher, something that could outwit the cryptanalysts. Although this cipher would not emerge until the end of the sixteenth century, its origins can be traced back to the fifteenth-century Florentine polymath Leon Battista Alberti. Born in 1404, Alberti was one of the leading figures of the Renaissance—a painter, composer, poet and philosopher, as well as the author of the first scientific analysis of perspective, a treatise on the housefly and a funeral oration for his dog. He is probably best known as an architect, having designed Rome's first Trevi Fountain and having written *De re aedificatoria,* the first printed book on architecture, which acted as a catalyst for the transition from Gothic to Renaissance design.

Sometime in the 1460s, Alberti was wandering through the gardens of the Vatican when he bumped into his friend Leonardo Dato, the pontifical secretary, who began chatting to him about some of the finer points of cryptography. This casual conversation prompted Alberti to write an essay on the subject, outlining what he believed to be a new form of cipher. At the time, all substitution ciphers required a single cipher alphabet for encrypting each message. However, Alberti proposed using two or more cipher alphabets and switching between them during encipherment, thereby confusing potential cryptanalysts.

Plain alphabet	a b c d e f g h i j k l m n o p q r s t u v w x y z
Cipher alphabet 1	F Z B V K I X A Y M E P L S D H J O R G N Q C U T W
Cipher alphabet 2	G O X B F W T H Q I L A P Z J D E S V Y C R K U H N

For example, here we have two possible cipher alphabets, and we could encrypt a message by alternating between them. To encrypt the message **hello**, we would encrypt the first letter according to the first cipher alphabet, so that **h** becomes **A**, but we would encrypt the second letter according to the second cipher alphabet, so that **e** becomes **F**. To encrypt the third letter we return to the first cipher alphabet, and to encrypt the fourth letter we return to the second alphabet. This means that the first **l** is enciphered as **P**, but the second **l** is enciphered as **A**. The final letter, **o**, is enciphered according to the first cipher alphabet and becomes **D**. The complete ciphertext reads **AFPAD**. The crucial advantage of Alberti's system is that the same letter in the plaintext does not necessarily appear as the same letter in the ciphertext, so the repeated l in **hello** is enciphered differently in each case. Similarly, the repeated A in the ciphertext represents a different plaintext letter in each case, first h and then l.

Blaise de Vigenère, a French diplomat born in 1523, became acquainted with the writings of Alberti when, at the age of twenty-six, he was sent to Rome on a two-year mission. To start with, his interest in cryptography was purely practical and was linked to his work. Then, at the age of thirty-nine, Vigenère decided that he had accumulated enough money to be able to abandon his career and concentrate on a life of study. It was only then that he examined Alberti's idea and turned it into a coherent and powerful new cipher, now known as the Vigenère cipher. The strength of the Vigenère cipher lies in its use of not one or two but twenty-six distinct cipher alphabets to encrypt a message. The first step in encipherment is to draw up a so-called *Vigenère square,* as shown in Table 3, a plaintext

Figure 10 Blaise de Vigenère.

alphabet followed by twenty-six cipher alphabets, each shifted by one letter with respect to the previous alphabet. Hence, row 1 represents a cipher alphabet with a Caesar shift of 1, which means that it could be used to implement a Caesar shift cipher in which every letter of the plaintext is replaced by the letter one place further on in the alphabet. Similarly, row 2 represents a cipher alphabet with a Caesar shift of 2, and so on. The top row of the square, in lowercase, represents the plaintext letters. You could encipher each plaintext letter according to any one of the twenty-six cipher alphabets. For example, if cipher alphabet number 2 is used, then the letter **a** is enciphered as **C**, but if cipher alphabet number 12 is used, then **a** is enciphered as **M**.

If the sender were to use just one of the cipher alphabets to encipher an entire message, this would effectively be a simple Caesar cipher, which would be a very weak form of encryption, easily deciphered by an enemy interceptor. However, in the Vigenère cipher a different row of the Vigenère square (a different cipher alphabet) is used to encrypt different letters of the message. In other words, the sender might encrypt the first letter according to row 5, the second according to row 14, the third according to row 21, and so on.

To unscramble the message, the intended receiver needs to know which row of the Vigenère square has been used to encipher each letter, so there must be an agreed system of switching between rows. This is achieved by using a keyword. To illustrate how a keyword is used with the Vigenère square to encrypt a sample message, let us encipher **divert troops to east ridge**, using the keyword **WHITE**. First of all, the keyword is spelled out above the message and repeated over and over again, so that each letter in the message is associated with a letter from the keyword, as shown on page 56. The ciphertext is then generated as follows. To encrypt the first letter, **d**, begin by identifying the key letter above it, **w**, which in turn defines a particular row in the Vigenère square. The row beginning with **w**, row 22, is the cipher alphabet that will be used to find the substitute letter for the plaintext **d**. We look to see where the column headed by **d** intersects the row beginning with **w**, which turns out to be at the letter **z**. Consequently,

Table 3 A Vigenère square.

Plain	a b c d e f g h i j k l m n o p q r s t u v w x y z
1	B C D E F G H I J K L M N O P Q R S T U V W X Y Z A
2	C D E F G H I J K L M N O P Q R S T U V W X Y Z A B
3	D E F G H I J K L M N O P Q R S T U V W X Y Z A B C
4	E F G H I J K L M N O P Q R S T U V W X Y Z A B C D
5	F G H I J K L M N O P Q R S T U V W X Y Z A B C D E
6	G H I J K L M N O P Q R S T U V W X Y Z A B C D E F
7	H I J K L M N O P Q R S T U V W X Y Z A B C D E F G
8	I J K L M N O P Q R S T U V W X Y Z A B C D E F G H
9	J K L M N O P Q R S T U V W X Y Z A B C D E F G H I
10	K L M N O P Q R S T U V W X Y Z A B C D E F G H I J
11	L M N O P Q R S T U V W X Y Z A B C D E F G H I J K
12	M N O P Q R S T U V W X Y Z A B C D E F G H I J K L
13	N O P Q R S T U V W X Y Z A B C D E F G H I J K L M
14	O P Q R S T U V W X Y Z A B C D E F G H I J K L M N
15	P Q R S T U V W X Y Z A B C D E F G H I J K L M N O
16	Q R S T U V W X Y Z A B C D E F G H I J K L M N O P
17	R S T U V W X Y Z A B C D E F G H I J K L M N O P Q
18	S T U V W X Y Z A B C D E F G H I J K L M N O P Q R
19	T U V W X Y Z A B C D E F G H I J K L M N O P Q R S
20	U V W X Y Z A B C D E F G H I J K L M N O P Q R S T
21	V W X Y Z A B C D E F G H I J K L M N O P Q R S T U
22	W X Y Z A B C D E F G H I J K L M N O P Q R S T U V
23	X Y Z A B C D E F G H I J K L M N O P Q R S T U V W
24	Y Z A B C D E F G H I J K L M N O P Q R S T U V W X
25	Z A B C D E F G H I J K L M N O P Q R S T U V W X Y
26	A B C D E F G H I J K L M N O P Q R S T U V W X Y Z

the letter **d** in the plaintext is represented by **Z** in the cipher-text.

Keyword	WH I T EWH I T EWH I T EWH I T EWH I
Plaintext	d i v e r t t r o o p s t o e a s t r i dg e
Ciphertext	Z P D X V P A Z H S L Z B H I WZ B K M Z N M

To encipher the second letter of the message, **i**, the process is repeated. The key letter above **i** is **H**, so it is encrypted via a different row in the Vigenère square: the **H** row (row 7), which is a new cipher alphabet. To encrypt **i**, we look to see where the column headed by **i** intersects the row beginning with **H**, which turns out to be at the letter **P**. Consequently, the letter **i** in the plaintext is represented by **P** in the ciphertext. Each letter of the keyword indicates a particular cipher alphabet within the Vigenère square, and because the keyword contains five letters, the sender encrypts the message by cycling through five rows of the Vigenère square. The fifth letter of the message is enciphered according to the fifth letter of the keyword, **E**, but to encipher the sixth letter of the message we have to return to the first letter of the keyword. A longer keyword, or perhaps a keyphrase, would bring more rows into the encryption process and increase the complexity of the cipher. Table 4 shows a Vigenère square, highlighting the five rows (i.e., the five cipher alphabets) defined by the keyword **WHITE**.

The great advantage of the Vigenère cipher is that it is invulnerable to the frequency analysis described in Chapter 1. For example, a cryptanalyst applying frequency analysis to a piece of ciphertext would usually begin by identifying the most common letter in the ciphertext, which in the case above is **Z**, and then assume that this represents the most common letter in English, **e**. In fact, the letter **Z** represents three different letters, **d**, **r** and **s**, but not **e**. This is clearly a problem for the cryptanalyst. The fact that a letter that appears several times in the ciphertext can represent a different plaintext letter on each occasion generates tremendous ambiguity for the cryptanalyst. Equally confusing is the fact that a letter that appears several times in the plaintext can be represented by different letters in the ciphertext. For example, the letter **o** is repeated in **troops**, but it is substituted by two different letters—the **oo** is enciphered as **HS**.

Table 4 A Vigenère square with the rows defined by the keyword **WHITE** highlighted. Encryption is achieved by switching among the five highlighted cipher alphabets, defined by **W, H, I, T** and **E**.

Plain	a b c d e f g h i j k l m n o p q r s t u v w x y z
1	B C D E F G H I J K L M N O P Q R S T U V W X Y Z A
2	C D E F G H I J K L M N O P Q R S T U V W X Y Z A B
3	D E F G H I J K L M N O P Q R S T U V W X Y Z A B C
4	E F G H I J K L M N O P Q R S T U V W X Y Z A B C D
5	F G H I J K L M N O P Q R S T U V W X Y Z A B C D E
6	G H I J K L M N O P Q R S T U V W X Y Z A B C D E F
7	H I J K L M N O P Q R S T U V W X Y Z A B C D E F G
8	I J K L M N O P Q R S T U V W X Y Z A B C D E F G H
9	J K L M N O P Q R S T U V W X Y Z A B C D E F G H I
10	K L M N O P Q R S T U V W X Y Z A B C D E F G H I J
11	L M N O P Q R S T U V W X Y Z A B C D E F G H I J K
12	M N O P Q R S T U V W X Y Z A B C D E F G H I J K L
13	N O P Q R S T U V W X Y Z A B C D E F G H I J K L M
14	O P Q R S T U V W X Y Z A B C D E F G H I J K L M N
15	P Q R S T U V W X Y Z A B C D E F G H I J K L M N O
16	Q R S T U V W X Y Z A B C D E F G H I J K L M N O P
17	R S T U V W X Y Z A B C D E F G H I J K L M N O P Q
18	S T U V W X Y Z A B C D E F G H I J K L M N O P Q R
19	T U V W X Y Z A B C D E F G H I J K L M N O P Q R S
20	U V W X Y Z A B C D E F G H I J K L M N O P Q R S T
21	V W X Y Z A B C D E F G H I J K L M N O P Q R S T U
22	W X Y Z A B C D E F G H I J K L M N O P Q R S T U V
23	X Y Z A B C D E F G H I J K L M N O P Q R S T U V W
24	Y Z A B C D E F G H I J K L M N O P Q R S T U V W X
25	Z A B C D E F G H I J K L M N O P Q R S T U V W X Y
26	A B C D E F G H I J K L M N O P Q R S T U V W X Y Z

As well as being invulnerable to frequency analysis, the Vigenère cipher has an enormous number of keys. The sender and receiver can agree on any word in the dictionary or any combination of words, or even fabricate words. A cryptanalyst would be unable to crack the message by searching all possible keys because the number of options is simply too great.

The traditional forms of substitution cipher, those that existed before the Vigenère cipher, were called monoalphabetic substitution ciphers because they used only one cipher alphabet per message. In contrast, the Vigenère cipher belongs to a class known as *polyalphabetic* because it employs several cipher alphabets per message.

In 1586 Vigenère published his work in *A Treatise on Secret Writing*. Although some people continued to use traditional ciphers (Appendix D), use of the Vigenère cipher spread during the seventeenth and eighteenth centuries, and the arrival of the telegraph in the nineteenth century suddenly made it popular within the business community.

The polyalphabetic Vigenère cipher was clearly the best way to ensure secrecy for important business communications that were transmitted via a telegraph operator, who would otherwise be able to read the contents of the message. The cipher was considered unbreakable, and became known as *le chiffre indéchiffrable*, the uncrackable cipher. Cryptographers had, for the time being at least, a clear lead over the cryptanalysts.

MR. BABBAGE VERSUS THE VIGENÈRE CIPHER

The most intriguing figure in nineteenth-century cryptanalysis is Charles Babbage, the eccentric British genius best known for developing the blueprint for the modern computer. He was born in 1791, the son of Benjamin Babbage, a wealthy London banker. When Charles married without his father's permission, he no longer had access to the Babbage fortune, but he still had enough money to be financially secure, and he pursued the life of a roving scholar, applying his mind to whatever problem tickled his fancy. His inventions include the speedometer and the cowcatcher, a device that could be fixed to the front of steam locomotives to clear cattle from railway tracks. In terms of scientific breakthroughs, he was the first to realize that the width of a tree ring depended on that year's weather, and he deduced that it was possible to determine past climates by studying ancient trees. He was also intrigued by statistics, and as a diversion he drew up a set of mortality tables, a basic tool for today's insurance industry.

The turning point in Babbage's scientific career came in 1821, when he and the astronomer John Herschel were examining a set of mathematical tables, the sort used as the basis for astronomical, engineering and navigational calculations. The two men were disgusted by the number of errors in the tables, which in turn would generate flaws in important calculations. One set of tables, the *Nautical Ephemeris for Finding Latitude and Longitude at Sea,* contained over a thousand errors. Indeed, many shipwrecks and engineering disasters were blamed on faulty tables.

These mathematical tables were calculated by hand, and the mistakes were simply the result of human error, causing Babbage to exclaim, "I wish to God these calculations had been executed by steam!" This marked the beginning of an extraordinary endeavor to build a machine capable of faultlessly calculating the tables to a high degree of accuracy. In 1823 Babbage designed Difference Engine No. 1, a magnificent calculator consisting of twenty-five thousand precision parts, to be built with government funding. Although Babbage was a brilliant innovator, he was not a great implementer. After ten years of toil, he abandoned Difference Engine No. 1, cooked up an entirely new design and set to work building Difference Engine No. 2.

When Babbage abandoned his first machine, the government lost confidence in him and decided to cut its losses by withdrawing from the project—it had already spent £17,470, enough to build a pair of battleships. It was probably this withdrawal of support that later prompted Babbage to make the following complaint: "Propose to an Englishman any principle, or any instrument, however admirable, and you will observe that the whole effort of the English mind is directed to find a difficulty, a defect, or an impossibility in it. If you speak to him of a machine for peeling a potato, he will pronounce it impossible: if you peel a potato with it before his eyes, he will declare it useless, because it will not slice a pineapple."

Lack of government funding meant that Babbage never completed Difference Engine No. 2. The scientific tragedy was

Figure 11 Charles Babbage.

that Babbage's machine would have offered a stepping-stone to the Analytical Engine, which, rather than merely calculating a specific set of tables, would have been able to solve a variety of mathematical problems depending on the instructions that it was given. In fact, the Analytical Engine provided a template for modern computers. The design included a "store" (memory) and a "mill" (processor), which would allow it to make decisions and repeat instructions, which are equivalent to the IF . . . THEN . . . and LOOP commands familiar in modern programming.

A century later, during the course of the Second World War, the first electronic incarnations of Babbage's machine would have a profound effect on cryptanalysis, but in his own lifetime, Babbage made an equally important contribution to codebreaking: He succeeded in breaking the Vigenère cipher, and in so doing he made the greatest breakthrough in cryptanalysis since the Arab scholars of the ninth century broke the monoalphabetic cipher by inventing frequency analysis. Babbage's work required no mechanical calculations or complex computations. Instead, he employed nothing more than sheer cunning.

Babbage had become interested in ciphers at a very young age. In later life, he recalled how his childhood hobby occasionally got him into trouble: "The bigger boys made ciphers, but if I got hold of a few words, I usually found out the key. The consequence of this ingenuity was occasionally painful: the owners of the detected ciphers sometimes thrashed me, though the fault lay in their own stupidity." These beatings did not discourage him, and he continued to be enchanted by cryptanalysis. He wrote in his autobiography that "deciphering is, in my opinion, one of the most fascinating of arts."

While most cryptanalysts had given up all hope of ever breaking the Vigenère cipher, Babbage was inspired to attempt a decipherment by an exchange of letters with John Hall Brock

Table 5 A Vigenère square used in combination with the keyword **KING**. The keyword defines four separate cipher alphabets, so that the letter **e** may be encrypted as **O, M, R** or **K**.

Plain	a b c d e f g h i j k l m n o p q r s t u v w x y z
1	B C D E F G H I J K L M N O P Q R S T U V W X Y Z A
2	C D E F G H I J K L M N O P Q R S T U V W X Y Z A B
3	D E F G H I J K L M N O P Q R S T U V W X Y Z A B C
4	E F G H I J K L M N O P Q R S T U V W X Y Z A B C D
5	F G H I J K L M N O P Q R S T U V W X Y Z A B C D E
6	G H I J K L M N O P Q R S T U V W X Y Z A B C D E F
7	H I J K L M N O P Q R S T U V W X Y Z A B C D E F G
8	I J K L M N O P Q R S T U V W X Y Z A B C D E F G H
9	J K L M N O P Q R S T U V W X Y Z A B C D E F G H I
10	K L M N O P Q R S T U V W X Y Z A B C D E F G H I J
11	L M N O P Q R S T U V W X Y Z A B C D E F G H I J K
12	M N O P Q R S T U V W X Y Z A B C D E F G H I J K L
13	N O P Q R S T U V W X Y Z A B C D E F G H I J K L M
14	O P Q R S T U V W X Y Z A B C D E F G H I J K L M N
15	P Q R S T U V W X Y Z A B C D E F G H I J K L M N O
16	Q R S T U V W X Y Z A B C D E F G H I J K L M N O P
17	R S T U V W X Y Z A B C D E F G H I J K L M N O P Q
18	S T U V W X Y Z A B C D E F G H I J K L M N O P Q R
19	T U V W X Y Z A B C D E F G H I J K L M N O P Q R S
20	U V W X Y Z A B C D E F G H I J K L M N O P Q R S T
21	V W X Y Z A B C D E F G H I J K L M N O P Q R S T U
22	W X Y Z A B C D E F G H I J K L M N O P Q R S T U V
23	X Y Z A B C D E F G H I J K L M N O P Q R S T U V W
24	Y Z A B C D E F G H I J K L M N O P Q R S T U V W X
25	Z A B C D E F G H I J K L M N O P Q R S T U V W X Y
26	A B C D E F G H I J K L M N O P Q R S T U V W X Y Z

Thwaites, a dentist from Bristol with a rather innocent view of ciphers. In 1854, Thwaites claimed to have invented a new cipher, which, in fact, was equivalent to the Vigenère cipher. He wrote to the *Journal of the Society of Arts* with the intention of patenting his idea, apparently unaware that he was several centuries too late. Babbage too wrote to the society, pointing out that "the cypher . . . is a very old one, and to be found in most books." Thwaites was unapologetic and challenged Babbage to break his cipher. Whether or not it was breakable was irrelevant to whether or not it was new, but Babbage's curiosity was sufficiently aroused for him to embark on a search for a weakness in the Vigenère cipher.

Cracking a difficult cipher is akin to climbing a sheer cliff face: The cryptanalyst is seeking any nook or cranny that could provide the slightest foothold. In a monoalphabetic cipher the cryptanalyst will latch on to the frequency of the letters, because the commonest letters, such as **e**, **t** and **a**, will stand out no matter how they have been disguised. In the polyalphabetic Vigenère cipher the frequencies are much more balanced, because the keyword is used to switch between cipher alphabets. Hence, at first sight, the rock face seems perfectly smooth.

Remember, the great strength of the Vigenère cipher is that the same letter will be enciphered in different ways. For example, if the keyword is **KING**, then every letter in the plaintext can potentially be enciphered in four different ways, because the keyword contains four letters. Each letter of the keyword defines a different cipher alphabet in the Vigenère square, as shown in Table 5. The **e** column of the square has been highlighted to show how it is enciphered differently, depending on which letter of the keyword is defining the encipherment:

If the **K** of **KING** is used to encipher **e**, then the resulting ciphertext letter is **O**.
If the **I** of **KING** is used to encipher **e**, then the resulting ciphertext letter is **M**.
If the **N** of **KING** is used to encipher **e**, then the resulting ciphertext letter is **R**.
If the **G** of **KING** is used to encipher **e**, then the resulting ciphertext letter is **K**.

Similarly, whole words will be enciphered in different ways: the word **the**, for example, could be enciphered as **DPR, BUK, GNO** or **ZRM**, depending on its position relative to the keyword. Although this makes cryptanalysis difficult, it is not impossible.

The important point to note is that if there are only four ways to encipher the word **the**, and the original message contains several instances of the word **the**, then it is inevitable that some of the four possible encipherments will be repeated in the ciphertext. This is demonstrated in the following example, in which the line **the sun and the man in the moon** has been enciphered using the Vigenère cipher and the keyword **KING**.

Keyword	K I N G K I N G K I N G K I N G K I N G K I N G
Plaintext	t h e s u n a n d t h e m a n i n t h e m o o n
Ciphertext	D P R Y E V N T N B U K W I A O X B U K W W B T

The word **the** is enciphered as **DPR** in the first instance, and then as **BUK** on the second and third occasions. The reason for the repetition of **BUK** is that the second **the** is displaced by eight letters with respect to the third **the**, and eight is a multiple of the length of the keyword, which is four letters long. In other words, the second **the** was enciphered according to its relationship to the keyword (**the** is directly below **ING**), and by the time we reach the third **the**, the keyword has cycled around exactly twice, to repeat the relationship, and hence repeat the encipherment.

Babbage realized that this sort of repetition provided him with exactly the foothold he needed in order to conquer the Vigenère cipher. He was able to define a series of relatively simple steps that could be followed by any cryptanalyst to crack the hitherto uncrackable cipher. To demonstrate his brilliant technique, let us imagine that we have intercepted the ciphertext shown in Figure 12. We know that it was enciphered using the Vigenère cipher, but we know nothing about the original message, and the keyword is a mystery.

The first stage in Babbage's cryptanalysis is to look for sequences of letters that appear more than once in the ciphertext.

WU B E F I Q L Z U R M V O F E H M Y M W T
I X C G T M P I F K R Z U P M V O I R Q M M
WO Z M P U L M B N Y V Q Q Q M V M V J L E
Y M H F E F N Z P S D L P P S D L P E V Q M
W C X Y M D A V Q E E F I Q C A Y T Q O W C
X Y M W M S E M E F C F W Y E Y Q E T R L I
Q Y C G M T W C W F B S M Y F P L R X T Q Y
E E X M R U L U K S G W F P T L R Q A E R L
U V P M V Y Q Y C X T W F Q L M T E L S F J
P Q E H M O Z C I W C I W F P Z S L M A E Z
I Q V L Q M Z V P P X A W C S M Z M O R V G
V V Q S Z E T R L Q Z P B J A Z V Q I Y X E
WWO I C C G D W H Q M M V O W S G N T J P
F P P A Y B I Y B J U T W R L Q K L L L M D
P Y V A C D C F Q N Z P I F P P K S D V P T
I D G X M Q Q V E B M Q A L K E Z M G C V K
U Z K I Z B Z L I U A M M V Z

Figure 12 The ciphertext, enciphered using the Vigenère cipher.

There are two ways that such repetitions could arise. The most likely is that the same sequence of letters in the plaintext has been enciphered using the same part of the key. Alternatively, there is a slight possibility that two different sequences of letters in the plaintext have been enciphered using different parts of the key, coincidentally leading to the identical sequence in the ciphertext. If we restrict ourselves to long sequences, then we largely discount the second possibility, and in this case we shall consider repeated sequences only if they consist of four letters or more. Table 6 is a log of such repetitions, along with the spacing between the repetition. For example, the sequence **E-F-I-Q** appears in the first line of the ciphertext and then in the fifth line, shifted forward by 95 letters.

As well as being used to encipher the plaintext into ciphertext, the keyword is used by the receiver to decipher the ciphertext back into plaintext. Hence, if we could identify the keyword, deciphering the text would be easy. At this stage we do not have enough information to work out the keyword, but Table 6 does provide some very good clues as to its length. Having listed which sequences repeat themselves and the spacing between these repetitions, the rest of the table is given over to identifying the *factors* of the spacing—the numbers that will divide into the spacing. For example, the sequence **W-C-X-Y-M** repeats itself after twenty letters, and the numbers 1, 2, 4, 5, 10 and 20 are factors, because they divide perfectly into 20 without leaving a remainder. These factors suggest six possibilities:

1. The key is 1 letter long and is recycled 20 times between encryptions.
2. The key is 2 letters long and is recycled 10 times between encryptions.
3. The key is 4 letters long and is recycled 5 times between encryptions.
4. The key is 5 letters long and is recycled 4 times between encryptions.
5. The key is 10 letters long and is recycled 2 times between encryptions.
6. The key is 20 letters long and is recycled 1 time between encryptions.

The first possibility can be excluded, because a key that is only 1 letter long gives rise to a monoalphabetic cipher—only one

Table 6 Repetitions and spacings in the ciphertext.

Repeated sequence	Repeat spacing	2	3	4	5	6	7	8	9	10	11	12	13	14	15	16	17	18	19	20
E-F-I-Q	95				✓														✓	
P-S-D-L-P	5				✓															
W-C-X-Y-M	20	✓		✓	✓					✓										✓
E-T-R-L	120	✓	✓	✓	✓	✓		✓		✓		✓			✓					✓

Possible length of key (or factors)

row of the Vigenère square would be used for the entire encryption, and the cipher alphabet would remain unchanged; it is unlikely that a cryptographer would do this. To indicate each of the other possibilities, a check mark is placed in the appropriate column of Table 6. Each check mark indicates a potential key length.

To identify whether the key is two, four, five, ten or twenty letters long, we need to look at the factors of all the other spacings. Because the keyword seems to be twenty letters or smaller, Table 6 lists those factors that are 20 or smaller for each of the other spacings. There is a clear tendency toward a spacing divisible by 5. In fact, every spacing is divisible by 5. The first repeated sequence, E-F-I-Q, can be explained by a keyword of length five recycled nineteen times between the first and second encryptions. The second repeated sequence, P-S-D-L-P, can be explained by a keyword of length five recycled just once between the first and second encryptions. The third repeated sequence, W-C-X-Y-M, can be explained by a keyword of length five recycled four times between the first and second encryptions. The fourth repeated sequence, E-T-R-L, can be explained by a keyword of length five recycled twenty-four times between the first and second encryptions. In short, everything is consistent with a five-letter keyword.

Assuming that the keyword is indeed five letters long, the next step is to work out the actual letters of the keyword. For the time being, let us call the keyword L_1-L_2-L_3-L_4-L_5, such that L_1 represents the first letter of the keyword, and so on. The process of encipherment would have begun with enciphering the first letter of the plaintext according to the first letter of the keyword, L_1. The letter L_1 defines one row of the Vigenère square and effectively provides a monoalphabetic substitution cipher alphabet for the first letter of the plaintext. However, when it comes to encrypting the second letter of the plaintext, the cryptographer would have used L_2 to define a different row of the Vigenère square, effectively providing a different monoalphabetic substitution cipher alphabet. The third letter of plaintext would be encrypted according to L_3, the fourth according to L_4, and the fifth according to L_5. Each letter of the keyword is providing a different cipher alphabet for encryption. However, the sixth letter of the plaintext would once again be encrypted according to L_1, the seventh letter of the plaintext would once again be encrypted according to L_2, and the cycle repeats itself thereafter. In other words, the polyalphabetic cipher consists of five monoalphabetic ciphers, each monoalphabetic cipher is responsible for encrypting one-fifth of the entire message and, most importantly, we already know how to cryptanalyze monoalphabetic ciphers.

We proceed as follows. We know that one of the rows of the Vigenère square, defined by L_1, provided the cipher alphabet to encrypt the first, sixth, eleventh, sixteenth, . . . letters of the message. Hence, if we look at the first, sixth, eleventh, sixteenth, . . . letters of the ciphertext, we should be able to use old-fashioned frequency analysis to work out the cipher alphabet in question. Figure 13 shows the frequency distribution of the letters that appear in the first, sixth, eleventh, sixteenth, . . . positions of the ciphertext, which are W, I, R, E, . . . At this point, remember that each cipher alphabet in the Vigenère square is simply a standard alphabet shifted by between 1 and 26 spaces. Hence, the frequency distribution in Figure 13 should have similar features to the frequency distribution of a standard alphabet, except that it will have been shifted by some distance. By comparing the L_1 distribution with the standard distribution, it should be possible to work out the shift. Figure 14 shows the standard frequency distribution for a piece of English plaintext.

The standard distribution has peaks, plateaus and valleys,

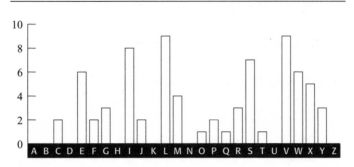

Figure 13 Frequency distribution for letters in the ciphertext encrypted using the L_1 cipher alphabet (number of occurrences).

and to match it with the L_1 cipher distribution we look for the most outstanding combination of features. For example, the three spikes at **R-S-T** in the standard distribution (Figure 14) and the long depression to its right that stretches across six letters from **U** to **Z** together form a very distinctive pair of features. The only similar features in the L_1 distribution (Figure 13) are the three spikes at **V-W-X**, followed by the depression stretching six letters from **Y** to **D**. This would suggest that all the letters encrypted according to L_1 have been shifted four

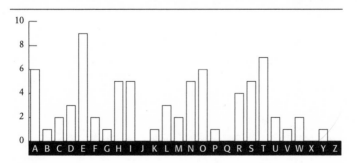

Figure 14 Standard frequency distribution (number of occurrences based on a piece of plaintext containing the same number of letters as in the ciphertext).

places, or that L_1 defines a cipher alphabet that begins E, F, G, H, . . . In turn, this means that the first letter of the keyword, L_1, is probably E. This hypothesis can be tested by shifting the L_1 distribution back four letters and comparing it with the standard distribution. Figure 15 shows both distributions for comparison. The match between the major peaks is very strong, implying that it is safe to assume that the keyword does indeed begin with E.

To summarize, searching for repetitions in the ciphertext has allowed us to identify the length of the keyword, which turned out to be five letters long. This allowed us to split the ciphertext into five parts, each one enciphered according to a monoalphabetic substitution as defined by one letter of the

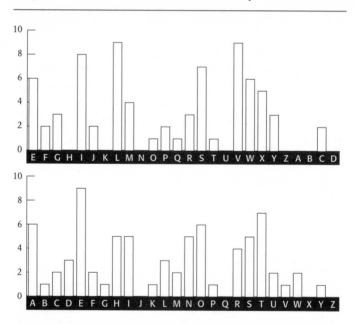

Figure 15 The L_1 distribution shifted back four letters (top), compared with the standard frequency distribution (bottom). All major peaks and troughs match.

keyword. By analyzing the fraction of the ciphertext that was enciphered according to the first letter of the keyword, we have been able to show that this letter, L_1, is probably E. This process is repeated in order to identify the second letter of the keyword. A frequency distribution is established for the second, seventh, twelfth, seventeenth, ... letters in the ciphertext. Again, the resulting distribution, shown in Figure 16, is compared with the standard distribution in order to deduce the shift.

This distribution is harder to analyze. There are no obvious candidates for the three neighboring peaks that correspond to R-S-T. However, the depression that stretches from G to L is very distinct and probably corresponds to the depression we expect to see stretching from U to Z in the standard distribution. If this were the case, we would expect the three R-S-T peaks to appear at D, E and F, but the peak at E is missing. For the time being, we shall dismiss the missing peak as a statistical glitch and go with our initial hunch, which is that the depression from G to L is a recognizably shifted feature. This would suggest that all the

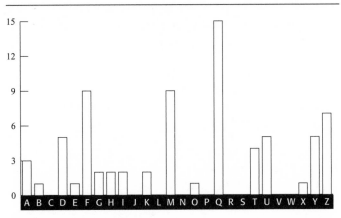

Figure 16 Frequency distribution for letters in the ciphertext encrypted using the L_2 cipher alphabet (number of occurrences).

letters encrypted according to L_2 have been shifted twelve places, or that L_2 defines a cipher alphabet that begins M, N, O, P, . . . and that the second letter of the keyword, L_2, is M. Once again, this hypothesis could be tested by shifting the L_2 distribution back twelve letters and comparing it with the standard distribution.

I shall not continue the analysis; suffice it to say that analyzing the third, eighth, thirteenth, . . . letters implies that the third letter of the keyword is I; analyzing the fourth, ninth, fourteenth, . . . letters implies that the fourth letter is L; and analyzing the fifth, tenth, fifteenth, . . . letters implies that the fifth letter is Y. The keyword is EMILY. It is now possible to reverse the Vigenère cipher and complete the cryptanalysis. The first letter of the ciphertext is W, and it was encrypted according to the first letter of the keyword, E. Working backward, we look at the Vigenère square and find W in the row beginning with E, and then we find which letter is at the top of that column. The letter is s, which must make it the first letter of the plaintext. By repeating this process, we see that the plaintext begins sittheedownandhavenoshamecheekbyjowl. By inserting suitable word breaks and punctuation, we eventually get:

> Sit thee down, and have no shame,
> Cheek by jowl, and knee by knee:
> What care I for any name?
> What for order or degree?
>
> Let me screw thee up a peg:
> Let me loose thy tongue with wine:
> Callest thou that thing a leg?
> Which is thinnest? thine or mine?
>
> Thou shalt not be saved by works:
> Thou hast been a sinner too:

Ruined trunks on withered forks,
Empty scarecrows, I and you!

Fill the cup, and fill the can:
Have a rouse before the morn:
Every moment dies a man,
Every moment one is born.

These are verses from a poem by Alfred, Lord Tennyson entitled "The Vision of Sin." The keyword happens to be the first name of Tennyson's wife, Emily Sellwood. I chose to use a section from this particular poem as an example for cryptanalysis because it inspired some curious correspondence between Babbage and the great poet. Being an avid statistician and compiler of mortality tables, Babbage was irritated by the lines "Every moment dies a man / Every moment one is born," which are the last lines of the plaintext above. Consequently, he offered a correction to Tennyson's "otherwise beautiful" poem:

> It must be manifest that if this were true, the population of the world would be at a standstill. . . . I would suggest that in the next edition of your poem you have it read—"Every moment dies a man, Every moment $1\frac{1}{16}$ is born." . . . The actual figure is so long I cannot get it onto a line, but I believe the figure $1\frac{1}{16}$ will be sufficiently accurate for poetry.
>
> I am, Sir, yours, etc.,
>
> Charles Babbage.

Babbage's successful cryptanalysis of the Vigenère cipher was probably achieved in 1854, soon after his spat with Thwaites, but his discovery went completely unrecognized because he never published it. The discovery came to light only in the twentieth century, when scholars examined Babbage's extensive notes. In the meantime, his technique was independently discovered by Friedrich Wilhelm Kasiski, a retired Prussian army officer. Ever since 1863, when he published his cryptanalytic breakthrough in *Die Geheimschriften und die Dechiffrirkunst* (Secret Writing and the Art of Deciphering), the technique has been known as the Kasiski test, and Babbage's contribution has been largely ignored.

And why did Babbage fail to publicize his cracking of such a vital cipher? He certainly had a habit of not finishing projects and not publishing his discoveries, which might suggest that this is just one more example of his lackadaisical attitude. However, there is an alternate explanation for his anonymity. His discovery occurred soon after the outbreak of the Crimean War, and one theory is that it gave the British a clear advantage over their Russian enemy. It is quite possible that the British military demanded that Babbage keep his work secret, thus providing them with a nine-year head start over the rest of the world. If this was the case, then it would fit in with the long-standing tradition of hushing up codebreaking achievements in the interests of national security, a practice that has continued into the twentieth century.

FROM AGONY COLUMNS TO BURIED TREASURE

The development of the telegraph, which had driven a commercial interest in cryptography, was also responsible for generating public interest in cryptography. The public became aware of the need to protect personal messages of a highly sensitive nature, and they would use encryption if necessary, even though it then took more time to send the message, which added to the cost of the telegram.

As people became comfortable with encipherment, they began to express their cryptographic skills in a variety of ways. For example, young lovers in Victorian England were often forbidden from publicly expressing their affection, and could not even communicate by letter in case their parents intercepted and read the contents. This resulted in lovers sending encrypted messages to each other via the personal columns of newspapers. These "agony columns," as they became known, provoked the curiosity of cryptanalysts, who would scan the notes and try to decipher their titillating contents. Charles Babbage is known to have indulged in this activity, along with his friend Sir Charles Wheatstone. On one occasion, Wheatstone deciphered a note in the *Times* from an Oxford student, suggesting to his true love that they elope. A few days later, Wheatstone inserted his own message, encrypted in the same cipher, advising the couple against this rebellious and rash action. Shortly afterward there appeared a third message, this time unencrypted and from the lady in question: "Dear Charlie, Write no more. Our cipher is discovered."

Another example of the public's familiarity with cryptography was the widespread use of pinprick encryption. The ancient Greek historian Aeneas the Tactician suggested conveying a secret message by pricking tiny holes under particular letters in an apparently innocuous page of text, just as there are dots under some letters in this paragraph. Those letters would spell out a secret message, easily read by the intended receiver. However, any intermediary who stared at the page would probably be oblivious to the barely perceptible pinpricks and would probably be unaware of the secret message. Two thousand years later, British letter writers used exactly the same method, not to achieve secrecy but to avoid paying excessive postage costs. Before the overhaul of the postage system in the mid-1800s, sending a letter cost about a shilling for every hundred miles, beyond the means of most people. However, newspapers could be posted free of charge, and this provided a loophole for thrifty Victorians. Instead of writing and sending letters, people began to use pinpricks to spell out a message on the front page of a newspaper. They could then send the newspaper through the post without having to pay a penny.

The public's growing fascination with cryptographic techniques meant that codes and ciphers soon found their way into nineteenth-century literature. In Jules Verne's *Journey to the Center of the Earth*, the decipherment of a parchment filled with runic characters prompts the first step on the epic journey. The characters are part of a substitution cipher that generates a Latin script, which in turn makes sense only when the letters are reversed: "Descend the crater of the volcano of Sneffels when the shadow of Scartaris comes to caress it before the calends of July, audacious voyager, and you will reach the center of the Earth." In 1885, Verne also used a cipher as a pivotal element in his novel *Mathias Sandorff.* In Britain, one of the finest writers of cryptographic fiction was Sir Arthur Conan Doyle. Not surprisingly, Sherlock Holmes was an expert in cryptography and, as he explained to Dr. Watson, was "the author of a trifling monograph upon the subject in which I analyze one hundred and sixty separate ciphers." The most famous of Holmes' decipherments is told in "The Adventure of the Dancing Men," which involves a cipher consisting of stick men, each pose representing a distinct letter.

On the other side of the Atlantic, Edgar Allan Poe was also developing an interest in cryptanalysis. Writing for Philadelphia's *Alexander Weekly Messenger,* he issued a challenge to readers, claiming that he could decipher any monoalphabetic substitution cipher. Hundreds of readers sent in their ciphertexts, and he successfully deciphered them all. Although this required nothing more than frequency analysis, Poe's readers were astonished by his achievements. One adoring fan proclaimed him "the most profound and skilful cryptographer who ever lived."

In 1843, hoping to exploit the interest he had generated, Poe wrote a short story about ciphers that is widely acknowledged by professional cryptographers to be the finest piece of fictional literature on the subject. "The Gold Bug" tells the story of William Legrand, who discovers an unusual beetle, the gold bug, and collects it using a scrap of paper lying nearby. That evening he sketches the gold bug upon the same piece of paper, and then holds his drawing up to the light of the fire to check its accuracy. However, his sketch is obliterated by an invisible ink, which has been developed by the heat of the flames. Legrand examines the characters that have emerged and becomes convinced that he has in his hands the encrypted directions for finding Captain Kidd's treasure. The remainder of the story is a classic demonstration of frequency analysis, resulting in the decipherment of Captain Kidd's clues and the discovery of his buried treasure.

Although "The Gold Bug" is pure fiction, there is a true nineteenth-century story containing many of the same elements. The case of the Beale ciphers involves Wild West escapades, a cowboy who amassed a vast fortune, a buried treasure worth $20 million and a mysterious set of encrypted papers describing its whereabouts. Much of what we know about this story, including the encrypted papers, is contained in a pamphlet published in 1885. Although only twenty-three pages long, the pamphlet has baffled generations of cryptanalysts and captivated hundreds of treasure hunters.

Figure 17 A section of the ciphertext from *The Adventures of the Dancing Men*, a Sherlock Holmes adventure by Sir Arthur Conan Doyle.

The story begins at the Washington Hotel in Lynchburg, Virginia, sixty-five years before the publication of the pamphlet. According to the pamphlet, the hotel owner, Robert Morriss, was held in high regard: "His kind disposition, strict probity, excellent management, and well ordered household, soon rendered him famous as a host, and his reputation extended even to other States." In January 1820 a stranger by the name of Thomas J. Beale rode into Lynchburg and checked into the Washington Hotel. "In person, he was about six feet in height," recalled Morriss, "with jet black eyes and hair of the same color, worn longer than was the style at the time. His form was symmetrical, and gave evidence of unusual strength and activity; but his distinguishing feature was a dark and swarthy complexion." Although Beale spent the rest of the winter with Morriss and was "extremely popular with every one, particularly the ladies," he never spoke about his background, his family or the purpose of his visit. Then, at the end of March, he left as suddenly as he had arrived.

Two years later, in January 1822, Beale returned to the Washington Hotel, "darker and swarthier than ever." Once again, he spent the rest of the winter in Lynchburg and disappeared in the spring, but not before he entrusted Morriss with a locked iron box, which he said contained "papers of value and importance." Morriss placed the box in a safe and thought nothing more about it or its contents until he received a letter from Beale, dated May 9, 1822, and sent from St. Louis. After a few pleasantries and a paragraph about an intended trip to the plains "to hunt the buffalo and encounter the savage grizzlies," Beale's letter revealed the significance of the box:

> It contains papers vitally affecting the fortunes of myself and many others engaged in business with me, and in the event of my death, its loss might be irreparable. You will, therefore, see the necessity of guarding it with vigilance and care to prevent

so great a catastrophe. Should none of us ever return you will please preserve carefully the box for the period of ten years from the date of this letter, and if I, or no one with authority from me, during that time demands its restoration, you will open it, which can be done by removing the lock. You will find, in addition to the papers addressed to you, other papers which will be unintelligible without the aid of a key to assist you. Such a key I have left in the hand of a friend in this place, sealed and addressed to yourself, and endorsed not to be delivered until June 1832. By means of this you will understand fully all you will be required to do.

Morriss dutifully continued to guard the box, waiting for Beale to collect it, but the swarthy man of mystery never returned to Lynchburg. He disappeared without explanation, never to be seen again. Ten years later, Morriss could have followed the letter's instructions and opened the box, but he seems to have been reluctant to break the lock. Beale's letter had mentioned that a note would be sent to Morriss in June 1832, and this was supposed to explain how to decipher the contents of the box. However, the note never arrived, and perhaps Morriss felt that there was no point opening the box if he could not decipher what was inside it. Eventually, in 1845, Morriss' curiosity got the better of him and he cracked open the lock. The box contained three sheets of enciphered characters, and a note written by Beale in plain English.

The intriguing note revealed the truth about Beale, the box and the ciphers. It explained that in April 1817, almost three years before his first meeting with Morriss, Beale and twenty-nine others had embarked on a journey across America. After traveling through the rich hunting grounds of the western plains, they arrived in Santa Fe, and spent the winter in the "little Mexican town." In March they headed north and began tracking an "immense herd of buffaloes," picking off as many

THE

BEALE PAPERS,

CONTAINING

AUTHENTIC STATEMENTS

REGARDING THE

TREASURE BURIED

IN ,

1819 AND 1821,

NEAR

BUFORDS, IN BEDFORD COUNTY, VIRGINIA,

AND

WHICH HAS NEVER BEEN RECOVERED.

PRICE FIFTY CENTS.

LYNCHBURG:
VIRGINIAN BOOK AND JOB PRINT,
1885.

Figure 18 The title page of *The Beale Papers,* the pamphlet that contains all we know about the mystery of the Beale treasure.

as possible along the way. Then, according to Beale, they struck lucky:

> One day, while following them, the party encamped in a small ravine, some 250 or 300 miles north of Santa Fé, and, with their horses tethered, were preparing their evening meal, when one of the men discovered in a cleft of the rocks something that had the appearance of gold. Upon showing it to the others it was pronounced to be gold, and much excitement was the natural consequence.

The letter went on to explain that Beale and his men, with help from the local tribe, mined the site for the next eighteen months, by which time they had accumulated a large quantity of gold, as well as some silver that was found nearby. In due course they agreed that their newfound wealth should be moved to a secure place, and decided to take it back home to Virginia, where they would hide it in a secret location. In 1820, Beale traveled to Lynchburg with the gold and silver, found a suitable location, and buried it. It was on this occasion that he first lodged at the Washington Hotel and made the acquaintance of Morriss. When Beale left at the end of the winter, he rejoined his men, who had continued to work the mine during his absence.

After another eighteen months Beale revisited Lynchburg with even more to add to his stash. This time there was an additional reason for his trip:

> Before leaving my companions on the plains it was suggested that, in case of an accident to ourselves, the treasure so concealed would be lost to their relatives, without some provision against such a contingency. I was, therefore, instructed to select some perfectly reliable person, if such could be found, who should, in the event of this proving acceptable to the party, be confided in to carry out their wishes in regard to their respective shares.

Beale believed that Morriss was a man of integrity, which is why he trusted him with the box containing the three enciphered sheets, the so-called Beale ciphers. Each enciphered sheet contained an array of numbers (reprinted here as Figures 19, 20 and 21), and deciphering the numbers would reveal all the relevant details; the first sheet described the treasure's location, the second outlined the contents of the treasure and the third listed the relatives of the men who should receive a share of the treasure. When Morriss read all of this, it was some twenty-three years after he had last seen Thomas Beale. Working on the assumption that Beale and his men were dead, Morriss felt obliged to find the gold and share it among their relatives. However, without the promised key, he was forced to decipher the ciphers from scratch, a task that troubled his mind for the next twenty years, and which ended in failure.

In 1862, at the age of eighty-four, Morriss knew that he was coming to the end of his life, and that he had to share the secret of the Beale ciphers, otherwise any hope of carrying out Beale's wishes would die with him. Morriss confided in a friend, but unfortunately the identity of this person remains a mystery. All we know about Morriss' friend is that it was he who wrote the pamphlet in 1885, so hereafter I will refer to him simply as *the author*. The author explained the reasons for his anonymity within the pamphlet:

> I anticipate for these papers a large circulation, and, to avoid the multitude of letters with which I should be assailed from all sections of the Union, propounding all sorts of questions, and requiring answers which, if attended to, would absorb my entire time, and only change the character of my work, I have decided upon withdrawing my name from the publication, after assuring all interested that I have given all that I know of the matter, and that I cannot add one word to the statements herein contained.

71, 194, 38, 1701, 89, 76, 11, 83, 1629, 48, 94, 63, 132, 16, 111, 95, 84, 341,
975, 14, 40, 64, 27, 81, 139, 213, 63, 90, 1120, 8, 15, 3, 126, 2018, 40, 74, 758,
485, 604, 230, 436, 664, 582, 150, 251, 284, 308, 231, 124, 211, 486, 225, 401,
370, 11, 101, 305, 139, 189, 17, 33, 88, 208, 193, 145, 1, 94, 73, 416, 918, 263,
28, 500, 538, 356, 117, 136, 219, 27, 176, 130, 10, 460, 25, 485, 18, 436, 65, 84,
200, 283, 118, 320, 138, 36, 416, 280, 15, 71, 224, 961, 44, 16, 401, 39, 88, 61,
304, 12, 21, 24, 283, 134, 92, 63, 246, 486, 682, 7, 219, 184, 360, 780, 18, 64,
463, 474, 131, 160, 79, 73, 440, 95, 18, 64, 581, 34, 69, 128, 367, 460, 17, 81,
12, 103, 820, 62, 116, 97, 103, 862, 70, 60, 1317, 471, 540, 208, 121, 890, 346,
36, 150, 59, 568, 614, 13, 120, 63, 219, 812, 2160, 1780, 99, 35, 18, 21, 136,
872, 15, 28, 170, 88, 4, 30, 44, 112, 18, 147, 436, 195, 320, 37, 122, 113, 6, 140,
8, 120, 305, 42, 58, 461, 44, 106, 301, 13, 408, 680, 93, 86, 116, 530, 82, 568, 9,
102, 38, 416, 89, 71, 216, 728, 965, 818, 2, 38, 121, 195, 14, 326, 148, 234, 18,
55, 131, 234, 361, 824, 5, 81, 623, 48, 961, 19, 26, 33, 10, 1101, 365, 92, 88,
181, 275, 346, 201, 206, 86, 36, 219, 324, 829, 840, 64, 326, 19, 48, 122, 85,
216, 284, 919, 861, 326, 985, 233, 64, 68, 232, 431, 960, 50, 29, 81, 216, 321,
603, 14, 612, 81, 360, 36, 51, 62, 194, 78, 60, 200, 314, 676, 112, 4, 28, 18, 61,
136, 247, 819, 921, 1060, 464, 895, 10, 6, 66, 119, 38, 41, 49, 602, 423, 962,
302, 294, 875, 78, 14, 23, 111, 109, 62, 31, 501, 823, 216, 280, 34, 24, 150,
1000, 162, 286, 19, 21, 17, 340, 19, 242, 31, 86, 234, 140, 607, 115, 33, 191, 67,
104, 86, 52, 88, 16, 80, 121, 67, 95, 122, 216, 548, 96, 11, 201, 77, 364, 218, 65,
667, 890, 236, 154, 211, 10, 98, 34, 119, 56, 216, 119, 71, 218, 1164, 1496,
1817, 51, 39, 210, 36, 3, 19, 540, 232, 22, 141, 617, 84, 290, 80, 46, 207, 411,
150, 29, 38, 46, 172, 85, 194, 39, 261, 543, 897, 624, 18, 212, 416, 127, 931, 19,
4, 63, 96, 12, 101, 418, 16, 140, 230, 460, 538, 19, 27, 88, 612, 1431, 90, 716,
275, 74, 83, 11, 426, 89, 72, 84, 1300, 1706, 814, 221, 132, 40, 102, 34, 868,
975, 1101, 84, 16, 79, 23, 16, 81, 122, 324, 403, 912, 227, 936, 447, 55, 86, 34,
43, 212, 107, 96, 314, 264, 1065, 323, 428, 601, 203, 124, 95, 216, 814, 2906,
654, 820, 2, 301, 112, 176, 213, 71, 87, 96, 202, 35, 10, 2, 41, 17, 84, 221, 736,
820, 214, 11, 60, 760.

Figure 19 The first Beale cipher.

115, 73, 24, 807, 37, 52, 49, 17, 31, 62, 647, 22, 7, 15, 140, 47, 29, 107, 79, 84, 56,
239, 10, 26, 811, 5, 196, 308, 85, 52, 160, 136, 59, 211, 36, 9, 46, 316, 554, 122, 106,
95, 53, 58, 2, 42, 7, 35, 122, 53, 31, 82, 77, 250, 196, 56, 96, 118, 71, 140, 287, 28,
353, 37, 1005, 65, 147, 807, 24, 3, 8, 12, 47, 43, 59, 807, 45, 316, 101, 41, 78, 154,
1005, 122, 138, 191, 16, 77, 49, 102, 57, 72, 34, 73, 85, 35, 371, 59, 196, 81, 92, 191,
106, 273, 60, 394, 620, 270, 220, 106, 388, 287, 63, 3, 6, 191, 122, 43, 234, 400, 106,
290, 314, 47, 48, 81, 96, 26, 115, 92, 158, 191, 110, 77, 85, 197, 46, 10, 113, 140,
353, 48, 120, 106, 2, 607, 61, 420, 811, 29, 125, 14, 20, 37, 105, 28, 248, 16, 159, 7,
35, 19, 301, 125, 110, 486, 287, 98, 117, 511, 62, 51, 220, 37, 113, 140, 807, 138,
540, 8, 44, 287, 388, 117, 18, 79, 344, 34, 20, 59, 511, 548, 107, 603, 220, 7, 66, 154,
41, 20, 50, 6, 575, 122, 154, 248, 110, 61, 52, 33, 30, 5, 38, 8, 14, 84, 57, 540, 217,
115, 71, 29, 84, 63, 43, 131, 29, 138, 47, 73, 239, 540, 52, 53, 79, 118, 51, 44, 63,
196, 12, 239, 112, 3, 49, 79, 353, 105, 56, 371, 557, 211, 515, 125, 360, 133, 143,
101, 15, 284, 540, 252, 14, 205, 140, 344, 26, 811, 138, 115, 48, 73, 34, 205, 316,
607, 63, 220, 7, 52, 150, 44, 52, 16, 40, 37, 158, 807, 37, 121, 12, 95, 10, 15, 35, 12,
131, 62, 115, 102, 807, 49, 53, 135, 138, 30, 31, 62, 67, 41, 85, 63, 10, 106, 807, 138,
8, 113, 20, 32, 33, 37, 353, 287, 140, 47, 85, 50, 37, 49, 47, 64, 6, 7, 71, 33, 4, 43, 47,
63, 1, 27, 600, 208, 230, 15, 191, 246, 85, 94, 511, 2, 270, 20, 39, 7, 33, 44, 22, 40, 7,
10, 3, 811, 106, 44, 486, 230, 353, 211, 200, 31, 10, 38, 140, 297, 61, 603, 320, 302,
666, 287, 2, 44, 33, 32, 511, 548, 10, 6, 250, 557, 246, 53, 37, 52, 83, 47, 320, 38, 33,
807, 7, 44, 30, 31, 250, 10, 15, 35, 106, 160, 113, 31, 102, 406, 230, 540, 320, 29, 66,
33, 101, 807, 138, 301, 316, 353, 320, 220, 37, 52, 28, 540, 320, 33, 8, 48, 107, 50,
811, 7, 2, 113, 73, 16, 125, 11, 110, 67, 102, 807, 33, 59, 81, 158, 38, 43, 581, 138,
19, 85, 400, 38, 43, 77, 14, 27, 8, 47, 138, 63, 140, 44, 35, 22, 177, 106, 250, 314,
217, 2, 10, 7, 1005, 4, 20, 25, 44, 48, 7, 26, 46, 110, 230, 807, 191, 34, 112, 147, 44,
110, 121, 125, 96, 41, 51, 50, 140, 56, 47, 152, 540, 63, 807, 28, 42, 250, 138, 582,
98, 643, 32, 107, 140, 112, 26, 85, 138, 540, 53, 20, 125, 371, 38, 36, 10, 52, 118,
136, 102, 420, 150, 112, 71, 14, 20, 7, 24, 18, 12, 807, 37, 67, 110, 62, 33, 21, 95,
220, 511, 102, 811, 30, 83, 84, 305, 620, 15, 2, 108, 220, 106, 353, 105, 106, 60, 275,
72, 8, 50, 205, 185, 112, 125, 540, 65, 106, 807, 188, 96, 110, 16, 73, 33, 807, 150,
409, 400, 50, 154, 285, 96, 106, 316, 270, 205, 101, 811, 400, 8, 44, 37, 52, 40, 241,
34, 205, 38, 16, 46, 47, 85, 24, 44, 15, 64, 73, 138, 807, 85, 78, 110, 33, 420, 505, 53,
37, 38, 22, 31, 10, 110, 106, 101, 140, 15, 38, 3, 5, 44, 7, 98, 287, 135, 150, 96, 33,
84, 125, 807, 191, 96, 511, 118, 440, 370, 643, 466, 106, 41, 107, 603, 220, 275, 30,
150, 105, 49, 53, 287, 250, 208, 134, 7, 53, 12, 47, 85, 63, 138, 110, 21, 112, 140,
485, 486, 505, 14, 73, 84, 575, 1005, 150, 200, 16, 42, 5, 4, 25, 42, 8, 16, 811, 125,
160, 32, 205, 603, 807, 81, 96, 405, 41, 600, 136, 14, 20, 28, 26, 353, 302, 246, 8,
131, 160, 140, 84, 440, 42, 16, 811, 40, 67, 101, 102, 194, 138, 205, 51, 63, 241, 540,
122, 8, 10, 63, 140, 47, 48, 140, 288.

Figure 20 The second Beale cipher.

17, 8, 92, 73, 112, 89, 67, 318, 28, 96, 107, 41, 631, 78, 146, 397, 118, 98, 114,
46, 348, 116, 74, 88, 12, 65, 32, 14, 81, 19, 76, 121, 216, 85, 33, 66, 15, 108,
8, 77, 43, 24, 122, 96, 117, 36, 211, 301, 15, 44, 11, 46, 89, 18, 136, 68, 317,
8, 90, 82, 304, 71, 43, 221, 198, 176, 310, 319, 81, 99, 264, 380, 56, 37, 319, 2,
4, 53, 28, 44, 75, 98, 102, 37, 85, 107, 117, 64, 88, 136, 48, 154, 99, 175, 89,
15, 326, 78, 96, 214, 218, 311, 43, 89, 51, 90, 75, 128, 96, 33, 28, 103, 84, 65,
6, 41, 246, 84, 270, 98, 116, 32, 59, 74, 66, 69, 240, 15, 8, 121, 20, 77, 89, 31,
1, 106, 81, 191, 224, 328, 18, 75, 52, 82, 117, 201, 39, 23, 217, 27, 21, 84, 35,
4, 109, 128, 49, 77, 88, 1, 81, 217, 64, 55, 83, 116, 251, 269, 311, 96, 54, 32,
20, 18, 132, 102, 219, 211, 84, 150, 219, 275, 312, 64, 10, 106, 87, 75, 47, 21,
9, 37, 81, 44, 18, 126, 115, 132, 160, 181, 203, 76, 81, 299, 314, 337, 351, 96,
1, 28, 97, 318, 238, 106, 24, 93, 3, 19, 17, 26, 60, 73, 88, 14, 126, 138, 234,
86, 297, 321, 365, 264, 19, 22, 84, 56, 107, 98, 123, 111, 214, 136, 7, 33, 45,
0, 13, 28, 46, 42, 107, 196, 227, 344, 198, 203, 247, 116, 19, 8, 212, 230, 31, 6,
28, 65, 48, 52, 59, 41, 122, 33, 117, 11, 18, 25, 71, 36, 45, 83, 76, 89, 92, 31,
5, 70, 83, 96, 27, 33, 44, 50, 61, 24, 112, 136, 149, 176, 180, 194, 143, 171,
05, 296, 87, 12, 44, 51, 89, 98, 34, 41, 208, 173, 66, 9, 35, 16, 95, 8, 113, 175,
0, 56, 203, 19, 177, 183, 206, 157, 200, 218, 260, 291, 305, 618, 951, 320, 18,
24, 78, 65, 19, 32, 124, 48, 53, 57, 84, 96, 207, 244, 66, 82, 119, 71, 11, 86, 77,
13, 54, 82, 316, 245, 303, 86, 97, 106, 212, 18, 37, 15, 81, 89, 16, 7, 81, 39, 96,
4, 43, 216, 118, 29, 55, 109, 136, 172, 213, 64, 8, 227, 304, 611, 221, 364, 819,
75, 128, 296, 1, 18, 53, 76, 10, 15, 23, 19, 71, 84, 120, 134, 66, 73, 89, 96, 230,
8, 77, 26, 101, 127, 936, 218, 439, 178, 171, 61, 226, 313, 215, 102, 18, 167,
62, 114, 218, 66, 59, 48, 27, 19, 13, 82, 48, 162, 119, 34, 127, 139, 34, 128,
29, 74, 63, 120, 11, 54, 61, 73, 92, 180, 66, 75, 101, 124, 265, 89, 96, 126, 274,
96, 917, 434, 461, 235, 890, 312, 413, 328, 381, 96, 105, 217, 66, 118, 22, 77,
4, 42, 12, 7, 55, 24, 83, 67, 97, 109, 121, 135, 181, 203, 219, 228, 256, 21, 34,
7, 319, 374, 382, 675, 684, 717, 864, 203, 4, 18, 92, 16, 63, 82, 22, 46, 55, 69,
4, 112, 134, 186, 175, 119, 213, 416, 312, 343, 264, 119, 186, 218, 343, 417,
45, 951, 124, 209, 49, 617, 856, 924, 936, 72, 19, 28, 11, 35, 42, 40, 66, 85, 94,
12, 65, 82, 115, 119, 236, 244, 186, 172, 112, 85, 6, 56, 38, 44, 85, 72, 32, 47,
3, 96, 124, 217, 314, 319, 221, 644, 817, 821, 934, 922, 416, 975, 10, 22, 18,
6, 137, 181, 101, 39, 86, 103, 116, 138, 164, 212, 218, 296, 815, 380, 412, 460,
95, 675, 820, 952.

Figure 21 The third Beale cipher.

To protect his identity, the author asked James B. Ward, a respected member of the local community and the county's road surveyor, to act as his agent and publisher.

Everything we know about the strange tale of the Beale ciphers is published in the pamphlet, and so it is thanks to the author that we have the ciphers and Morriss' account of the story. In addition to this, the author is also responsible for successfully deciphering the second Beale cipher. Like the first and third ciphers, the second cipher consists of a page of numbers, and the author assumed that each number represented a letter. However, the range of numbers far exceeds the number of letters in the alphabet, so the author realized that he was dealing with a cipher that uses several numbers to represent the same letter. One cipher that fulfills this criterion is the so-called *book cipher*, in which a book, or any other piece of text, is the key.

First, the cryptographer sequentially numbers every word in the book (or keytext). Thereafter, each number acts as a substitute for the initial letter of its associated word. [1]For [2]example, [3]if [4]the [5]sender [6]and [7]receiver [8]agreed [9]that [10]this [11]sentence [12]was [13]to [14]be [15]the [16]keytext, [17]then [18]every [19]word [20]would [21]be [22]numerically [23]labeled, [24]each [25]number [26]providing [27]the [28]basis [29]for [30]encryption. Next, a list would be drawn up matching each number to the initial letter of its associated word:

1 = f	11 = s	21 = b
2 = e	12 = w	22 = n
3 = i	13 = t	23 = l
4 = t	14 = b	24 = e
5 = s	15 = t	25 = n
6 = a	16 = k	26 = p

7 = r	17 = t	27 = t
8 = a	18 = e	28 = b
9 = t	19 = w	29 = f
10 = t	20 = w	30 = e

A message can now be encrypted by substituting letters in the plaintext for numbers according to the list. In this list, the plaintext letter **f** would be substituted with **1**, and the plaintext letter **e** could be substituted with either **2, 18, 24** or **30**. Because our keytext is such a short sentence, we do not have numbers that could replace rare letters such as **x** and **z**, but we do have enough substitutes to encipher the word **beale**, which could be **14–2–8–23–18**. If the intended receiver has a copy of the keytext, then deciphering the encrypted message is trivial. However, if a third party intercepts only the ciphertext, then cryptanalysis depends on somehow identifying the keytext. The author of the pamphlet wrote, "With this idea, a test was made of every book I could procure, by numbering its letters and comparing the numbers with those of the manuscript; all to no purpose, however, until the Declaration of Independence afforded the clue to one of the papers, and revived all my hopes."

The Declaration of Independence turned out to be the keytext for the second Beale cipher, and by numbering the words in the Declaration it is possible to unravel it. Figure 22 shows the start of the Declaration of Independence, with every tenth word numbered to help the reader see how the decipherment works. Figure 20 shows the ciphertext—the first number is **115**, and the 115th word in the Declaration is *instituted*, so the first number represents **i**. The second number in the ciphertext is **73**, and the 73rd word in the Declaration is *hold*, so the second number represents **h**. Here is the whole decipherment, as printed in the pamphlet:

> I have deposited in the county of Bedford, about four miles from Buford's, in an excavation or vault, six feet below the surface of the ground, the following articles, belonging jointly to the parties whose names are given in number "3," herewith:
>
> The first deposit consisted of one thousand and fourteen pounds of gold, and three thousand eight hundred and twelve pounds of silver, deposited November, 1819. The second was made December, 1821, and consisted of nineteen hundred and seven pounds of gold, and twelve hundred and eighty-eight pounds of silver; also jewels, obtained in St. Louis in exchange for silver to save transportation, and valued at $13,000.
>
> The above is securely packed in iron pots, with iron covers. The vault is roughly lined with stone, and the vessels rest on solid stone, and are covered with others. Paper number "1" describes the exact locality of the vault, so that no difficulty will be had in finding it.

It is worth noting that there are some errors in the ciphertext. For example, the decipherment includes the words "four miles," which relies on the 95th word of the Declaration of Independence, beginning with the letter *u*. However, the 95th word is *inalienable*. This could be the result of Beale's sloppy encryption, or it could be that Beale had a copy of the Declaration in which the 95th word was *unalienable*, which does appear in some versions dating from the early nineteenth century. Either way, the successful decipherment clearly indicated the value of the treasure—at least $20 million at today's bullion prices.

Not surprisingly, once the author knew the value of the treasure, he spent increasing amounts of time analyzing the other two cipher sheets, particularly the first Beale cipher, which describes the treasure's location. Despite strenuous efforts, he failed, and the ciphers brought him nothing but sorrow:

When, in the course of human events, it becomes [10]necessary for one people to dissolve the political bands which [20]have connected them with another, and to assume among the [30]powers of the earth, the separate and equal station to [40]which the laws of nature and of nature's God entitle [50]them, a decent respect to the opinions of mankind requires [60]that they should declare the causes which impel them to [70]the separation.

We hold these truths to be self-evident, [80]that all men are created equal, that they are endowed [90]by their Creator with certain inalienable rights, that among these [100]are life, liberty and the pursuit of happiness; That to [110]secure these rights, governments are instituted among men, deriving their [120]just powers from the consent of the governed; That whenever [130]any form of government becomes destructive of these ends, it [140]is the right of the people to alter or to [150]abolish it, and to institute a new government, laying its [160]foundation on such principles and organizing its powers in such [170]form, as to them shall seem most likely to effect [180]their safety and happiness. Prudence, indeed, will dictate that governments [190]long established should not be changed for light and transient [200]causes; and accordingly all experience hath shewn, that mankind are [210]more disposed to suffer, while evils are sufferable, than to [220]right themselves by abolishing the forms to which they are [230]accustomed.

But when a long train of abuses and usurpations, [240]pursuing invariably the same object evinces a design to reduce [250]them under absolute despotism, it is their right, it is [260]their duty, to throw off such government, and to provide [270]new Guards for their future security. Such has been the [280]patient sufferance of these Colonies; and such is now the [290]necessity which constrains them to alter their former systems of [300]government. The history of the present King of Great Britain [310]is a history of repeated injuries and usurpations, all having [320]in direct object the establishment of an absolute tyranny over [330]these States. To prove this, let facts be submitted to [340]a candid world.

Figure 22 The first three paragraphs of the Declaration of Independence, with every tenth word numbered. This is the key for deciphering the second Beale cipher.

In consequence of the time lost in the above investigation, I have been reduced from comparative affluence to absolute penury, entailing suffering upon those it was my duty to protect, and this, too, in spite of their remonstrations. My eyes were at last opened to their condition, and I resolved to sever at once, and forever, all connection with the affair, and retrieve, if possible, my errors. To do this, as the best means of placing temptation beyond my reach, I determined to make public the whole matter, and shift from my shoulders my responsibility to Mr. Morriss.

Thus the ciphers, along with everything else known by the author, were published in 1885. Although a warehouse fire destroyed most of the pamphlets, those that survived caused quite a stir in Lynchburg. Among the most ardent treasure hunters attracted to the Beale ciphers were the Hart brothers, George and Clayton. For years they pored over the two remaining ciphers, mounting various forms of cryptanalytic attack, occasionally fooling themselves into believing that they had a solution. A false line of attack will sometimes generate a few tantalizing words within a sea of gibberish, which then encourages the cryptanalyst to devise a series of caveats to excuse the gibberish. To an unbiased observer the decipherment is clearly nothing more than wishful thinking, but to the all-consumed treasure hunter it makes complete sense. One of the Harts' tentative decipherments encouraged them to use dynamite to excavate a particular site; unfortunately, the resulting crater yielded no gold. Although Clayton Hart gave up in 1912, George continued working on the Beale ciphers until 1952.

Professional cryptanalysts have also embarked on the Beale treasure trail. Herbert O. Yardley, who founded the U.S. Cipher Bureau (known as the American Black Chamber) at the end of the First World War, was intrigued by the Beale ciphers, as was Colonel William Friedman, the dominant figure in American cryptanalysis during the first half of the twentieth century. While he was in charge of the Signal Intelligence Service, he made the Beale ciphers part of the training program, presumably because, as his wife once said, he believed the ciphers to be of "diabolical ingenuity, specifically designed to lure the unwary reader." The Friedman archive, established after his death in 1969 at the George C. Marshall Research Center, is frequently consulted by military historians, but the great majority of visitors are eager Beale devotees, hoping to follow up some of the great man's leads. More recently, one of the major figures in the hunt for the Beale treasure has been Carl Hammer, retired director of computer science at Sperry Univac and one of the pioneers of computer cryptanalysis. According to Hammer, "the Beale ciphers have occupied at least 10 percent of the best cryptanalytic minds in the country. And not a dime of this effort should be begrudged. The work—even the lines that have led into blind alleys—has more than paid for itself in advancing and refining computer research."

You might be surprised by the strength of the unbroken Beale ciphers, especially bearing in mind that when we left the ongoing battle between codemakers and codebreakers, it was the codebreakers who were on top. Babbage and Kasiski had invented a way of breaking the Vigenère cipher, and codemakers were struggling to find something to replace it. How did Beale come up with something that is so formidable? The answer is that the Beale ciphers were created under circumstances that gave the cryptographer a great advantage. The messages were not intended to be part of a series, and because they related to such a valuable treasure, Beale might have been prepared to create a special keytext for the first and third ciphers. Indeed, if the keytext was penned by Beale himself, this would explain why searches of published material have not revealed it.

We can imagine that Beale might have written a two-thousand-word private essay on the subject of buffalo hunting, of which there was only one copy. Only the holder of this essay, the unique keytext, would be able to decipher the first and third Beale ciphers. Beale mentioned that he had left the key in "the hand of a friend" in St. Louis, but if the friend lost or destroyed the key, then cryptanalysts might never be able to crack the Beale ciphers.

Creating a keytext specifically for one message is much more secure than using a key based on a published book, but it is practical only if the sender has the time to create the keytext and is able to convey it to the intended recipient, requirements that are not feasible for routine, day-to-day communications. In Beale's case, he could compose his keytext at leisure, deliver it to his friend in St. Louis whenever he happened to be passing through, and then have it posted or collected at some arbitrary time in the future, whenever the treasure was to be reclaimed.

It is possible that the treasure was found many years ago and that the discoverer spirited it away without being spotted by local residents. Beale enthusiasts with a fondness for conspiracy theories have suggested that the National Security Agency (NSA) has already found the treasure. America's central government cipher facility has access to the most powerful computers and some of the most brilliant minds in the world, and they may have discovered something about the ciphers that has eluded everybody else. The lack of any announcement would be in keeping with the NSA's hush-hush reputation—it has been proposed that NSA stands not for "National Security Agency," but rather for "Never Say Anything" or "No Such Agency."

Finally, we cannot exclude the possibility that the Beale ciphers are an elaborate hoax and that Beale never existed. Skeptics have suggested that the unknown author, inspired by Poe's "The Gold Bug," fabricated the whole story and published the pamphlet as a way of profiting from the greed of others.

One of the foremost nonbelievers is the cryptographer Louis Kruh, who claims to have found evidence that the pamphlet's author also wrote Beale's letters, the one supposedly sent from St. Louis and the one supposedly contained in the box. He performed a textual analysis on the words attributed to the author and the words attributed to Beale to see if there were any similarities. Kruh compared aspects such as the percentage of sentences beginning with *the, of* and *and,* the average number of commas and semicolons per sentence, and the writing style—the use of negatives, negative passives, infinitives, relative clauses and so on. In addition to the author's words and Beale's letters, the analysis also took in the writing of three other nineteenth-century Virginians. Of the five sets of writing, those authored by Beale and the pamphlet's author bore the closest resemblance, suggesting that they may have been written by the same person. In other words, this suggests that the author faked the letters attributed to Beale and fabricated the whole story.

On the other hand, evidence favoring the validity of the ciphers comes from historical research, which can be used to verify the story of Thomas Beale. Peter Viemeister, a local historian, has gathered much of the research in his book *The Beale Treasure—History of a Mystery.* Viemeister began by asking if there was any evidence that Thomas Beale actually existed. Using the census of 1790 and other documents, Viemeister has identified several Thomas Beales who were born in Virginia and whose backgrounds fit the few known details. Viemeister has also attempted to confirm the other details in the pamphlet, such as Beale's trip to Santa Fe and his discovery of gold. For example, there is a Cheyenne legend dating from around 1820 that tells of gold and silver being taken from the West and buried in eastern mountains. Also, the 1820 postmaster's list in St. Louis contains a Thomas Beall, which fits in with the pamphlet's claim that Beale passed through the city in 1820 on his journey westward after leaving Lynchburg. The pamphlet also says that Beale sent a letter from St. Louis in 1822. So there does seem to be a basis for the tale of the Beale ciphers, and consequently it continues to enthrall cryptanalysts and treasure hunters.

Having read the tale of the Beale ciphers, you might be encouraged to take up the challenge yourself. The lure of an unbroken nineteenth-century cipher, together with a treasure worth $20 million, might prove irresistible. However, before you set off on the treasure trail, take heed of the advice given by the author of the pamphlet:

> Before giving the papers to the public, I would say a word to those who may take an interest in them, and give them a little advice, acquired by bitter experience. It is, to devote only such time as can be spared from your legitimate business to the task, and if you can spare no time, let the matter alone. . . . Again, never, as I have done, sacrifice your own and your family's interests to what may prove an illusion; but, as I have already said, when your day's work is done, and you are comfortably seated by your good fire, a short time devoted to the subject can injure no one, and may bring its reward.

via Galveston

JAN

GERMAN LEGATION

MEXICO CITY

13042   13401   8501   115   3528   0491

18222   21560   10247   11518   23677   13605   3494

5905   11311

3

The Mechanization of Secrecy

The Zimmermann telegram,
the Enigma machine and
how cryptography changed
the courses of
World Wars I and II

At the end of the nineteenth century, cryptography was in disarray. Ever since Babbage and Kasiski had destroyed the security of the Vigenère cipher, cryptographers had been searching for a new cipher, something that would reestablish secret communication, thereby allowing businessmen and the military to utilize the immediacy of the telegraph without their communications being stolen and deciphered. Furthermore, at the turn of the century, the Italian physicist Guglielmo Marconi invented an even more powerful form of telecommunication, which made the need for secure encryption even more pressing.

In 1894, Marconi began experimenting with a curious property of electrical circuits. Under certain conditions, if one circuit carried an electric current, this could induce a current in another isolated circuit some distance away. By enhancing the design of the two circuits, increasing the power and adding aerials, Marconi could soon transmit and receive pulses of information across distances of up to 1.5 miles. He had invented radio. The telegraph had already been established for half a century, but it required a wire to transport a message between sender and receiver. Marconi's system had the great advantage of being wireless—the signal traveled, as if by magic, through the air.

In 1896, in search of financial backing for his idea, Marconi emigrated to Britain, where he filed his first patent. Continuing his experiments, he increased the range of his radio communications, first transmitting a message about 9 miles across the Bristol Channel, and then nearly 33 miles across the English Channel to France. At the same time he began to look for commercial applications for his invention, pointing out to potential backers the two main advantages of radio: It did not require the construction of expensive telegraph lines, and it had the potential to send messages between otherwise isolated locations. He pulled off a magnificent publicity stunt in 1899, when he equipped two ships with radios so that journalists covering the America's Cup, the world's most important yacht race, could send reports back to New York for the following day's newspapers.

Marconi's invention tantalized the military, who viewed it with a mixture of desire and trepidation. The tactical advantages of radio are obvious: It allows direct communication between any two points without the need for a wire between the locations. Laying such a wire is often impractical, sometimes impossible. Previously, a naval commander based in port had no way of communicating with his ships, which might disappear for months on end, but radio would enable him to coordinate a fleet wherever the ships might be. Similarly, radio would allow generals to direct their campaigns, keeping them in continual contact with battalions, regardless of their movements. All this is made possible by the nature of radio waves, which emanate in all directions, and reach receivers wherever they may be. However, this all-pervasive property of radio is also its greatest military weakness, because messages will inevitably reach the enemy as well as the intended recipient. Consequently, reliable encryption became a necessity. If the enemy was going to be able to intercept every radio message, then cryptographers had to find a way of preventing them from deciphering these messages.

The mixed blessings of radio—ease of communication and ease of interception—were brought into sharp focus at the outbreak of the First World War. Both sides were eager to exploit the power of radio, but were also unsure of how to guarantee security. Together, the advent of radio and the Great War intensified the need for effective encryption. The hope was that there would be a breakthrough, some new cipher that would reestablish secrecy for military commanders. However, between 1914 and 1918 there was to be no great discovery, merely a catalog of cryptographic failures. Codemakers conjured up several new ciphers, but one by one they were broken. It was Germany that suffered most from these security breaches. The supremacy of the Allied codebreakers and their influence on the Great War are best illustrated by the decipherment of a German telegram that was intercepted by the British on January 17, 1917.

At the beginning of 1917, Germany was planning a new naval offensive against the British, but it was concerned that this might result in accidental damage to, and the sinking of, American ships. Up until this point, America had remained neutral, but the German offensive and inadvertent attacks on American ships might bring America into the war, which Germany was anxious to avoid. Hence the German foreign minister, Arthur Zimmermann, planned to forge an alliance with Mexico. If America entered the war, then Germany would help

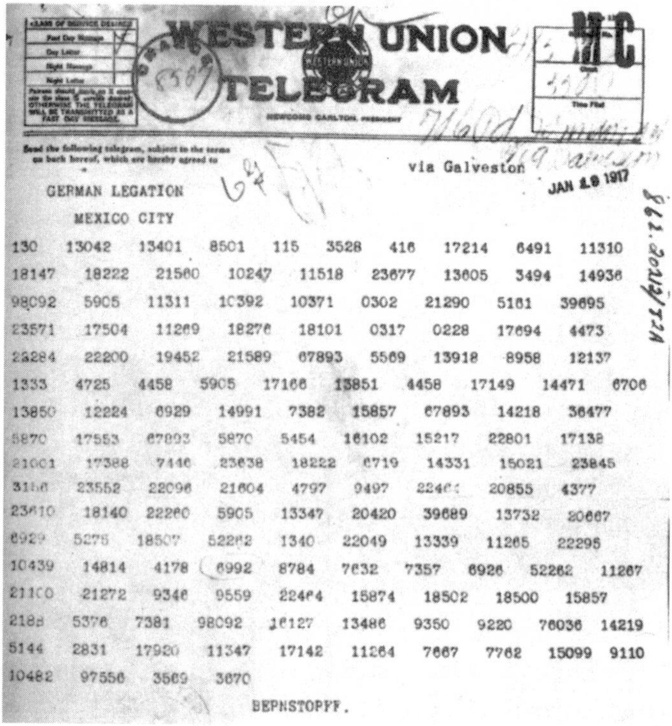
WESTERN UNION TELEGRAM

via Galveston

JAN 19 1917

GERMAN LEGATION

MEXICO CITY

130 13042 13401 8501 115 3528 416 17214 6491 11310
18147 18222 21560 10247 11518 23677 13605 3494 14936
98092 5905 11311 10392 10371 0302 21290 5161 39695
23571 17504 11269 18276 18101 0317 0228 17694 4473
22284 22200 19452 21589 67893 5569 13918 8958 12137
1333 4725 4458 5905 17166 13851 4458 17149 14471 6706
13850 12224 6929 14991 7382 15857 67893 14218 36477
5870 17553 67893 5870 5454 16102 15217 22801 17138
21001 17388 7446 23638 18222 6719 14331 15021 23845
3156 23552 22096 21604 4797 9497 22464 20855 4377
23610 18140 22260 5905 13347 20420 39689 13732 20667
6929 5275 18507 52262 1340 22049 13339 11265 22295
10439 14814 4178 6992 8784 7632 7357 6926 52262 11267
21100 21272 9346 9559 22464 15874 18502 18500 15857
2188 5376 7381 98092 16127 13486 9350 9220 76036 14219
5144 2831 17920 11347 17142 11264 7667 7762 15099 9110
10482 97556 3569 3670

BERNSTORFF.

Figure 23 The Zimmermann telegram, as forwarded by von Bernstorff, the German ambassador in Washington, to Eckhardt, the German ambassador in Mexico City.

Mexico recapture territory lost to America, thereby forcing America to keep most of its troops at home, as opposed to sending them to European battlefronts.

On January 16, Zimmermann encapsulated his offer in a telegram to the German ambassador in Washington, who would then retransmit it to the German ambassador in Mexico, who would deliver it to the Mexican president. Figure 23 shows the telegram, its contents encrypted with a diplomatic code. The telegram contained the following proposal:

We shall endeavor in spite of this to keep the United States neutral. In the event of this not succeeding, we make Mexico a proposal of alliance on the following basis: make war together, make peace together, generous financial support, and an understanding on our part that Mexico is to reconquer the lost territory in Texas, New Mexico and Arizona. The settlement in detail is left to you.

Zimmermann

Zimmermann had to encrypt his telegram because Germany was aware that the Allies were intercepting all its transatlantic communications, a consequence of Britain's first offensive action of the war. Before dawn on the first day of the First World War, the British ship *Telconia* approached the German coast under cover of darkness, dropped anchor, and hauled up a clutch of undersea cables. These were Germany's transatlantic cables—its communication links to the rest of the world. By the time the sun had risen, they had been severed. This act of sabotage was aimed at destroying Germany's most secure means of communication, thereby forcing German messages to be sent via insecure radio links or via cables owned by other countries. Zimmermann sent his encrypted telegram via routes that touched England, so the Zimmermann telegram, as it would become known, soon fell into British hands.

The intercepted telegram was immediately sent to Room 40, the Admiralty's cipher bureau, named after the office in which it was initially housed. Room 40 was a strange mixture of linguists, classical scholars and puzzle addicts, capable of the most ingenious feats of cryptanalysis. For example, the Reverend Montgomery, a gifted translator of German theological works, had deciphered a secret message hidden in a postcard addressed to Sir Henry Jones, 184 King's Road, Tighnabruaich, Scotland. The postcard had been sent from Turkey, so Sir Henry had assumed that it was from his son, a prisoner of the Turks. However, he was puzzled because the postcard was blank, and the address was peculiar—the village of Tighnabruaich was so tiny that none of the houses had numbers, and there was no King's Road. Eventually, Montgomery spotted the postcard's cryptic message. The address alluded to the Bible, First Book of Kings, chapter 18, verse 4: "Obadiah took a hundred prophets, and hid them fifty in a cave, and fed them with bread and water." Sir Henry's son was simply reassuring his family that he was being well looked after by his captors.

When the encrypted Zimmermann telegram arrived in Room 40, it was Montgomery who was made responsible for decrypting it, along with Nigel de Grey, who in peacetime had been with the publishing firm of William Heinemann. They saw immediately that they were dealing with a form of encryption used only for high-level diplomatic communications, and tackled the telegram with some urgency. The decipherment was far from trivial, but they were able to draw upon previous analyses of other, similarly encrypted telegrams. Within a few hours the codebreaking duo had been able to recover a few chunks of text, enough to see that they were working with a message of the utmost importance. Montgomery and de Grey persevered with their task, and within a few days they could discern the outline of Zimmermann's terrible plans. They realized the dreadful implications of the new German naval offensive, but at the same time they could see that the German foreign minister was encouraging an attack on America, which was likely to provoke President Wilson into abandoning America's neutrality. The telegram contained the deadliest of threats, but also the possibility of America joining the Allies.

Montgomery and de Grey took the deciphered telegram to Admiral Sir William Hall, director of naval intelligence, expecting him to pass the information to the Americans, thereby drawing them into the war. However, Admiral Hall merely placed the decipherment in his safe. He reckoned that there was no point in releasing the telegram if the German naval offensive would in any case draw America into the war.

On February 1, as ordered by the Kaiser, Germany instigated the new offensive. On February 2, Woodrow Wilson held a cabinet meeting to decide the American response. On February 3, he spoke to Congress and announced that America would continue to remain neutral, acting as a peacemaker, not a combatant. This was contrary to Allied and German expectations. American reluctance to join the Allies left Admiral Hall with no choice but to exploit the Zimmermann telegram.

Figure 24 "Exploding in his Hands," a cartoon by Rollin Kirby published on March 3, 1917, in *The World*.

On February 23, Arthur Balfour, the British secretary of state for foreign affairs, summoned the American ambassador, Walter Page, and presented him with the Zimmermann telegram, later calling this "the most dramatic moment in all my life." Four days later, President Wilson saw for himself the "eloquent evidence," as he called it, proof that Germany was encouraging direct aggression against America.

At the beginning of the year, Wilson had said that it would be a "crime against civilization" to lead his nation to war, but by April 2, 1917, he had changed his mind: "I advise that the Congress declare the recent course of the Imperial German Government to be in fact nothing less than war against the government and people of the United States, and that it formally accept the status of belligerent which has thus been thrust upon it." A single breakthrough by Room 40 cryptanalysts had succeeded where three years of intensive diplomacy had failed. Barbara Tuchman, American historian and author of *The Zimmermann Telegram,* offered the following analysis:

> Had the telegram never been intercepted or never been published, inevitably the Germans would have done something else that would have brought us in eventually. But the time was already late and, had we delayed much longer, the Allies might have been forced to negotiate. To that extent the Zimmermann telegram altered the course of history. . . . In itself the Zimmermann telegram was only a pebble on the long road of history. But a pebble can kill a Goliath, and this one killed the American illusion that we could go about our business happily separate from other nations. In world affairs it was a German Minister's minor plot. In the lives of the American people it was the end of innocence.

THE DEVELOPMENT OF CIPHER MACHINES

The First World War saw a series of victories for codebreakers, culminating in the decipherment of the Zimmermann telegram. Ever since the cracking of the Vigenère cipher in the nineteenth century, codebreakers had maintained the upper hand over the codemakers. In the years following the war, there was a concerted effort to find new, secure encryption systems. Cryptographers turned to technology to help guarantee security. Rather than relying on pencil-and-paper ciphers, they focused their attention on the mechanization of secrecy.

Although primitive, the earliest cryptographic machine was the cipher disc, invented in the fifteenth century by the Italian architect Leon Alberti, one of the fathers of the polyalphabetic cipher. He took two copper discs, one slightly larger than the other, and inscribed the alphabet around the edge of both. By placing the smaller disc on top of the larger one and fixing them with a needle to act as an axis, he constructed something similar to the cipher disc shown in Figure 25. The two discs can be independently rotated so that the two alphabets can have different relative positions, and can thus be used to encrypt a message with a simple Caesar shift. For example, to encrypt a message with a Caesar shift of one place, position the outer A next to the inner B—the outer disc is the plain alphabet, and the inner disc represents the cipher alphabet. Each letter in the plaintext message is looked up on the outer disc, and the corresponding letter on the inner disc is written down as part of the ciphertext. To send a message with a Caesar shift of five places, simply rotate the discs so that the outer A is next to the inner F, and then use the cipher disc in its new setting. Even though the cipher disc is a very basic device, it does ease encipherment, and it endured for five centuries. The version shown in Figure 25 was used in the Civil War.

The cipher disc can be thought of as a scrambler, taking each plaintext letter and transforming it into something else. The mode of operation described so far is straightforward, and the resulting cipher is relatively simple to break, but the cipher disc can be used in a more complicated way. Its inventor, Alberti, suggested changing the setting of the disc during the message, which in effect generates a polyalphabetic cipher instead of a monoalphabetic cipher. For example, Alberti could have used his disc to encipher the word **goodbye**, using the keyword **LEON**. He would begin by setting his disc according to the first letter of the keyword, moving the outer **A** next to the inner **L**. Then he would encipher the first letter of the message, **g**, by finding it on the outer disc and noting the corresponding letter on the inner disc, which is **R**. To encipher the second letter of the message, he would reset his disc according to the second letter of the keyword, moving the outer **A** next to the inner **E**.

Figure 25 A Confederate cipher disc used in the Civil War.

Then he would encipher **o** by finding it on the outer disc and noting the corresponding letter on the inner disc, which is **S**. The encryption process continues with the cipher disc being set according to the keyletter **O**, then **N**, then back to **L**, and so on. Alberti has effectively encrypted a message using the Vigenère cipher with his first name acting as the keyword. The cipher disc speeds up encryption and reduces errors compared with performing the encryption via a Vigenère square.

The important feature of using the cipher disc in this way is the fact that the disc is changing its mode of scrambling during encryption. Although this extra level of complication makes the cipher harder to break, it does not make it unbreakable, because we are simply dealing with a mechanized version of the Vigenère cipher, and the Vigenère cipher was broken by Babbage and Kasiski. However, five hundred years after Alberti, a more complex reincarnation of his cipher disc would lead to a new generation of ciphers, an order of magnitude more difficult to crack than anything previously used.

In 1918, the German inventor Arthur Scherbius and his close friend Richard Ritter founded the company of Scherbius & Ritter, an innovative engineering firm that dabbled in everything from turbines to heated pillows. Scherbius was in charge of research and development, and was constantly looking for new opportunities. One of his pet projects was to replace the inadequate systems of cryptography used in the First World War by swapping traditional codes and ciphers with a form of encryption that exploited twentieth-century technology. Having studied electrical engineering in Hanover and Munich, he developed a piece of cryptographic machinery that was essentially an electrical version of Alberti's cipher disc. Called Enigma, Scherbius' invention would become the most fearsome system of encryption in history.

Scherbius' Enigma machine consisted of a number of

ingenious components, which he combined into a formidable and intricate cipher machine. However, if we break the machine down into its constituent parts and rebuild it in stages, then its underlying principles will become apparent. The basic form of Scherbius' invention consists of three elements connected by wires: a keyboard for inputting each plaintext letter, a scrambling unit that encrypts each plaintext letter into a corresponding ciphertext letter, and a display board consisting of various lamps for indicating the ciphertext letter. Figure 26 shows a stylized layout of the machine, limited to a six-letter alphabet for simplicity. In order to encrypt a plaintext letter, the operator presses the appropriate plaintext letter on the keyboard, which sends an electric pulse through the central scrambling unit and out the other side, where it illuminates the corresponding ciphertext letter on the lampboard.

The scrambler, a thick disc riddled with wires, is the most important part of the machine. From the keyboard, the wires enter the scrambler at six points, and then make a series of twists and turns within the scrambler before emerging at six points on the other side. The internal wirings of the scrambler determine how the plaintext letters will be encrypted. For example, in Figure 26 the wirings dictate that:

Typing in **a** will illuminate the letter **B**, which means that **a** is encrypted as **B**
Typing in **b** will illuminate the letter **A**, which means that **b** is encrypted as **A**
Typing in **c** will illuminate the letter **D**, which means that **c** is encrypted as **D**
Typing in **d** will illuminate the letter **F**, which means that **d** is encrypted as **F**
Typing in **e** will illuminate the letter **E**, which means that **e** is encrypted as **E**
Typing in **f** will illuminate the letter **C**, which means that **f** is encrypted as **C**

The message **cafe** would be encrypted as **DBCE**. With this basic setup, the scrambler essentially defines a cipher alphabet, and the machine can be used to implement a simple monoalphabetic substitution cipher.

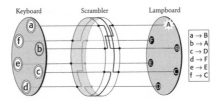

Figure 26 A simplified version of the Enigma machine with an alphabet of just six letters. The most important element of the machine is the scrambler. By typing in **b** on the keyboard, a current passes into the scrambler, follows the path of the internal wiring, and then emerges so as to illuminate the **A** lamp. In short, **b** is encrypted as **A**. The box to the right indicates how each of the six letters is encrypted.

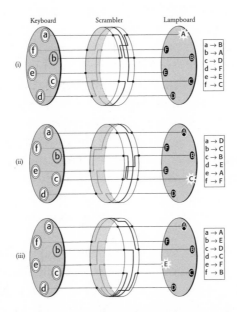

Figure 27 Every time a letter is typed into the keyboard and encrypted, the scrambler rotates by one place, thus changing how each letter is potentially encrypted. In (i) the scrambler encrypts **b** as **A**, but in (ii) the new scrambler orientation encrypts **b** as **C**. In (iii) after rotating one more place, the scrambler encrypts **b** as **E**. After encrypting four more letters, and rotating four more places, the scrambler returns to its original orientation.

However, Scherbius' idea was for the scrambler disc to automatically rotate by one-sixth of a revolution each time a letter is encrypted (or one-twenty-sixth of a revolution for a complete alphabet of twenty-six letters). Figure 27(i) shows the same arrangement as in Figure 26; once again, typing in the letter **b** will illuminate the letter **A**. However, this time, immediately after typing a letter and illuminating the lampboard, the scrambler revolves by one-sixth of a revolution to the position shown in Figure 27(ii). Typing in the letter **b** again will now illuminate a different letter, namely, **C**. Immediately afterward, the scrambler rotates once more, to the position shown in Figure 27(iii). This time, typing in the letter **b** will illuminate **E**. Typing the letter **b** six times in a row would generate the ciphertext **ACEBDC**. In other words, the cipher alphabet changes after each encryption, and the encryption of the letter **b** is constantly changing. With this rotating setup, the scrambler essentially defines six cipher alphabets, and the machine can be used to implement a polyalphabetic cipher.

The rotation of the scrambler is the most important feature of Scherbius' design. However, as it stands, the machine suffers from one obvious weakness. Typing **b** six times will return the scrambler to its original position, and typing **b** again and again will repeat the pattern of encryption. In general, cryptographers try to avoid repetition because it leads to regularity and structure in the ciphertext, symptoms of a weak cipher. This problem can be alleviated by introducing a second scrambler disc.

Figure 28 is a schematic of a cipher machine with two scramblers. Because of the difficulty of drawing a three-dimensional scrambler with three-dimensional internal wirings, Figure 28 shows only a two-dimensional representation. Each time a letter is encrypted, the first scrambler rotates by one space, or in terms of the two-dimensional diagram, each wiring shifts down one place. In contrast, the second scrambler disc remains

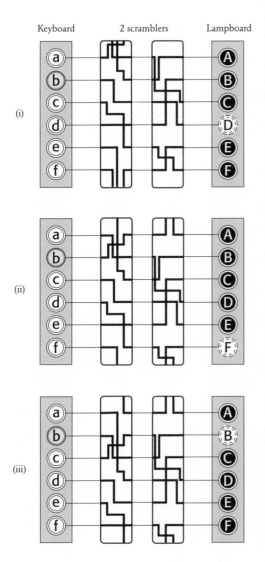

Keyboard   2 scramblers   Lampboard

(i)

(ii)

(iii)

Figure 28 On adding a second scrambler, the pattern of encryption does not repeat until thirty-six letters have been enciphered, at which point both scramblers have returned to their original positions. To simplify the diagram, the scramblers are represented in just two dimensions; instead of rotating one place, the wirings move down one place. If a wire appears to leave the top or bottom of a scrambler, its path can be followed by continuing from the corresponding wire at the bottom or top of the same scrambler. In (i), **b** is encrypted as **D**. After encryption, the first scrambler rotates by one place, also nudging the second scrambler forward one place—this happens only once during each complete revolution of the first wheel. This new setting is shown in (ii) in which **b** is encrypted as **F**. After encryption, the first scrambler rotates by one place, but this time the second scrambler remains fixed. This new setting is shown in (iii) in which **b** is encrypted as **B**.

stationary for most of the time. It moves only after the first scrambler has made a complete revolution. You could imagine that the first scrambler is fitted with a tooth, and it is only when this tooth reaches a certain point that it knocks the second scrambler forward one place.

In Figure 28(i), the first scrambler is in a position where it is just about to knock forward the second scrambler. Typing in and encrypting a letter moves the mechanism to the configuration shown in Figure 28(ii), in which the first scrambler has moved one place, and the second scrambler has also been knocked forward one place. Typing in and encrypting another letter again moves the first scrambler forward one place, Figure 28(iii), but this time the second scrambler has remained stationary. The second scrambler will not move again until the first scrambler completes one revolution, which will take another five encryptions. This arrangement is similar to a car odometer—the rotor representing tenths of miles turns quite quickly, and when it completes one revolution by reaching 9, it knocks the rotor representing single miles forward one place.

The advantage of adding a second scrambler is that the pattern of encryption is not repeated until the second scrambler is back where it started, which requires six complete revolutions of the first scrambler, or the encryption of 6 × 6, or 36 letters in total. In other words, there are 36 distinct scrambler settings, which is equivalent to switching between 36 cipher alphabets. With a full alphabet of 26 letters, the cipher machine would switch between 26 × 26, or 676 cipher alphabets. So by combining scramblers (sometimes called rotors), it is possible to build an encryption machine that is switching between a greater number of cipher alphabets. The operator types in a particular letter, which, depending on the scrambler arrangement, can be encrypted according to any one of hundreds of cipher alphabets. Then the scrambler arrangement changes, so that when the next letter is typed into the machine, it is encrypted according to a different cipher alphabet. Furthermore, all of this is done with great efficiency and accuracy, thanks to the automatic movement of scramblers and the speed of electricity.

Before explaining in detail how Scherbius intended his encryption machine to be used, it is necessary to describe two more elements of the Enigma, which are shown in Figure 29. First, Scherbius' standard encryption machine employed a third scrambler for extra complexity—for a full alphabet these three scramblers would provide $26 \times 26 \times 26$, or 17,576, distinct scrambler arrangements. Second, Scherbius added a *reflector*. The reflector is a bit like a scrambler, inasmuch as it is a disc with internal wirings, but it differs because it does not rotate and the wires enter on one side and then reemerge on the same side. With the reflector in place, the operator types in a letter, which sends an electrical signal through the three scramblers. When the reflector receives the incoming signal it sends it back through the same three scramblers, but along a different route. For example, with the setup in Figure 29, typing the letter **b** would send a signal through the three scramblers and into the reflector, whereupon the signal would return back through the wirings to arrive at the letter **D**. The signal does not actually emerge through the keyboard, as it might

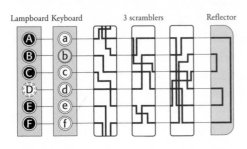

Lampboard Keyboard   3 scramblers   Reflector

Figure 29 Scherbius' design of the Enigma included a third scrambler and a reflector that sends the current back through the scramblers. In this particular setting, typing in **b** eventually illuminates **D** on the lampboard, shown here adjacent to the keyboard.

seem from Figure 29, but instead is diverted to the lampboard. At first sight the reflector seems to be a pointless addition to the machine, because its static nature means that it does not add to the number of cipher alphabets. However, its benefits become clear when we see how the machine was actually used to encrypt and decrypt a message.

Imagine that an operator wants to send a secret message. Before encryption begins, he must first rotate the scramblers to some starting position. There are 17,576 possible arrangements and therefore 17,576 possible starting positions. The initial setting of the scramblers will determine how the message is encrypted. We can think of the Enigma machine in terms of a general cipher system, and the initial settings are what determine the exact details of the encryption. In other words, the initial settings provide the key. The initial settings are usually dictated by a codebook, which lists the key for each day, and which is available to everybody within the communications network. Distributing the codebook requires time and effort, but because only one key per day is required, it could be arranged for a codebook containing twenty-eight keys to be sent out just once every four weeks. Once the scramblers have been set according to the codebook's daily requirement, the sender can begin encrypting. He types in the first letter of the message, sees which letter is illuminated on the lampboard and notes it down as the first letter of the ciphertext. Then, the first scrambler having automatically stepped forward by one place, the sender inputs the second letter of the message, and so on. Once he has generated the complete ciphertext, he hands it to a radio operator, who transmits it to the intended receiver.

In order to decipher the message, the receiver needs to have another Enigma machine and a copy of the codebook that contains the initial scrambler settings for that day. He sets up the machine according to the book, types in the ciphertext letter by letter, and the lampboard indicates the plaintext. In other words, the sender types in the plaintext to generate the ciphertext, and then the receiver types in the ciphertext to generate the plaintext—encipherment and decipherment are mirror processes. The ease of decipherment is a consequence of the reflector. From Figure 29 we can see that if we type in **b** and follow the electrical path, we come back to **D**. Similarly, if we type in **D** and follow the path, then we come back to **b**. The machine encrypts a plaintext letter into a ciphertext letter, and as long as the machine is in the same setting, it will decrypt the ciphertext letter back into the plaintext letter.

It is clear that the key, and the codebook that contains it, must never be allowed to fall into enemy hands. It is quite possible that the enemy might capture an Enigma machine, but without knowing the initial settings used for encryption, they cannot easily decrypt an intercepted message. Without the codebook, the enemy cryptanalyst must resort to checking all the possible keys, which means trying all the 17,576 possible initial scrambler settings. The desperate cryptanalyst will set up the captured Enigma machine with a particular scrambler arrangement, input a short piece of the ciphertext, and see if the output makes any sense. If not, he will change to a different scrambler arrangement and try again. If he can check one scrambler arrangement each minute and works night and day, it will take almost two weeks to check all the settings. This is a moderate level of security, but if the enemy sets a dozen people on the task, then all the settings can be checked within a day. Scherbius therefore decided to improve the security of his invention by increasing the number of initial settings and thus the number of possible keys.

He could have increased security by adding more scramblers (each new scrambler increases the number of keys by a factor of 26), but this would have increased the size of the Enigma machine. Instead, he added two other features. First, he simply made the scramblers removable and interchangeable. So, for example, the first scrambler disc could be moved to the third position, and the third scrambler disc to the first position. The arrangement of the scramblers affects the encryption, so the exact arrangement is crucial to encipherment and decipherment. There are six different ways to arrange the three scramblers, so this feature increases the number of keys, or the number of possible initial settings, by a factor of six.

The second new feature was the insertion of a *plugboard* between the keyboard and the first scrambler. The plugboard allows the sender to insert cables that have the effect of swapping some of the letters before they enter the scrambler. For example, a cable could be used to connect the **a** and **b** sockets of the plugboard, so that when the cryptographer wants to encrypt the letter **b**, the electrical signal actually follows the path through the scramblers that previously would have been the path for the letter **a**, and vice versa. The Enigma operator had

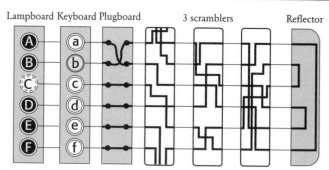

Figure 30 The plugboard sits between the keyboard and the first scrambler. By inserting cables it is possible to swap pairs of letters, so that, in this case, **b** is swapped with **a**. Now, **b** is encrypted by following the path previously associated with the encryption of **a**. In the real twenty-six letter Enigma, the user would have six cables for swapping six pairs of letters.

six cables, which meant that six pairs of letters could be swapped, leaving fourteen letters unplugged and unswapped. The letters swapped by the plugboard are part of the machine's setting, and so must be specified in the codebook. Figure 30 shows the layout of the machine with the plugboard in place. Because the diagram deals only with a six-letter alphabet, only one pair of letters, **a** and **b**, have been swapped.

Now that we know all the main elements of Scherbius' Enigma machine, we can work out the number of keys by combining the number of possible plugboard cablings with the number of possible scrambler arrangements and orientations. The following list shows each variable of the machine and the corresponding number of possibilities for each one:

Scrambler orientations. Each of the three scramblers can be set in one of 26 orientations. There are therefore $26 \times 26 \times 26$ settings: 17,576

Scrambler arrangements. The three scramblers (1, 2 and 3) can be positioned in any of the following six orders: 123, 132, 213, 231, 312, 321:   6

Plugboard. The number of ways of connecting, thereby swapping, 6 pairs of letters out of 26 is enormous:
100,391,791,500

Total. The total number of keys is the multiple of these three numbers: $17,576 \times 6 \times 100,391,791,500$

$$\approx 10,000,000,000,000,000$$

As long as sender and receiver have agreed on the plugboard cablings, the order of the scramblers and their respective orientations, all of which specify the key, they can encrypt and decrypt messages easily. However, an enemy interceptor who does not know the key would have to check every single one of the 10,000,000,000,000,000 possible keys in order to crack the ciphertext. To put this into context, a persistent cryptanalyst who is capable of checking one setting every minute would need longer than the age of the universe to check every setting. (In fact, I have ignored the effect of one aspect of the Enigma machine, known as the ring setting, so the number of possible keys is even larger, and the time to break Enigma even longer.)

Since by far the largest contribution to the number of keys comes from the plugboard, you might wonder why Scherbius bothered with the scramblers. On its own, the plugboard would provide a trivial cipher, because it would do nothing more than act as a monoalphabetic substitution cipher, just swapping around a few letters. The problem with the plugboard is that the swaps do not change once encryption begins, so on its own it would generate a ciphertext that could be broken by frequency analysis. The scramblers contribute a smaller number of keys, but their setup is continually changing, which

Figure 31 Arthur Scherbius.

means that the resulting ciphertext cannot be broken by frequency analysis. By combining the scramblers with the plugboard, Scherbius protected his machine against frequency analysis, and at the same time gave it an enormous number of possible keys.

Scherbius took out his first patent in 1918. His cipher machine was contained in a compact box measuring only 13.5 × 11 × 6 inches, but it weighed a hefty 26 pounds. Figure 32 shows an Enigma machine with the outer lid open, ready for use. It is possible to see the keyboard where the plaintext letters are typed in, and above it the lampboard, which displays the resulting ciphertext letter. Below the keyboard is the plugboard; there are more than six pairs of letters swapped by the plugboard, because this particular Enigma machine is a slightly later modification of the original model, which is the version that has been described so far. Figure 33 shows an Enigma with the cover plate removed to reveal more features, in particular the three scramblers.

Scherbius believed his cipher machine was invincible, and because the memories of security failures haunted the German military, he soon persuaded them to adopt Enigma. By 1925 Scherbius began mass-producing Enigmas, which went into military service the following year. They were subsequently used by the government and by state-run organizations such as the railways.

Over the next two decades, the German military would buy over thirty thousand Enigma machines. Scherbius' invention provided the most secure system of cryptography in the world, and at the outbreak of the Second World War the German military's communications were protected by an unparalleled level of encryption. At times, it seemed that the Enigma machine would play a vital role in ensuring Nazi victory, but instead it was ultimately part of Hitler's downfall. Scherbius did

Figure 32 An army Enigma machine ready for use.

Figure 33 An Enigma machine with the inner lid opened, revealing the three scramblers.

not live long enough to see the successes and failures of his cipher system. In 1929, while driving a team of horses, he lost control of his carriage and crashed into a wall, dying on May 13 from internal injuries.

CRACKING THE ENIGMA

In the years that followed the First World War, the British cryptanalysts in Room 40 continued to monitor German communications. In 1926 they began to intercept messages that baffled them completely. Enigma had arrived, and as the number of Enigma machines increased, Room 40's ability to gather intelligence diminished rapidly. The Americans and the French also tried to tackle the Enigma cipher, but their attempts were equally dismal, and they soon gave up hope of breaking it. Germany now had the most secure communications in the world.

The speed with which the Allied cryptanalysts abandoned hope of breaking Enigma was in sharp contrast to their perseverance just a decade earlier in the First World War. Confronted with the prospect of defeat, the Allied cryptanalysts had worked night and day to penetrate German ciphers. It would appear that fear was the main driving force, and that adversity is one of the foundations of successful codebreaking. However, in the wake of the First World War the Allies no longer feared anybody. Germany had been crippled by defeat, and the Allies were in a dominant position; as a result, they seemed to lose their cryptanalytic zeal.

One nation, however, could not afford to relax. After the First World War, Poland reestablished itself as an independent state, but it was concerned about threats to its newfound sovereignty. To the east lay Russia, a nation ambitious to spread its communism, and to the west lay Germany, intent upon regaining territory ceded to Poland after the war. Sandwiched between these two enemies, the Poles were desperate for intelligence information, and they formed a new cipher bureau, the Biuro Szyfrów. If necessity is the mother of invention, then perhaps adversity is the mother of cryptanalysis.

In charge of deciphering German messages was Captain Maksymilian Ciezki, a committed patriot who had grown up in the town of Szamotuly, a center of Polish nationalism. Ciezki had no access to a military Enigma machine, and without knowing the wirings of the military machine, he had no chance of deciphering messages being sent by the German army. He became so despondent that at one point he even employed a clairvoyant in a frantic attempt to conjure some sense from the enciphered intercepts. Not surprisingly, the clairvoyant failed to make the breakthrough the Biuro Szyfrów needed. Instead, it was left to a disaffected German, Hans-Thilo Schmidt, to make the first step toward breaking the Enigma cipher.

Hans-Thilo Schmidt was born in 1888 in Berlin, the second son of a distinguished professor and his aristocratic wife. Schmidt embarked on a career in the German army and fought in the First World War, but he was not considered worthy enough to remain in the army after the drastic cuts implemented as part of the Treaty of Versailles. He then tried to make his name as a businessman, but his soap factory was forced to close because of the postwar depression and hyperinflation, leaving him and his family destitute.

The humiliation of Schmidt's failures was compounded by the success of his elder brother, Rudolph, who had also fought in the war, and who was retained in the army afterward. During the 1920s Rudolph rose through the ranks and was eventually promoted to chief of staff of the Signal Corps. He was responsible for ensuring secure communications, and in fact it was Rudolph who officially sanctioned the army's use of the Enigma cipher.

After his business collapsed, Hans-Thilo was forced to ask his brother for help, and Rudolph arranged a job for him in Berlin at the Chiffrierstelle, the office responsible for administering Germany's encrypted communications. This was Enigma's command center, a top-secret establishment dealing with highly sensitive information. When Hans-Thilo moved to his new job, he left his family behind in Bavaria, where the cost of living was affordable. He was living alone in expensive Berlin, impoverished and isolated, envious of his perfect brother and resentful toward a nation that had rejected him. The result was inevitable. By selling secret Enigma information to foreign powers, Hans-Thilo Schmidt could earn money and gain revenge, damaging his country's security and undermining his brother's organization.

On November 8, 1931, Schmidt arrived at the Grand Hotel in Verviers, Belgium, for a liaison with a French secret agent code-named Rex. In exchange for 10,000 marks (equivalent to $30,000 in today's money), Schmidt allowed Rex to photograph two documents: "Gebrauchsanweisung für die Chiffriermaschine Enigma" and "Schlüsselanleitung für die Chiffriermaschine Enigma." These documents were essentially instructions for using the Enigma machine, and although there was no explicit description of the wirings inside each scrambler, they contained the information needed to deduce those wirings.

Thanks to Schmidt's treachery, it was now possible for the Allies to create an accurate replica of the German military Enigma machine. However, this was not enough to enable them to decipher messages encrypted by Enigma. The strength of the cipher depends not on keeping the machine secret, but on keeping the initial setting of the machine (the key) secret. If a cryptanalyst wants to decipher an intercepted message, then, in addition to having a replica of the Enigma machine, he still has to find which of the millions of billions of possible keys was used to encipher it. A German memorandum put it thus: "It is assumed in judging the security of the cryptosystem that the enemy has at his disposition the machine."

The French secret service was clearly up to scratch, having found an informant in Schmidt, and having obtained the documents that suggested the wirings of the military Enigma machine. In comparison, French cryptanalysts were inadequate, and seemed unwilling and unable to exploit this newly acquired information. The Bureau du Chiffre did not even bother trying to build a replica of the military Enigma machine, because they were convinced that achieving the next stage, finding the key required to decipher a particular Enigma message, was impossible.

As it happened, ten years earlier the French had signed an agreement of military cooperation with the Poles. The Poles had expressed an interest in anything connected with Enigma, so in accordance with their decade-old agreement the French simply handed the photographs of Schmidt's documents to their allies and left the hopeless task of cracking Enigma to the Biuro Szyfrów. The Biuro realized that the documents were only a starting point, but unlike the French, they had the fear of invasion to spur them on. The Poles convinced themselves that there must be a shortcut to finding the key to an Enigma-encrypted message and that if they applied sufficient effort, ingenuity and wit, they could find that shortcut.

As well as revealing the internal wirings of the scramblers, Schmidt's documents also explained in detail the layout of the codebooks used by the Germans. Each month, Enigma operators received a new codebook, which specified which key should be used for each day. For example, on the first day of the month, the codebook might specify the following *day key:*

1. *Plugboard settings:*	A/L - P/R - T/D - B/W - K/F - O/Y
2. *Scrambler arrangement:*	2–3–1
3. *Scrambler orientations:*	Q-C-W

Together, the scrambler arrangement and orientations are known as the scrambler settings. To implement this particular day key, the Enigma operator would set up his Enigma machine as follows:

1. *Plugboard settings:* Swap the letters A and L by connecting them via a lead on the plugboard, and similarly swap P and R, then T and D, then B and W, then K and F, and lastly O and Y.

2. *Scrambler arrangement:* Place the second scrambler in the first slot of the machine, the third scrambler in the second slot and the first scrambler in the third slot.

3. *Scrambler orientations:* Each scrambler has an alphabet engraved on its outer rim, which allows the operator to set it in a particular orientation. In this case, the operator would rotate the scrambler in slot 1 so that Q is facing upward, rotate the scrambler in the second slot so that C is facing upward, and rotate the scrambler in the third slot so that W is facing upward.

One way of encrypting messages would be for the sender to encrypt all the day's traffic according to the day key. This would mean that for a whole day all Enigma operators would set their machines according to the same day key. Then, each time a message needed to be sent, it would be typed into the machine; the enciphered output would be recorded and handed to the radio operator for transmission. At the other end, the receiving radio operator would record the incoming message and hand it to the Enigma operator, who would type it into his machine, which would already be set to the same day key. The output would be the original message.

This process is reasonably secure, but it is weakened by the repeated use of a single day key to encrypt the hundreds of messages that might be sent each day. In general, it is true that if a single key is used to encipher an enormous quantity of material, then it is easier for a cryptanalyst to deduce it. A large amount of identically encrypted material provides a cryptanalyst with a correspondingly larger chance of identifying the key. For example, harking back to simpler ciphers, it is much easier to break a monoalphabetic cipher with frequency analysis if there are several pages of encrypted material, as opposed to just a couple of sentences.

As an extra precaution, the Germans therefore took the clever step of using the day key settings to transmit a new *message key* for each message. The message keys would have the same plugboard settings and scrambler arrangement as the day keys but different scrambler orientations. Because the new scrambler orientation would not be in the codebook, the sender had to transmit it securely to the receiver according to the following process. First, the sender sets his machine according to the agreed day key, which includes a scrambler orientation, say, QCW. Next, he randomly picks a new scrambler orientation for the message key, say, PGH. He then enciphers PGH according to the day key. The message key is typed into the Enigma twice, just to provide a double check for the receiver. For example, the sender might encipher the message key PGHPGH as KIVBJE. Note that the two PGH's are enciphered differently (the first as KIV, the second as BJE), because the Enigma scramblers are rotating after each letter, and changing the overall mode of encryption. The sender then changes his machine to the **PGH** setting and encrypts the main message according to this message key. At the receiver's end, the machine is initially set according to the day key, **QCW**. The first six letters of the incoming message, **KIVBJE**, are typed in and reveal **PGHPGH**. The receiver then knows to reset his scramblers to **PGH**, the message key, and can then decipher the main body of the message.

This is equivalent to the sender and receiver agreeing on a main cipher key. Then, instead of using this single main cipher key to encrypt every message, they use it merely to encrypt a new cipher key for each message, and then encrypt the actual message according to the new cipher key. Had the Germans not employed message keys, then everything—perhaps thousands of messages containing millions of letters—would have been sent using the same day key. However, if the day key is used only to transmit the message keys, then it encrypts only a limited amount of text. If there are one thousand message keys sent in a day, then the day key encrypts only six thousand letters. And because each message key is picked at random and is used to encipher only one message, it encrypts a limited amount of text, perhaps just a few hundred characters.

At first sight the system seemed to be invulnerable, but the Polish cryptanalysts were undaunted. They were prepared to explore every avenue in order to find a weakness in the Enigma machine and its use of day and message keys. The Biuro organized a course on cryptography and invited twenty mathematicians, each of them sworn to an oath of secrecy. The mathematicians were all from the university at Poznán. Although not the most respected academic institution in Poland, it had the advantage of being located in the west of the country, in territory that had been part of Germany until 1918. These mathematicians were therefore fluent in German.

Three of the twenty demonstrated an aptitude for solving

ciphers and were recruited into the Biuro. The most gifted of them was Marian Rejewski, a timid twenty-three-year-old who had previously studied statistics in order to pursue a career in insurance.

Rejewski's strategy for attacking Enigma focused on the fact that repetition is the enemy of security: Repetition leads to patterns, and cryptanalysts thrive on patterns. The most obvious repetition in the Enigma encryption was the message key, which was enciphered twice at the beginning of every message. If the operator chose the message key ULJ, then he would encrypt it twice, so that ULJULJ might be enciphered as PEFNWZ, which he would then send at the start before the actual message. The Germans had demanded this repetition in order to avoid mistakes caused by radio interference or operator error. But they did not foresee that this would jeopardize the security of the machine.

Each day, Rejewski would find himself with a new batch of intercepted messages. They all began with the six letters of the repeated three-letter message key, all encrypted according to the same agreed day key. For example, he might receive four messages that began with the following encrypted message keys:

	1st	2nd	3rd	4th	5th	6th
1st message	L	O	K	R	G	M
2nd message	M	V	T	X	Z	E
3rd message	J	K	T	M	P	E
4th message	D	V	Y	P	Z	X

In each message, the first and fourth letters are encryptions of the same letter, namely, the first letter of the message key. Also, the second and fifth letters are encryptions of the same letter, namely, the second letter of the message key, and the third and sixth letters are encryptions of the same letter, namely, the third

letter of the message key. For example, in the first message, L
and R are encryptions of the same letter, the first letter of the
message key. The reason why this same letter is encrypted differently, first as L and then as R, is that between the two encryptions the first Enigma scrambler has moved on three steps,
changing the overall mode of scrambling.

The fact that L and R are encryptions of the same letter allowed Rejewski to deduce some slight constraint on the initial
setup of the machine. The initial scrambler setting, which is
unknown, encrypted the first letter of the day key, which is also
unknown, into L, and then another scrambler setting, three
steps forward from the initial setting, which is still unknown,
encrypted the same letter of the day key, which is also still unknown, into R.

This constraint might seem vague, as it is full of unknowns,
but at least it demonstrates that the letters L and R are inti-
mately related by the initial setting of the Enigma machine, the
day key. As each new message is intercepted, it is possible to
identify other relationships between the first and fourth letters
of the repeated message key. All these relationships are reflec-
tions of the initial setting of the Enigma machine. For example, the second message above tells us that M and X are related,
the third tells us that J and M are related, and the fourth that D
and P are related. Rejewski began to summarize these relationships by tabulating them. For the four messages we have so far,
the table would reflect the relationships between (L,R), (M,X),
(J,M) and (D,P):

1st letter	A B C D E F G H I J K L M N O P Q R S T U V W X Y Z
4th letter	P M R X

If Rejewski had access to enough messages in a single day, then
he would be able to complete the alphabet of relationships. The
following table shows such a completed set of relationships:

1st letter	A B C D E F G H I J K L M N O P Q R S T U V W X Y Z
4th letter	F Q H P L W O G B M V R X U Y C Z I T N J E A S D K

Rejewski had no idea of the day key, and he had no idea which message keys were being chosen, but he did know that they resulted in this table of relationships. Had the day key been different, then the table of relationships would have been completely different. The next question was whether there existed any way of determining the day key by looking at the table of relationships. Rejewski began to look for patterns within the table, structures that might indicate the day key. Eventually, he began to study one particular type of pattern, which featured chains of letters. For example, in the table, A on the top row is linked to F on the bottom row, so next he would look up F on the top row. It turns out that F is linked to W, and so he would look up W on the top row. And it turns out that W is linked to A, which is where we started. The chain has been completed.

With the remaining letters in the alphabet, Rejewski would generate more chains. He listed all the chains, and noted the number of links in each one:

A → F → W → A	3 links
B → Q → Z → K → V → E → L → R → I → B	9 links
C → H → G → O → Y → D → P → C	7 links
J → M → X → S → T → N → U → J	7 links

So far, we have only considered the links between the first and fourth letters of the six-letter repeated key. In fact, Rejewski would repeat this whole exercise for the relationships between the second and fifth letters, and the third and sixth letters, identifying the chains in each case and the number of links in each chain.

Rejewski noticed that the chains changed each day. Sometimes there were lots of short chains, sometimes just a few long chains. And, of course, the letters within the chains changed. The characteristics of the chains were clearly a result of the day key setting—a complex consequence of the plugboard settings, the scrambler arrangement and the scrambler orientations. However, there remained the question of how Rejewski could determine the day key from these chains. Which of 10,000,000,000,000,000 possible day keys was related to a particular pattern of chains? The number of possibilities was simply too great.

It was at this point that Rejewski had a profound insight. Although the plugboard and scrambler settings both affect the details of the chains, their contributions can to some extent be disentangled. In particular, there is one aspect of the chains that is wholly dependent on the scrambler settings and has nothing to do with the plugboard settings: the number of links in the chains, which is purely a consequence of the scrambler settings. For instance, let us take the example above and pretend that the day key required the letters S and G to be swapped as part of the plugboard settings. If we change this element of

Figure 34 Hans-Thilo Schmidt.

Figure 35 Marian Rejewski.

the day key, by removing the cable that swaps **S** and **G**, and use it to swap, say, **T** and **K** instead, then the chains would change to the following:

A → F → W → A	3 links
B → Q → Z → T → V → E → L → R → I → B	9 links
C → H → S → O → Y → D → P → C	7 links
J → M → X → G → K → N → U → J	7 links

Some of the letters in the chains have changed, but, crucially, the number of links in each chain remains constant. Rejewski had identified a facet of the chains that was solely a reflection of the scrambler settings.

The total number of scrambler settings is the number of scrambler arrangements (6) multiplied by the number of scrambler orientations (17,576), which comes to 105,456. So, instead of having to worry about which of the 10,000,000,000,000,000 day keys was associated with a particular set of chains, Rejewski could busy himself with a drastically simpler problem: Which of the 105,456 scrambler settings was associated with the number of links within a set of chains? This number is still large, but it is roughly one hundred billion times smaller than the total number of possible day keys. In short, the task has become one hundred billion times easier, certainly within the realm of human endeavor.

Rejewski proceeded as follows. Thanks to Hans-Thilo Schmidt's espionage, he had access to replica Enigma machines. His team began the laborious chore of checking each of 105,456 scrambler settings and cataloging the chain lengths that were generated by each one. It took an entire year to complete the catalog, but once the Biuro had accumulated the data, Rejewski could finally begin to unravel the Enigma cipher.

Each day, he would look at the encrypted message keys, the first six letters of all the intercepted messages, and use the information to build his table of relationships. This would allow him to trace the chains and establish the number of links in each chain. For example, analyzing the first and fourth letters might result in four chains with three, nine, seven and seven links. Analyzing the second and fifth letters might also result in four chains, with two, three, nine and twelve links. Analyzing the third and sixth letters might result in five chains with five, five, five, three and eight links. As yet, Rejewski still had no idea of the day key, but he knew that it resulted in three sets of chains with the following number of chains and links in each one:

4 chains from the 1st and 4th letters, with 3, 9, 7 and 7 links

4 chains from the 2nd and 5th letters, with 2, 3, 9 and 12 links

5 chains from the 3rd and 6th letters, with 5, 5, 5, 3 and 8 links

Rejewski could now go to his catalog, which contained every scrambler setting indexed according to the sort of chains it would generate. Having found the catalog entry that contained the right number of chains with the appropriate number of links in each one, he immediately knew the scrambler settings for that particular day key. The chains were effectively fingerprints, the evidence that betrayed the initial scrambler arrangement and orientations. Rejewski was working just like a detective who might find a fingerprint at the scene of a crime and then use a database to match it to a suspect.

Although he had identified the scrambler part of the day key, Rejewski still had to establish the plugboard settings. There are about a hundred billion possibilities for the plugboard settings, but this was a relatively straightforward task. Rejewski would begin by setting the scramblers in his Enigma replica according to the newly established scrambler part of the day key. He would then remove all cables from the plugboard, so that the plugboard had no effect. Finally, he would take a piece of intercepted ciphertext and type it into the Enigma machine. This would largely result in gibberish, because the plugboard cablings were unknown and missing. However, every so often vaguely recognizable phrases would appear, such as **alliveinbelrin**—presumably, this should be "arrive in Berlin." If this assumption is correct, then it would imply that the letters **R** and **L** should be connected and swapped by a plugboard cable, while **A, I, V, E, B** and **N** should not. By analyzing other phrases, it would be possible to identify the other five pairs of letters that had been swapped by the plugboard. Having established the plugboard settings, and having already discovered the scrambler settings, Rejewski had the complete day key, and could then decipher any message sent that day.

Rejewski had vastly simplified the task of finding the day key by divorcing the problem of finding the scrambler settings from the problem of finding the plugboard settings. On their own, both of these problems were solvable. Originally, we estimated that it would take more than the lifetime of the universe to check every possible Enigma key. However, Rejewski had spent only a year compiling his catalog of chain lengths, and thereafter he could find the day key before the day was out. Once he had the day key, he possessed the same information as the intended receiver and so could decipher messages just as easily.

Following Rejewski's breakthrough, German communications became transparent. Poland was not at war with Germany, but there was a threat of invasion, so Polish relief at conquering Enigma was nevertheless immense. If they could find out what the German generals had in mind for them, there was a chance that they could defend themselves. The Polish nation had depended on Rejewski, and he did not disappoint his country. Rejewski's attack on Enigma is one of the truly great accomplishments of cryptanalysis. I have had to sum up his work in just a few pages, and so have omitted many of the technical details, and all of the dead ends. Enigma is a complicated cipher machine, and breaking it required immense intellectual force. My simplifications should not mislead you into underestimating Rejewski's extraordinary achievement.

The Polish success in breaking the Enigma cipher can be attributed to three factors: fear, mathematics and espionage. Without the fear of invasion, the Poles would have been discouraged by the apparent invulnerability of the Enigma cipher. Without mathematics, Rejewski would not have been able to analyze the chains. And without Schmidt, code-named Asche, and his documents, the wirings of the scramblers would not have been known, and cryptanalysis could not even have begun. Rejewski did not hesitate to express the debt he owed Schmidt: "Asche's documents were welcomed like manna from heaven, and all doors were immediately opened."

The Poles successfully used Rejewski's technique for several years. When Hermann Göring visited Warsaw in 1934, he was totally unaware of the fact that his communications were being intercepted and deciphered. As he and other German dignitaries laid a wreath at the Tomb of the Unknown Soldier next to the offices of the Biuro Szyfrów, Rejewski could stare down at them from his window, content in the knowledge that he could read their most secret communications.

Even when the Germans made a minor alteration to the way they transmitted messages, Rejewski fought back. His old catalog of chain lengths was useless, but rather than rewriting the catalog, he devised a mechanized version of his cataloging system, which could automatically search for the correct scrambler settings. Rejewski's invention was an adaptation of the Enigma machine, able to rapidly check each of the 17,576 settings until it spotted a match. Because of the six possible scrambler arrangements, it was necessary to have six of Rejewski's machines working in parallel, each one representing one of the possible arrangements. Together, they formed a unit that was about three feet high, capable of finding the day key in roughly two hours. The units were called *bombes,* a name that might reflect the ticking noise they made while checking scrambler settings. Alternatively, it is said that Rejewski got his inspiration for the machines while at a cafe eating a bombe, an ice cream shaped into a hemisphere. The bombes effectively mechanized the process of decipherment. It was a natural response to Enigma, which was a mechanization of encipherment.

For most of the 1930s, Rejewski and his colleagues worked tirelessly to uncover the Enigma keys. Month after month, the team would have to deal with the stresses and strains of cryptanalysis, continually having to fix mechanical failures in the bombes, continually having to deal with the never-ending supply of encrypted intercepts. Their lives became dominated by the pursuit of the day key, that vital piece of information that would reveal the meaning of the encrypted messages. However, unknown to the Polish codebreakers, much of their work was unnecessary. The chief of the Biuro, Major Gwido Langer, already had the Enigma day keys, but he kept them hidden, tucked away in his desk.

Langer, via the French, was still receiving information from Schmidt. The German spy's underhanded activities did not end in 1931 with the delivery of the two documents on the operation of Enigma, but continued for another seven years. He met the French secret agent Rex on twenty occasions, often in secluded alpine chalets where privacy was guaranteed. At every meeting, Schmidt handed over one or more codebooks, each one containing a month's worth of day keys. These were the codebooks that were distributed to all German Enigma operators, and they contained all the information that was needed to encipher and decipher messages. In total, he provided codebooks that contained thirty-eight months' worth of day keys. The keys would have saved Rejewski an enormous amount of time and effort, eliminating the necessity for bombes and sparing manpower that could have been used in other sections of the Biuro. However, the remarkably astute Langer decided not to tell Rejewski that the keys existed. By depriving Rejewski of the keys, Langer believed he was preparing him for the inevitable time when the keys would no longer be available. He knew that if war broke out, it would be impossible for Schmidt to continue to attend covert meetings, and Rejewski would then be forced to be self-sufficient. Langer thought that Rejewski should practice self-sufficiency in peacetime, as preparation for what lay ahead.

Rejewski's skills eventually reached their limit in December 1938, when German cryptographers increased Enigma's security. Enigma operators were all given two new scramblers, so that the scrambler arrangement might involve any three of the five available scramblers. Previously there were only three scramblers (labeled 1, 2 and 3) to choose from, and only six ways to arrange them, but now that there were two extra scramblers (labeled 4 and 5) to choose from, the number of arrangements rose to sixty, as shown in Table 7. Rejewski's first challenge was to work out the internal wirings of the two new scramblers. More worryingly, he also had to build ten times as many bombes, each representing a different scrambler arrangement. The sheer cost of building such a battery of bombes was fifteen times the Biuro's entire annual equipment budget. The following month, the situation worsened when the number of plugboard cables increased from six to ten. Instead of twelve letters being swapped before entering the scramblers, there were now twenty swapped letters. The number of possible keys increased to 159,000,000,000,000,000,000.

In 1938, Polish interceptions and decipherments had been at their peak, but by the beginning of 1939, the new scramblers and extra plugboard cables stemmed the flow of intelligence. Rejewski, who had pushed forward the boundaries of crypt-analysis in previous years, was confounded. He had proved that Enigma was not an unbreakable cipher, but without the re-sources required to check every scrambler setting, he could not find the day key, and decipherment was impossible. Under such desperate circumstances, Langer might have been tempted to hand over the keys that had been obtained by Schmidt, but the keys were no longer being delivered. Just before the introduc-tion of the new scramblers, Schmidt had broken off contact with the agent Rex. For seven years he had supplied keys that were superfluous because of Polish innovation. Now, just when the Poles needed the keys, they were no longer available.

The new invulnerability of Enigma was a devastating blow to Poland, because Enigma was not merely a means of com-munication, but was at the heart of Hitler's blitzkrieg strategy. The concept of blitzkrieg (the word means "lightning war")

Table 7 Possible arrangements with five scramblers.

Arrangements with three scramblers	Extra arrangements available with two extra scramblers								
123	124	125	134	135	142	143	145	152	153
132	154	214	215	234	235	241	243	245	251
213	253	254	314	315	324	325	341	342	345
231	351	352	354	412	413	415	421	423	425
312	431	432	435	451	452	453	512	513	514
321	521	523	524	531	532	534	541	542	543

Figure 36 General Heinz Guderian's command-post vehicle. An Enigma machine can be seen in use at bottom left.

involved rapid, intense, coordinated attack, which meant that large tank divisions would have to communicate with each other and with infantry and artillery. Furthermore, land forces would be backed up by air support from dive-bombing Stukas, which would rely on effective and secure communication between the front-line troops and the airfields. The philosophy of blitzkrieg was "speed of attack through speed of communications." If the Poles could not break Enigma, they had no hope of stopping the German onslaught, which was clearly only a matter of months away. Germany already occupied the Sudetenland, and on April 27, 1939, it withdrew from its nonaggression treaty with Poland. Hitler's anti-Polish speeches became increasingly vicious. Langer was determined that if Poland was invaded, then its cryptanalytic breakthroughs, which had so far been kept secret from the Allies, should not be lost. If Poland could not benefit from Rejewski's work, then at least the Allies should have the chance to try to build on it. Perhaps Britain and France, with their extra resources, could fully exploit the concept of the bombe.

On June 30, Major Langer telegraphed his French and British counterparts, inviting them to Warsaw to discuss some urgent matters concerning Enigma. On July 24, senior French and British cryptanalysts arrived at the Biuro's headquarters, not knowing quite what to expect. Langer ushered them into a room in which stood an object covered with a black cloth. He pulled away the cloth, dramatically revealing one of Rejewski's bombes. The audience were astonished as they heard how Rejewski had been breaking Enigma for years. The Poles were a decade ahead of anybody else in the world. The French were particularly astonished, because the Polish work had been based on the results of French espionage. The French had handed the information from Schmidt to the Poles because they believed it to be of no value, but the Poles had proved them wrong.

As a final surprise, Langer offered the British and French two spare Enigma replicas and blueprints for the bombes, which were to be shipped in diplomatic bags to Paris. From there, on August 16, one of the Enigma machines was forwarded to London. It was smuggled across the Channel as part of the baggage of the playwright Sacha Guitry and his wife, the actress Yvonne Printemps, so as not to arouse the suspicion of German spies who would be monitoring the ports. Two weeks later, on September 1, Hitler invaded Poland, and the war began.

THE GEESE THAT NEVER CACKLED

The Poles had proved that Enigma was not a perfect cipher, and they had also demonstrated to the Allies the value of employing mathematicians as codebreakers. In Britain, Room 40 had always been dominated by linguists and classicists, but now there was a concerted effort to balance the staff with mathematicians and scientists. They were recruited largely via the old-boy network, with those inside Room 40 contacting their former Oxford and Cambridge colleges. There was also an old-girl network that recruited women undergraduates from places such as Newnham College and Girton College, Cambridge.

The new recruits were not brought to Room 40 in London, but instead went to Bletchley Park, Buckinghamshire, the home of the Government Code and Cypher School (GC&CS), a newly formed codebreaking organization that was taking over from Room 40. Bletchley Park could house a much larger staff, which was important because a deluge of encrypted intercepts was expected as soon as the war started. During the First World War, Germany had transmitted two million words a month, but it was anticipated that the greater availability of radios in the Second World War could result in the transmission of two million words a day.

At the center of Bletchley Park was a large Victorian Tudor-Gothic mansion built by the nineteenth-century financier Sir Herbert Leon. The mansion, with its library, dining hall and ornate ballroom, provided the central administration for the whole of the Bletchley operation. Commander Alastair Denniston, the director of GC&CS, had a ground-floor office overlooking the gardens, a view that was soon spoiled by the construction of numerous huts. These makeshift wooden buildings housed the various codebreaking activities. Initially, Bletchley Park had a staff of only two hundred, but within five years the mansion and the huts would house seven thousand men and women.

During the autumn of 1939, the scientists and mathematicians at Bletchley learned the intricacies of the Enigma cipher and rapidly mastered the Polish techniques. Bletchley had more staff and resources than the Polish Biuro Szyfrów and was thus able to cope with the larger selection of scramblers and the fact that Enigma was now ten times harder to break. Every twenty-four hours, the British codebreakers went through the same routine. At midnight, German Enigma operators would change to a new day key, at which point whatever breakthroughs Bletchley had achieved the previous day could no longer be used to decipher messages. The codebreakers now had to begin the task of trying to identify the new day key. It could take several hours, but as soon as they had discovered the Enigma settings for that day, the Bletchley staff could begin to decipher the German messages that had already accumulated, revealing information that was invaluable to the war effort.

Surprise is an invaluable weapon for a commander to have at his disposal. But if Bletchley could break into Enigma, German plans would become transparent and the British would be able to read the minds of the German high command. If the British could pick up news of an imminent attack, they could send reinforcements or take evasive action. If they could decipher

German discussions of their own weaknesses, the Allies would be able to focus their offensives. The Bletchley decipherments were of the utmost importance. For example, when Germany invaded Denmark and Norway in April 1940, Bletchley provided a detailed picture of German operations. Similarly, during the Battle of Britain, the cryptanalysts were able to give advance warning of bombing raids, including times and locations.

Once they had mastered the Polish techniques, the Bletchley cryptanalysts began to invent their own shortcuts for finding the Enigma keys. For example, they cottoned on to the fact that the German Enigma operators would occasionally choose obvious message keys. For each message, the operator was supposed to select a different message key, three letters chosen at random. However, in the heat of battle, rather than straining their imaginations to pick a random key, the overworked operators would sometimes pick three consecutive letters from the Enigma keyboard (Figure 32), such as **QWE** or **BNM**. These

Figure 37 In August 1939, Britain's senior codebreakers visited Bletchley Park to assess its suitability for the new Government Code and Cypher School. To avoid arousing suspicion from locals, they claimed to be part of Captain Ridley's shooting party.

predictable message keys became known as *cillies*. Another type of cilly was the repeated use of the same message key, perhaps the initials of the operator's girlfriend—indeed, one such set of initials, CIL, may have been the origin of the term. Before cracking Enigma the hard way, it became routine for the cryptanalysts to try out the cillies, and their hunches would sometimes pay off.

As the Enigma machine continued to evolve during the course of the war, the cryptanalysts were continually forced to innovate, to redesign and refine the bombes and to devise wholly new strategies. Part of the reason for their success was the bizarre combination of mathematicians, scientists, linguists, classicists, chess grandmasters and puzzle addicts within each hut. An intractable problem would be passed around the hut until it reached someone who had the right mental tools to solve it. However, if there is one figure who deserves to be singled out, it is the mathematician Alan Turing, who identified Enigma's greatest weakness and ruthlessly exploited it. Thanks to Turing, it became possible to crack the Enigma cipher under even the most difficult circumstances.

At the outbreak of war, Turing left his post at Cambridge University and joined the codebreakers at Bletchley Park, spending much of his time in the Bletchley think tank, formerly Sir Herbert Leon's apple, pear and plum store. The think tank was where the cryptanalysts brainstormed their way through new problems or anticipated how to tackle problems that might arise in the future. Turing focused on what would happen if the German military changed their system of exchanging message keys. Bletchley's early successes relied on Rejewski's work, which exploited the fact that Enigma operators encrypted each message key twice (for example, if the message key was **YGB**, the operator would encipher **YGBYGB**). This repetition was supposed to ensure that the receiver did not make a mistake, but it created a chink in the security of Enigma. British cryptanalysts guessed it would not be long before the Germans noticed that the repeated key was compromising the Enigma cipher, at which point the Enigma operators would be told to abandon the repetition, thus confounding Bletchley's current codebreaking techniques. It was Turing's job to find an alternative way to attack Enigma, one that did not rely on a repeated message key.

As the weeks passed, Turing realized that Bletchley was building up a vast library of decrypted messages, and he noticed that many of them conformed to a rigid structure. By studying old decrypted messages, he believed he could sometimes predict part of the contents of an undeciphered message, based on when it was sent and its source. For example, experience showed that the Germans sent a regular enciphered weather report shortly after 6 A.M. each day. So an encrypted message intercepted at 6:05 A.M. would be almost certain to contain **wetter**, the German word for "weather." The rigorous protocol used by any military organization meant that such

Figure 38 Alan Turing.

messages were highly regimented in style, so Turing could even be confident about the location of **wetter** within the encrypted message. For example, experience might tell him that the first six letters of a particular ciphertext corresponded to the plain-text letters **wetter**. When a piece of plaintext can be associated with a piece of ciphertext, this combination is known as a *crib*.

Turing proved that the crib placed severe constraints on the setup of the machine used to encrypt the message. In other words, it was possible to home in on the message key, and then the day key, the latter of which could be used to decipher other messages sent on the same day. It was still necessary to check thousands of Enigma scrambler settings in order to see which one satisfied the constraints, so Turing designed a machine for performing this task. It was called a bombe, after the Polish codebreaking machine that had helped to give Bletchley Park a head start against the Enigma cipher.

While waiting for the first of the bombes to be manufac-tured and delivered, Turing continued his day-to-day work at Bletchley. News of his breakthrough soon spread among the other senior cryptanalysts, who recognized that he was a sin-gularly gifted codebreaker. According to Peter Hilton, a fellow Bletchley codebreaker, "Alan Turing was obviously a genius, but he was an approachable, friendly genius. He was always willing to take time and trouble to explain his ideas; but he was no narrow specialist, so that his versatile thought ranged over a vast area of the exact sciences."

However, everything at the Government Code and Cypher School was top secret, so nobody outside of Bletchley Park was aware of Turing's remarkable achievement. For example, his parents had absolutely no idea that Alan was even a codebreaker, let alone Britain's foremost cryptanalyst. He had once told his mother that he was involved in some form of military research, but he did not elaborate. She was merely disappointed that this had not resulted in a more respectable haircut for her scruffy son. Although Bletchley was run by the military, they had conceded that they would have to tolerate the scruffiness and eccentricities of these "professor types." Turing rarely bothered to shave, his nails were stuffed with dirt and his clothes were a mass of creases.

By the end of 1941, there were fifteen bombes in operation, exploiting cribs, checking scrambler settings and revealing keys, each one clattering like a million knitting needles. If everything was going well, a bombe might find an Enigma key within an hour. Once the plugboard cablings and the scrambler settings (the message key) had been established for a particular message, it was easy to deduce the day key. All the other messages sent that same day could then be deciphered.

Even though the bombes represented a vital breakthrough in cryptanalysis, decipherment had not become a formality. There were many hurdles to overcome before the bombes could even begin to look for a key. For example, to operate a bombe you first needed a crib. The senior codebreakers would give cribs to the bombe operators, but there was no guarantee that the codebreakers had guessed the correct meaning of the ciphertext. And even if they did have the right crib, it might be in the wrong place—the cryptanalysts might have guessed that an encrypted message contained a certain phrase, but associated that phrase with the wrong piece of the ciphertext. However, there was a neat trick for checking whether a crib was in the correct position.

In the following crib, the cryptanalyst is confident that the plaintext is right, but he is not sure if he has matched it with the correct letters in the ciphertext.

| Guessed plaintext | w e t t e r n u l l s e c h s |
| Known ciphertext | I P R E N L W K M J J S X C P L E J W Q |

One of the features of the Enigma machine was its inability to encipher a letter as itself, which was a consequence of the reflector. The letter a could never be enciphered as A, the letter b could never be enciphered as B, and so on. The particular crib on the previous page must therefore be misaligned, because the first e in wetter is matched with an E in the ciphertext. To find the correct alignment, we simply slide the plaintext and the ciphertext relative to each other until no letter is paired with itself. If we shift the plaintext one place to the left, the match still fails, because this time the first s in sechs is matched with S in the ciphertext. However, if we shift the plaintext one place to the right, there are no illegal encipherments. This crib is therefore likely to be in the right place, and could be used as the basis for a bombe decipherment:

Guessed plaintext	w e t t e r n u l l s e c h s
Known ciphertext	I P R E N L W K M J J S X C P L E J W Q

The military intelligence derived from cracking the German Enigma was part of an intelligence-gathering operation codenamed Ultra. The Ultra files, which also contained decipherment of Italian and Japanese messages, gave the Allies a clear advantage in all the major arenas of the war. In North Africa, Ultra helped to destroy German supply lines and informed the Allies of the status of General Rommel's forces, enabling the Eighth Army to fight back against the German advances. Ultra also warned of the German invasion of Greece, allowing British troops to retreat without suffering heavy losses. In fact, Ultra provided accurate reports on the enemy's situation throughout the entire Mediterranean region. This information was particularly valuable when the Allies landed in Italy and Sicily in 1943. In 1944, Ultra played a major role in the Allied invasion of Europe. For example, in the months before D-Day the Bletchley decipherments provided a detailed picture of German troop concentrations along the French coast.

Crucially, the information had to be used in such a way as not to arouse the suspicion of the German military. In order to maintain the Ultra secret, Churchill's commanders took a variety of precautions. For example, the Enigma decipherments gave the locations of numerous U-boats, but it would have been unwise to attack every single one of them, because a sudden, unexplained increase in successful British attacks would suggest to Germany that its communications were being deciphered. Consequently, a number of U-boat coordinates were not passed on to the commanders at sea, allowing some of them to escape. Other U-boats were attacked only after a spotter plane had been sent out first, thus justifying the approach of a destroyer some hours later. Alternatively, the Allies might send fake messages describing sightings of U-boats, which likewise provided sufficient explanation for the ensuing attack.

Despite this policy of minimizing telltale signs that Enigma had been broken, British actions did sometimes raise concerns among Germany's security experts. On one occasion Bletchley

Figure 39 A bombe in action.

deciphered an Enigma message giving the exact location of a group of German tankers and supply ships, nine in total. Those responsible for exploiting the Ultra intelligence decided not to sink all the ships, in case this aroused German suspicion. Instead, they informed destroyers of the exact location of just seven of the ships, which should have allowed the *Gedania* and the *Gonzenheim* to escape unharmed. The seven targeted ships were indeed sunk, but Royal Navy destroyers accidentally encountered the two ships that were supposed to be spared, and sank them too. The destroyers did not know about Enigma or the policy of not arousing suspicion—they merely believed they were doing their duty. Back in Berlin, Admiral Kurt Fricke instigated an investigation into this and similar attacks, exploring the possibility that the British had broken the Enigma cipher. The report concluded that the numerous losses were either the result of natural misfortune or caused by a British spy who had infiltrated the German navy. The breaking of Enigma was considered impossible and inconceivable.

Stuart Milner-Barry, one of the Bletchley Park cryptanalysts, wrote: "I do not imagine that any war since classical times, if ever, has been fought in which one side read consistently the main military and naval intelligence of the other." It has been argued, albeit controversially, that Bletchley's achievements were the decisive factor in the Allied victory. What is certain is that the British codebreakers significantly shortened the war. This becomes evident by rerunning the Battle of the Atlantic and speculating what might have happened without the benefit of the Ultra intelligence. To begin with, more ships and supplies would certainly have been lost to the dominant U-boat fleet, and that would have compromised the vital link to America and forced the Allies to divert manpower and resources into the building of new ships. Historians have estimated that this would have delayed Allied plans by several months, which would have meant postponing the D-Day invasion until at least the following year. This would have cost lives on both sides.

However, cryptanalysis is a clandestine activity, so Bletchley's accomplishments remained a closely guarded secret even after 1945. Having successfully deciphered messages during the war, Britain wanted to continue its intelligence operations and was reluctant to divulge its capabilities. In fact, Britain had captured thousands of Enigma machines and distributed them among its former colonies, who believed that the cipher was as secure as it had seemed to the Germans. The British did nothing to disabuse them of this belief, and routinely deciphered their secret communications in the years that followed.

Consequently, the thousands of men and women who had contributed to the creation of Ultra received no recognition for their achievements. Most of the codebreakers returned to their civilian lives, sworn to secrecy, unable to reveal their pivotal role in the Allied war effort. While those who had fought conventional battles could talk of their heroic achievements, those who had fought intellectual battles of no less significance had to endure the embarrassment of having to evade questions about their wartime activities. According to Gordon Welchman, one of the young cryptanalysts working with him at Bletchley received a scathing letter from his old headmaster, accusing him of being a disgrace to his school for not being at the front. Derek Taunt, another cryptanalyst, summed up the true contribution of his colleagues: "Our happy band may not have been with King Harry on St. Crispin's Day, but we had certainly not been abed and have no reason to think ourselves accurs't for having been where we were."

After three decades of silence, the cloud of secrecy over Bletchley Park was dispersed in the early 1970s. Captain F. W. Winterbotham, who had been responsible for distributing the Ultra intelligence, badgered the British government, arguing that the Commonwealth countries had stopped using the Enigma cipher and that there was now nothing to be gained by concealing the fact that Britain had broken it. The intelligence services reluctantly agreed, and permitted him to write a book about Bletchley Park. Published in the summer of 1974, Winterbotham's *The Ultra Secret* meant that Bletchley codebreakers could at last get the recognition they deserved.

Tragically, Alan Turing did not live long enough to receive any public recognition. Before the war Turing had shown himself to be a mathematical genius, publishing work that had laid down the ground rules for computers. At Bletchley Park he turned his mind to cracking Enigma, arguably making the single most important contribution to finding the flaws in the German cipher machine. After the war, instead of being acclaimed a hero, he was persecuted for his homosexuality. In 1952, while reporting a burglary to the police, he naively revealed that he was having a homosexual relationship. The police felt they had no option but to charge him with "Gross Indecency contrary to Section II of the Criminal law Amendment Act 1885." The newspapers reported the subsequent trial and conviction, and Turing was publicly humiliated.

Turing's secret had been exposed, and his sexuality was now public knowledge. The British government withdrew his security clearance. He was forbidden to work on research projects relating to the development of the computer. He was forced to consult a psychiatrist and to undergo hormone treatment, which made him impotent and obese. Over the next two years he became severely depressed, and on June 7, 1954, he went to his bedroom, carrying with him a jar of cyanide solution and an apple. He dipped the apple in the cyanide and took several bites. At the age of just forty-two, one of the true geniuses of cryptanalysis committed suicide.

4

The Language Barrier

The impenetrability of unknown languages, the Navajo code talkers of World War II and the decipherment of Egyptian hieroglyphs

While British codebreakers were breaking the German Enigma cipher and altering the course of the war in Europe, American codebreakers were having an equally important influence on events in the Pacific arena by cracking the various Japanese ciphers such as Purple. For example, in June 1942 the Americans deciphered a message outlining a Japanese plan to draw U.S. naval forces to the Aleutian Islands by faking an attack, which would allow the Japanese navy to take their real objective, Midway Island. Although American ships played along with the plan by leaving Midway, they never strayed far away. When American cryptanalysts intercepted and deciphered the Japanese order to attack Midway, the ships were able to return swiftly and defend the island in one of the most important battles of the entire Pacific war. According to Admiral Chester Nimitz, the American victory at Midway "was essentially a victory of intelligence. In attempting surprise, the Japanese were themselves surprised."

To protect their own communications, American forces

used mechanical devices similar to the Enigma cipher. Unlike Enigma, these machines were never cracked, but during the Pacific campaign, American commanders began to realize that cipher machines had a fundamental drawback. Although electromechanical encryption offered relatively high levels of security, it was painfully slow. Messages had to be typed into the machine letter by letter, the output had to be noted down letter by letter, and then the completed ciphertext had to be transmitted by the radio operator. The radio operator who received the enciphered message then had to pass it on to a cipher expert, who would carefully select the correct key and type the ciphertext into a cipher machine, to decipher it letter by letter.

The time and space required for this delicate operation is available at headquarters or on board a ship, but machine encryption was not ideally suited to more hostile and intense environments, such as the islands of the Pacific. One war correspondent described the difficulties of communication during the heat of jungle battle: "When the fighting became confined to a small area, everything had to move on a split-second schedule. There was not time for enciphering and deciphering. At such times, the King's English became a last resort—the profaner the better." Unfortunately for the Americans, many Japanese soldiers had attended American colleges and were fluent in English, including the profanities. Valuable information about American strategy and tactics was falling into the hands of the enemy.

One of the first to react to this problem was Philip Johnston, an engineer based in Los Angeles, who was too old to fight but still wanted to contribute to the war effort. At the beginning of 1942 he began to formulate an encryption system inspired by his childhood experiences. The son of a Protestant missionary, Johnston had grown up on the Navajo reservations of Arizona, and as a result, he had become fully immersed in Navajo culture.

He was one of the few people outside the tribe who could speak their language fluently, which allowed him to act as an interpreter for discussions between the Navajo and government agents. His work in this capacity culminated in a visit to the White House, when, as a nine-year-old, Johnston translated for two Navajos who were appealing to President Theodore Roosevelt for fairer treatment for their community. Fully aware of how impenetrable the language was for those outside the tribe, Johnston was struck by the notion that Navajo, or any other Native American language, could act as a virtually unbreakable code. If each battalion in the Pacific employed a pair of Native Americans as radio operators, secure communication could be guaranteed. This would be much simpler than a mechanical encryption device and much harder to crack.

He took his idea to Lieutenant Colonel James E. Jones, the area signal officer at Camp Elliott, just outside San Diego. Merely by throwing a few Navajo phrases at the bewildered officer, Johnston was able to persuade him that the idea was worthy of serious consideration. Two weeks later he returned with two Navajos, ready to conduct a test demonstration in front of senior marine officers. The Navajos were isolated from each other, and one was given six typical messages in English, which he translated into Navajo and transmitted to his colleague via a radio. The Navajo receiver translated the messages back into English, wrote them down, and handed them over to the officers, who compared them with the originals. The game of Navajo whispers proved to be flawless, and the marine officers authorized a pilot project and ordered recruitment to begin immediately.

At the time of America's entry into the Second World War, the Navajo were living in harsh conditions and being treated as an inferior people. Yet their tribal council supported the war effort and declared their loyalty: "There exists no purer concentration of Americanism than among the First Americans." The Navajos were so eager to fight that some of them lied about their age, or gorged themselves on bunches of bananas and swallowed great quantities of water in order to reach the minimum weight requirement of 120 pounds. Similarly, there was no difficulty in finding suitable candidates to serve as Navajo code talkers, as they were to become known. Within four months of the bombing of Pearl Harbor, twenty-nine Navajos, some as young as fifteen, began an eight-week communications course with the Marine Corps.

Before training could begin, the Marine Corps had to overcome a problem that had plagued the only other code to have been based on a Native American language. In northern France during the First World War, Captain E. W. Horner of Company D, 141st Infantry, ordered that eight men from the Choctaw tribe be employed as radio operators. Obviously, none of the enemy understood their language, so the Choctaw provided secure communications. However, this encryption system was fundamentally flawed because the Choctaw language had no equivalent for modern military jargon. A specific technical term in a message might therefore have to be translated into a vague Choctaw expression, with the risk that this could be misinterpreted by the receiver.

The same problem would have arisen with the Navajo language, but the Marine Corps planned to construct a lexicon of Navajo terms to replace otherwise untranslatable English words, thus removing any ambiguities. The trainees helped to compile the lexicon, tending to choose words describing the natural world to indicate specific military terms. Thus, the names of birds were used for planes, and fish for ships. For example, an owl (**Da-he-tih-hi**) was a fighter plane, a frog (**Chal**) meant an amphibious vehicle and an iron fish (**Besh-lo**) meant a submarine. Commanding officers became "war chiefs," platoons were "mud-clans," fortifications turned into "cave dwellings" and mortars were known as "guns that squat."

Even though the complete lexicon contained 274 words, there was still the problem of translating less predictable words and the names of people and places. The solution was to devise an encoded phonetic alphabet for spelling out difficult words. For example, the word *Pacific* would be spelled out as "pig, ant, cat, ice, fox, ice, cat," which would then be translated into Navajo as **bi-sodih, wol-la-chee, moasi, tkin, ma-e, tkin, moasi.** The complete Navajo alphabet is given in Table 8. Within eight weeks, the trainee code talkers had learned the entire lexicon and alphabet, thus preventing the need for codebooks, which might fall into enemy hands. For the Navajos, committing everything to memory was trivial—traditionally their language had no written script, so they were used to memorizing their folk stories and family histories. As William McCabe, one of the trainees, said, "In Navajo everything is in the memory— songs, prayers, everything. That's the way we were raised."

At the end of their training, the Navajos were put to the test. Senders translated a series of messages from English into Navajo and transmitted them, and then receivers translated the messages back into English, using the memorized lexicon and alphabet when necessary. The results were word-perfect. To check the strength of the system, a recording of the transmissions was given to navy intelligence, the unit that had cracked Purple, the toughest Japanese cipher. After three weeks of intense cryptanalysis, the naval codebreakers were still baffled by the messages. They called the Navajo language a "weird succession of guttural, nasal, tongue-twisting sounds . . . we couldn't even transcribe it, much less crack it." The Navajo code was judged a success. Two Navajo soldiers, John Benally and Johnny Manuelito, were asked to stay and train the next batch of recruits, while the other twenty-seven Navajo code talkers were assigned to four regiments and sent to the Pacific.

Japanese forces had attacked Pearl Harbor on December 7, 1941, and not long afterward, they dominated large parts of the western Pacific. Japanese troops overran the American garrison on Guam on December 10; they took Guadalcanal, one of the islands in the Solomon chain, on December 13; Hong Kong fell on December 25; and U.S. troops on the Philippines surrendered on January 2, 1942. The Japanese planned to consolidate their control of the Pacific the following summer by building an airfield on Guadalcanal, creating a base for bombers that would enable them to destroy Allied supply lines, thus making any Allied counterattack almost impossible. Admiral Ernest King, chief of American naval operations, urged an attack on the island before the airfield was completed, and on August 7 the First Marine Division spearheaded an

Table 8 The Navajo alphabet code.

A	Ant	**Wol-la-chee**	N	Nut	**Nesh-chee**
B	Bear	**Shush**	O	Owl	**Ne-as-jah**
C	Cat	**Moasi**	P	Pig	**Bi-sodih**
D	Deer	**Be**	Q	Quiver	**Ca-yeilth**
E	Elk	**Dzeh**	R	Rabbit	**Gah**
F	Fox	**Ma-e**	S	Sheep	**Dibeh**
G	Goat	**Klizzie**	T	Turkey	**Than-zie**
H	Horse	**Lin**	U	Ute	**No-da-ih**
I	Ice	**Tkin**	V	Victor	**A-keh-di-glini**
J	Jackass	**Tkele-cho-gi**	W	Weasel	**Gloe-ih**
K	Kid	**Klizzie-yazzi**	X	Cross	**Al-an-as-dzoh**
L	Lamb	**Dibeh-yazzi**	Y	Yucca	**Tsah-as-zih**
M	Mouse	**Na-as-tso-si**	Z	Zinc	**Besh-do-gliz**

invasion of Guadalcanal. The initial landing parties included the first group of code talkers to see action.

Although the Navajos were confident that their skills would be a blessing to the marines, their first attempts generated only confusion. Many of the regular signal operators were unaware of this new code, and they sent panic messages all over the island, stating that the Japanese were broadcasting on American frequencies. The colonel in charge immediately halted Navajo communications until he could convince himself that the system was worth pursuing. One of the code talkers recalled how the Navajo code was eventually brought back into service:

> The colonel had an idea. He said he would keep us on one condition: that I could out-race his "white code"—a mechanical ticking cylinder thing. We both sent messages, by white cylinder and by my voice. Both of us received answers and the race was to see who could decode his answer first. I was asked, "How long will it take you? Two hours?" "More like two minutes," I answered. The other guy was still decoding when I got the roger on my return message in about four and a half minutes. I said, "Colonel, when are you going to give up on that cylinder thing?" He didn't say anything. He just lit up his pipe and walked away.

The code talkers soon proved their worth on the battlefield. During one episode on the island of Saipan, a battalion of marines took over positions previously held by Japanese soldiers, who had retreated. Suddenly a salvo exploded nearby. They were under friendly fire from fellow Americans who were unaware of their advance. The marines radioed back in English explaining their position, but the salvos continued because the attacking American troops suspected that the messages were from Japanese impersonators trying to fool them. It was only when a Navajo message was sent that the attackers saw their mistake and halted the assault. A Navajo message could never be faked and could always be trusted.

The reputation of the code talkers soon spread, and by the end of 1942 there was a request for eighty-three more men. The Navajo were to serve in all six Marine Corps divisions, and were sometimes borrowed by other American forces. Their war of words soon turned the Navajos into heroes. Other soldiers would offer to carry their radios and rifles, and they were even given personal bodyguards, partly to protect them from their own comrades. On at least three occasions code talkers were mistaken for Japanese soldiers and captured by fellow Americans. They were released only when colleagues from their own battalion vouched for them.

The impenetrability of the Navajo code was a result of the fact that Navajo belongs to the Na-Dene family of languages,

Figure 40 The first twenty-nine Navajo code talkers pose for a traditional graduation photograph.

which has no link with any Asian or European language. For example, a Navajo verb is conjugated not solely according to its subject, but also according to its object. The verb ending depends on which category the object belongs to: long (e.g., pipe, pencil), slender and flexible (e.g., snake, thong), granular (e.g., sugar, salt), bundled (e.g., hay), viscous (e.g., mud, feces) and many others. The verb will also incorporate adverbs, and will reflect whether or not the speaker has experienced what he or she is talking about or whether it is hearsay. Consequently, a single verb can be equivalent to a whole sentence, making it virtually impossible for foreigners to disentangle its meaning.

As the war in the Pacific intensified, and as the Americans advanced from the Solomon Islands to Okinawa, the Navajo code talkers played an increasingly vital role. During the first

Figure 41 Corporal Henry Bake Jr. (left) and Private First Class George H. Kirk using the Navajo code in the dense jungles of Bougainville in 1943.

days of the attack on Iwo Jima, more than eight hundred Navajo messages were sent, all without error. According to Major General Howard Conner, "without the Navajos, the marines would never have taken Iwo Jima." The contribution of the Navajo code talkers is all the more remarkable when you consider that, in order to fulfill their duties, they often had to confront and defy their own deeply held spiritual fears. The Navajo believe that the spirits of the dead, *chindi*, will seek revenge on the living unless ceremonial rites are performed on the body. The war in the Pacific was particularly bloody, with corpses strewn across the battlefields, and yet the code talkers summoned up the courage to carry on regardless of the *chindi* that haunted them. In Doris Paul's book *The Navajo Code Talkers*, one of the Navajo recounts an incident that typifies their bravery, dedication and composure:

> If you so much as held up your head six inches you were gone, the fire was so intense. And then in the wee hours, with no relief on our side or theirs, there was a dead standstill. It must have gotten so that this one Japanese couldn't take it anymore. He got up and yelled and screamed at the top of his voice and dashed over our trench, swinging a long samurai sword. I imagine he was shot from 25 to 40 times before he fell.
>
> There was a buddy with me in the trench. But that Japanese had cut him across the throat, clear through to the cords on the back of his neck. He was still gasping through his windpipe. And the sound of him trying to breathe was horrible. He died, of course. When the Jap struck, warm blood spattered all over my hand that was holding a microphone. I was calling in code for help. They tell me that in spite of what happened, every syllable of my message came through.

Altogether, there were 420 Navajo code talkers. Although their bravery as fighting men was acknowledged, their special role in securing communications was classified information. The government forbade them to talk about their work, and their unique contribution was not made public. Just like Turing and the cryptanalysts at Bletchley Park, the Navajo were ignored for decades. Eventually, in 1968, the Navajo code was declassified, and the following year the code talkers held their first reunion. Then, in 1982, they were honored when the U.S. government named August 14 National Navajo Code Talkers Day. However, the greatest tribute to the work of the Navajo is the simple fact that their code is one of very few throughout history that was never broken. Lieutenant General Seizo Arisue, the Japanese chief of intelligence, admitted that although they had broken the American air force code, they had failed to make any headway on the Navajo code.

DECIPHERING LOST LANGUAGES AND ANCIENT SCRIPTS

The success of the Navajo code was based largely on the simple fact that the mother tongue of one person is utterly meaningless to anybody unacquainted with it. In many ways, the task that confronted Japanese cryptanalysts is similar to that faced by archaeologists attempting to decipher a long-forgotten language, perhaps written in an extinct script. If anything, the archaeological challenge is much more severe. For example, while the Japanese had a continuous stream of Navajo words they could attempt to identify, the information available to the archaeologist can sometimes be just a small collection of clay tablets. Furthermore, the archaeological codebreaker often has no idea of the context or contents of an ancient text, clues that military codebreakers can normally rely on to help them crack a cipher.

Deciphering ancient texts seems an almost hopeless pursuit, yet many men and women have devoted themselves to this difficult enterprise. Their obsession is driven by the desire to understand the writings of our ancestors, allowing us to speak their words and catch a glimpse of their thoughts and lives. Perhaps this appetite for cracking ancient scripts is best summarized by Maurice Pope, the author of *The Story of Decipherment:* "Decipherments are by far the most glamorous achievements of scholarship. There is a touch of magic about unknown writing, especially when it comes from the remote past, and a corresponding glory is bound to attach itself to the person who first solves its mystery."

The decipherment of ancient scripts is not part of the ongoing evolutionary battle between codemakers and codebreakers, because although there are codebreakers in the shape of archaeologists, there are no codemakers. That is to say, in most cases of archaeological decipherment there was no deliberate attempt by the original scribe to hide the meaning of the text. The remainder of this chapter, which is about the decipherment of Egyptian hieroglyphs, is therefore a slight detour from the book's main theme. However, the principles of archaeological decipherment are essentially the same as those of conventional military cryptanalysis. Indeed, many military codebreakers have been attracted by the challenge of unraveling an ancient script. This is probably because archaeological decipherments make a refreshing change from military codebreaking, offering a purely intellectual puzzle rather than a military challenge. In other words, the motivation is curiosity rather than animosity.

The cracking of Egyptian hieroglyphs is the most famous, and arguably the most romantic, of all archaeological decipherments. For centuries, hieroglyphs remained a mystery, and archaeologists could do no more than speculate about their meaning. However, thanks to a classic piece of codebreaking, the hieroglyphs were eventually deciphered, and ever since, archaeologists have been able to read firsthand accounts of the history, culture and beliefs of the ancient Egyptians. The deciphion of hieroglyphs has bridged the millennia between ourselves and the civilization of the pharaohs.

The earliest hieroglyphs date back to 3000 B.C., and this form of ornate writing endured for the next three and a half millennia. Although the elaborate symbols of hieroglyphs were ideal for the walls of majestic temples (the Greek word *hieroglyphica* means "sacred carvings"), they were overly complicated for keeping track of mundane transactions. Hence, evolving in parallel with hieroglyphs was hieratic, an everyday script in which each hieroglyph was replaced by a stylized representation that was quicker and easier to write. In about 600 B.C., hieratic was replaced by an even simpler script known as demotic, the name being derived from the Greek *demotika*, meaning "popular," which reflects its secular function. Hieroglyphs, hieratic and demotic are essentially the same script—one could almost regard them as merely different fonts.

All three forms of writing are phonetic, which is to say that the characters largely represent distinct sounds, just like the letters in the English alphabet. For over three thousand years, the ancient Egyptians used these scripts in every aspect of their lives, just as we use writing today. Then, toward the end of the fourth century A.D., within a generation, the Egyptian scripts vanished. The last datable examples of ancient Egyptian writing are to be found on the island of Philae. A hieroglyphic temple inscription was carved in A.D. 394, and a piece of demotic graffiti has been dated to A.D. 450. The spread of Christianity was responsible for the extinction of the Egyptian scripts, with the Church outlawing their use in order to eliminate any link with Egypt's pagan past. The ancient scripts were replaced with Coptic, a script consisting of twenty-four letters from the Greek alphabet supplemented by six demotic characters used for Egyptian sounds not expressed in Greek. The dominance of Coptic was so complete that the ability to read hieroglyphs, demotic and hieratic vanished. The ancient Egyptian language continued to be spoken, and evolved into what became known as the Coptic language, but in due course both the Coptic language and script were displaced by the spread of Arabic in the eleventh century. The final linguistic link to Egypt's ancient kingdoms had been broken, and the knowledge needed to read the tales of the pharaohs was lost.

Interest in hieroglyphs was reawakened in the seventeenth century, when Pope Sixtus V reorganized the city of Rome according to a new network of avenues, erecting obelisks brought from Egypt at each intersection. Scholars attempted to decipher the meanings of the hieroglyphs on the obelisks but were hindered by a false assumption: Nobody was prepared to accept that hieroglyphics represented phonetic characters, or *phonograms*. Everybody assumed they were picture writing.

In 1652 the German Jesuit priest Athanasius Kircher published a dictionary of interpretations entitled *Œdipus ægyptiacus,* and used it to produce a series of weird and wonderful translations. A handful of hieroglyphs, which we now know merely represent the name of the pharaoh Apries, were translated by Kircher as "the benefits of the divine Osiris are to be procured by means of sacred ceremonies and of the chain of the Genii, in order that the benefits of the Nile may be obtained." Today Kircher's translations seem absurd, but their impact on other would-be decipherers was immense, because Kircher was more than just an Egyptologist. He wrote a book on cryptography, constructed a musical fountain, invented the magic lantern (a precursor of cinema) and lowered himself into the crater of Vesuvius, earning himself the title of "father of vulcanology." The Jesuit priest was widely acknowledged to be the most respected scholar of his age, and consequently his ideas were to influence generations of future Egyptologists.

A century and a half after Kircher, in the summer of 1798, the antiquities of ancient Egypt came under renewed scrutiny when Napoleon Bonaparte dispatched a team of historians, scientists and draftsmen to follow in the wake of his invading army. These academics, or "Pekinese dogs," as the soldiers called them, did a remarkable job of mapping, drawing, transcribing, measuring and recording everything they witnessed. In 1799, the French scholars encountered the single most famous slab of stone in the history of archaeology, found by a troop of French soldiers stationed at Fort Julien in the town of Rosetta in the Nile Delta. The soldiers had been given the task of demolishing an ancient wall to clear the way for an extension to the fort. Built into the wall was a stone bearing a remarkable set of inscriptions: The same piece of text had been inscribed on the stone three times, in Greek, demotic and hieroglyphs. The Rosetta stone, as it became known, appeared to be the equivalent of a cryptanalytic crib, just like the cribs that helped the codebreakers at Bletchley Park to break Enigma. The Greek, which could easily be read, was in effect a piece of plaintext that could be compared with the demotic and hieroglyphic ciphertexts. The Rosetta stone was potentially a way to unravel the meaning of the ancient Egyptian symbols.

The scholars immediately recognized the stone's significance and sent it to the National Institute in Cairo for detailed study. However, before the institute could embark on any serious research, it became clear that the French army was on the verge of being defeated by the advancing British forces. The French moved the Rosetta stone from Cairo to the relative safety of Alexandria, but ironically, when the French finally surrendered, Article XVI of the Treaty of Capitulation handed all the antiquities in Alexandria to the British, whereas those in Cairo were allowed to return to France. In 1802, the priceless slab of black basalt (measuring about forty-six inches in height, thirty inches

Figure 42 The Rosetta stone, inscribed in 196 B.C. and rediscovered in 1799, contains the same text written in three different scripts: hieroglyphs at the top, demotic in the middle and Greek at the bottom.

in width and twelve inches in thickness, and weighing about sixteen hundred pounds) was sent to Portsmouth on board HMS *L'Egyptienne,* and later that year it took up residence at the British Museum, where it has remained ever since.

The translation of the Greek soon revealed that the Rosetta stone bore a decree from the general council of Egyptian priests issued in 196 B.C. The text records the benefits that the pharaoh Ptolemy had bestowed upon the people of Egypt, and details the honors that the priests had, in return, piled upon the pharaoh. For example, they declared that "a festival shall be kept for King Ptolemy, the ever-living, the beloved of Ptah, the god Epiphanes Eucharistos, yearly in the temples throughout the land from the first of Thoth for five days, in which they shall wear garlands and perform sacrifices and libations and the other usual honors." If the other two inscriptions contained the identical decree, the decipherment of the hieroglyphic and demotic symbols would seem to be straightforward. However, three significant hurdles remained. First, the Rosetta stone is seriously damaged, as can be seen in Figure 42. The Greek text consists of fifty-four lines, of which the last twenty-six are damaged. The demotic consists of thirty-two lines, of which the beginnings of the first fourteen lines are damaged (note that demotic and hieroglyphs are written from right to left). The hieroglyphic text is in the worst condition, with half the lines missing completely and the remaining fourteen lines (corresponding to the last twenty-eight lines of the Greek text) partly missing. The second barrier to decipherment is that the two Egyptian scripts convey the ancient Egyptian language, which nobody had spoken for at least eight centuries. Although it was possible to find a set of Egyptian symbols that corresponded to a set of Greek words, which would enable archaeologists to work out the meaning of the Egyptian symbols, it was impossible to establish the sound of the Egyptian words.

Unless archaeologists knew how the Egyptian words were spoken, they could not deduce the phonetics of the symbols. Finally, the intellectual legacy of Kircher still encouraged archaeologists to think of Egyptian writing in terms of semagrams, representing whole ideas, rather than phonograms, representing sounds. Hence few people even considered attempting a phonetic decipherment of hieroglyphs.

One of the first scholars to question the prejudice that hieroglyphs were picture writing was the English prodigy and polymath Thomas Young. Born in 1773 in Milverton, Somerset, Young was able to read fluently at the age of two. By the age of fourteen he had studied Greek, Latin, French, Italian, Hebrew, Chaldean, Syriac, Samaritan, Arabic, Persian, Turkish and Ethiopic, and when he became a student at Emmanuel College, Cambridge, his brilliance gained him the nickname

Figure 43 Thomas Young.

"Phenomenon Young." At Cambridge he studied medicine, but it was said that he was interested only in the diseases, not the patients who had them. Gradually he began to concentrate more on research and less on caring for the sick.

Young performed an extraordinary series of medical experiments, many of them with the object of explaining how the human eye works. He established that color perception is the result of three separate types of receptors, each one sensitive to one of the three primary colors. Then, by placing metal rings around a living eyeball, he showed that focusing did not require distortion of the whole eye, and proposed that the internal lens did all the work. His interest in optics led him toward physics and another series of discoveries. He published "The Undulatory Theory of Light," a classic paper on the nature of light; he created a new and better explanation of tides; he formally defined the concept of energy and he published groundbreaking papers on the subject of elasticity. Young seemed to be able to tackle problems in almost any subject, but this was not entirely to his advantage. His mind was so easily fascinated that he would leap from subject to subject, embarking on a new problem before polishing off the last one.

When Young heard about the Rosetta stone, it became an irresistible challenge. In the summer of 1814 he set off on his annual holiday to the coastal resort of Worthing, taking with him a copy of the three inscriptions. Young's breakthrough came when he focused on a set of hieroglyphs surrounded by a loop, called a *cartouche*. His hunch was that these hieroglyphs were ringed because they represented something of great significance, possibly the name of the pharaoh Ptolemy, because his Greek name, Ptolemaios, was mentioned in the Greek text. If this were the case, it would enable Young to discover the phonetics of the corresponding hieroglyphs, because a pharaoh's name would be pronounced roughly the same regardless of the language. The

Ptolemy cartouche is repeated six times on the Rosetta stone, sometimes in a so-called standard version, and sometimes in a longer, more elaborate version. Young assumed that the longer version was the name of Ptolemy with the addition of titles, so he concentrated on the symbols that appeared in the standard version, guessing sound values for each hieroglyph (Table 9).

Although he did not know it at the time, Young managed to correlate most of the hieroglyphs with their correct sound values. Fortunately, he had placed the first two hieroglyphs (□, △), which appeared one above the other, in their correct phonetic order. The scribe has positioned the hieroglyphs in this way for aesthetic reasons, at the expense of phonetic clarity. Scribes tended to write in such a way as to avoid gaps and maintain visual harmony; sometimes they would even swap letters around, in direct contradiction to any sensible phonetic spelling, merely to increase the beauty of an inscription. After this decipherment, Young discovered a cartouche in an inscription copied from the temple of Karnak at Thebes that he suspected was the name of a Ptolemaic queen, Berenika (or Berenice). He repeated his strategy; the results are shown in Table 10.

Table 9 Young's decipherment of ⟨cartouche⟩, the cartouche of Ptolemaios (standard version) from the Rosetta stone.

Hieroglyph	Young's sound value	Actual sound value
□	p	p
△	t	t
⟨glyph⟩	optional	o
⟨glyph⟩	lo or ole	l
⟨glyph⟩	ma or m	m
⟨glyph⟩	i	i or y
⟨glyph⟩	osh or os	s

Of the thirteen hieroglyphs in both cartouches, Young had identified half of them perfectly, and he got another quarter partly right. He had also correctly identified the feminine termination symbol, placed after the names of queens and goddesses. Although he could not have known the level of his success, the appearance of 𓏤𓏤 in both cartouches, representing i on both occasions, should have told Young that he was on the right track, and given him the confidence he needed to press ahead with further decipherments. However, his work suddenly ground to a halt. It seems that he had too much reverence for Kircher's argument that hieroglyphs were symbolic, and he was not prepared to shatter that theory. He excused his own phonetic discoveries by noting that the Ptolemaic dynasty was descended from Lagus, a general of Alexander the Great. In other words, the Ptolemys were foreigners, and Young hypothesized that their names would have to be spelled out phonetically because there would not be a single natural symbol within the standard list of hieroglyphs. He summarized his thoughts by comparing hieroglyphs with Chinese characters, which Europeans were only just beginning to understand:

Table 10 Young's decipherment of ⟨𓃀𓏏𓇋𓇋𓈖𓆭𓎡⟩, the cartouche of Berenika from the temple of Karnak.

Hieroglyph	Young's sound value	Actual sound value
𓃀	bir	b
⟬⟭	e	r
𓈖	n	n
𓏤𓏤	i	i
𓎡	optional	k
𓄿	ke or ken	a
𓏏	feminine termination	feminine termination

It is extremely interesting to trace some of the steps by which alphabetic writing seems to have arisen out of hieroglyphical; a process which may indeed be in some measure illustrated by the manner in which the modern Chinese express a foreign combination of sounds, the characters being rendered simply "phonetic" by an appropriate mark, instead of retaining their natural signification; and this mark, in some modern printed books, approaching very near to the ring surrounding the hieroglyphic names.

Young called his achievements "the amusement of a few leisure hours." He lost interest in hieroglyphs and brought his work to a conclusion by summarizing it in an article for the 1819 *Supplement to the Encyclopaedia Britannica*.

Meanwhile, in France a promising young linguist, Jean-François Champollion, was prepared to take Young's ideas to their natural conclusion. Although he was still only in his late twenties, Champollion had been fascinated by hieroglyphs for

Figure 44 Jean-François Champollion.

the best part of two decades. The obsession began in 1800, when the French mathematician Jean-Baptiste Fourier, who had been one of Napoleon's original "Pekinese dogs," introduced the ten-year-old Champollion to his collection of Egyptian antiquities, many of them decorated with bizarre inscriptions. Fourier explained that nobody could interpret this cryptic writing, whereupon the boy promised that one day he would solve the mystery. Just seven years later, at the age of seventeen, he presented a paper entitled "Egypt Under the Pharaohs." It was so innovative that he was immediately elected to the Academy in Grenoble. When he heard that he had become a teenage professor, Champollion was so overwhelmed that he immediately fainted.

Champollion continued to astonish his peers, mastering Latin, Greek, Hebrew, Ethiopic, Sanskrit, Zend, Pahlavi, Arabic, Syrian, Chaldean, Persian and Chinese, all in order to arm himself for an assault on hieroglyphs. His obsession is illustrated by an incident in 1808, when he bumped into an old

Table 11 Champollion's decipherment of ⬚ and ⬚, the cartouches of Ptolemaios and Cleopatra from the Bankes obelisk.

Hieroglyph	Sound value		Hieroglyph	Sound value
□	p		◿	c
◠	t		🐦	l
🪶	o		〡	e
🐦	l		🪶	o
⊂	m		□	p
◊◊	e		🦅	a
〡	s		⬅	t
			⬭	r
			🦅	a

friend in the street. The friend casually mentioned that Alexandre Lenoir, a well-known Egyptologist, had published a complete decipherment of hieroglyphs. Champollion was so devastated that he collapsed on the spot. (He appears to have had quite a talent for fainting.) His whole reason for living seemed to depend on being the first to read the script of the ancient Eygptians. Fortunately for Champollion, Lenoir's decipherments were as fantastical as Kircher's seventeenth-century attempts, and the challenge remained.

In 1822, Champollion applied Young's approach to other cartouches. The British naturalist W. J. Bankes had brought an obelisk with Greek and hieroglyphic inscriptions to Dorset, and had recently published a lithograph of these bilingual texts, which included cartouches of Ptolemy and Cleopatra. Champollion obtained a copy, and managed to assign sound values to individual hieroglyphs (Table 11). The letters p, t, o, I and e are common to both names; in four cases they are represented by the same hieroglyph in both Ptolemy and Cleopatra, and only in one case, t, is there a discrepancy. Champollion assumed that the t sound could be represented by two hieroglyphs, just as the hard c sound in English can be represented by c or k, as in *cat* and *kid*. Inspired by his success, Champollion began to address cartouches without a bilingual translation, substituting whenever possible the hieroglyph sound values that he had derived from the Ptolemy and Cleopatra cartouches. His first mystery cartouche (Table 12) contained one of the greatest names of ancient times. It was obvious to Champollion that the cartouche, which seemed to read a-l-?-s-e-?-t-r-?, represented the name **alksentrs**—Alexandros in Greek, or Alexander in English. It also became apparent to Champollion that the scribes were not fond of using vowels, and would often omit them; the scribes assumed that readers would have no problem filling in the missing vowels. With three new hieroglyphs under his belt, the young scholar studied other inscriptions and deciphered a series of cartouches. However, all this progress was merely extending Young's work. All these names, such as Alexander and Cleopatra, were still foreign, supporting the theory that phonetics was invoked only for words outside the traditional Egyptian lexicon.

Then, on September 14, 1822, Champollion received reliefs from the temple of Abu Simbel, containing cartouches that predated the period of Greco-Roman domination. The significance of these cartouches was that they were old enough to contain traditional Egyptian names, yet they were still spelled out—clear evidence against the theory that spelling was used only for foreign names. Champollion concentrated on a cartouche containing just four hieroglyphs: ⟨☉�𓈖𓏏𓏏⟩. The first two symbols were unknown, but the repeated pair at the end, 𓏏𓏏, were known from the cartouche of Alexander (**alksentrs**) to both represent the letter **s**. This meant that the cartouche represented (?-?-**s**-**s**). At this point, Champollion brought to bear his vast linguistic knowledge. Although Coptic, the direct de-

Table 12 Champollion's decipherment of ⟨𓃭𓇋𓐠𓈖𓏏𓂋𓋴⟩, the cartouche of Alksentrs (Alexander).

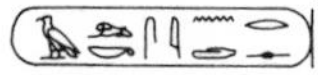

Hieroglyph	Sound value
𓄿	a
𓃭	l
⌒	?
 𓈖	s
 𓏭	e
〰	?
⌐	t
⌒	r
—	?

scendant of the ancient Egyptian language, had ceased to be a living language in the eleventh century A.D., it still existed in a fossilized form in the liturgy of the Christian Coptic Church. Champollion had learned Coptic as a teenager and was so fluent that he used it to record entries in his journal. However, until this moment, he had never considered that Coptic might also be the language of hieroglyphs.

Champollion wondered whether the first sign in the cartouche, ☉, might be a semagram representing the sun, that is, whether a picture of the sun was the symbol for the word *sun*. Then, in an act of intuitive genius, he assumed the sound value of the semagram to be that of the Coptic word for sun, **ra**. This gave him the sequence (**ra-?-s-s**). Only one pharaonic name seemed to fit. Allowing for the irritating omission of vowels, and assuming that the missing letter was **m**, then surely this had to be the name of Rameses, one of the greatest pharaohs, and one of the most ancient. The spell was broken. Even ancient traditional names were phonetically spelled. Champollion dashed into his brother's office and proclaimed, *"Je tiens l'affaire!"* ("I've got it!"), but once again his intense passion for hieroglyphs got the better of him. He promptly collapsed and was bedridden for the next five days.

Champollion had demonstrated that the scribes sometimes exploited the *rebus* principle. In a rebus, still found in some puzzle books, long words are broken into their phonetic components, which are then represented by semagrams. For example, the word *belief* can be broken down into two syllables, *be-lief,* which can then be rewritten as *bee-leaf.* Instead of writing the word alphabetically, it can be represented by the image of a bee followed by the image of a leaf. In the example discovered by Champollion, only the first syllable (**ra**) is represented by a rebus image, a picture of the sun, while the remainder of the word is spelled more conventionally.

The significance of the sun semagram in the Rameses cartouche is enormous, because it clearly restricts the possibilities for the language spoken by the scribes. For example, the scribes could not have spoken Greek, because this would have meant that the cartouche would be pronounced "helios-meses," because *helios* is the Greek word for "sun." The cartouche makes sense only if the scribes spoke a form of Coptic, because the cartouche would then be pronounced "ra-meses."

Although this was just one more cartouche, its decipherment clearly demonstrated the four principles of hieroglyphics. First, the language of the script is at least related to Coptic, and indeed, examination of other hieroglyphs showed that it was Coptic pure and simple. Second, semagrams are used to represent some words; for example, the word *sun* is represented by a picture of the sun. Third, some long words are built wholly or partly using the rebus principle. Finally, for most of their writing, the ancient scribes relied on a conventional phonetic alphabet. This final point is the most important one, and Champollion called phonetics the "soul" of hieroglyphs.

Using his deep knowledge of Coptic, Champollion began an unhindered and prolific decipherment of hieroglyphs beyond the cartouches. Within two years he identified phonetic values for the majority of hieroglyphs, and discovered that some of them represented combinations of two or even three consonants. This sometimes gave scribes the option of spelling a word using several simple hieroglyphs or with just a few multiconsonant hieroglyphs.

Champollion sent his initial results in a letter to Monsieur Dacier, the permanent secretary of the French Académie des Inscriptions. Then in 1824, at the age of thirty-four, Champollion published all his achievements in a book entitled *Précis du système hiéroglyphique*. For the first time in fourteen centuries it was possible to read the history of the pharaohs as written by their scribes. For linguists, here was an opportunity to study the evolution of a language and a script across a period of over three thousand years. Hieroglyphs could be understood and traced from the third millennium B.C. through to the fourth century A.D.

For several years, politics and envy prevented Champollion's magnificent achievement from being universally accepted. Thomas Young was a particularly bitter critic. On some occasions Young denied that hieroglyphs could be largely phonetic; at other times he accepted the argument but complained that he himself had reached this conclusion before Champollion and that the Frenchman had merely filled in the gaps. Much of Young's hostility resulted from Champollion's failure to give him any credit, even though it is likely that Young's initial breakthrough provided the inspiration for the full decipherment.

In July 1828 Champollion embarked on his first expedition to Egypt, which lasted eighteen months. It was a remarkable opportunity for him to witness firsthand the inscriptions he had previously seen only in drawings. Thirty years earlier, Napoleon's expedition had guessed wildly at the meaning of the hieroglyphs that adorned the temples, but now Champollion could simply read them character by character and reinterpret them correctly. His visit came just in time. Three years later, having written up the notes, drawings and translations from his Egyptian expedition, he suffered a severe stroke. The fainting spells he had suffered throughout his life were perhaps symptomatic of a more serious illness, made worse by his obsessive and intense study. He died on March 4, 1832, at the age of forty-one.

Alice and Bob Go Public

Modern cryptography,
the solution to the so-called
key-distribution problem
and the secret history of
nonsecret encryption

During the Second World War, British codebreakers had the upper hand over German codemakers, mainly because the men and women at Bletchley Park, following the lead of the Poles, developed some of the earliest codebreaking technology. In addition to Turing's bombes, which were used to crack the Enigma cipher, the British also invented another codebreaking device, Colossus, to combat an even stronger form of encryption, the German Lorenz cipher. Of the two types of codebreaking machine, it was Colossus that would determine the development of cryptography during the latter half of the twentieth century.

The Lorenz cipher was used to encrypt communications between Hitler and his generals. The encryption was performed by the Lorenz SZ40 machine, which operated in a similar way to the Enigma machine, but the Lorenz was far more complicated, and it provided the Bletchley codebreakers with an even greater challenge. However, two of Bletchley's codebreakers, John Tiltman and Bill Tutte, discovered a weakness in the way that the Lorenz cipher was used, a flaw that Bletchley could exploit and thereby read Hitler's messages.

Breaking the Lorenz cipher required a mixture of searching, matching, statistical analysis and careful judgment, all of which was beyond the technical abilities of the bombes. The bombes were able to carry out a specific task at high speed, but they were not flexible enough to deal with the subtleties of Lorenz. Lorenz-encrypted messages had to be broken by hand, which took weeks of painstaking effort, by which time the messages were largely out of date. Eventually, Max Newman, a Bletchley mathematician, came up with a way to mechanize the cryptanalysis of the Lorenz cipher. Drawing heavily on the ideas of Alan Turing, Newman designed a machine that was capable of adapting itself to different problems, what we today would call a programmable computer.

Implementing Newman's design was deemed technically impossible, so Bletchley's senior officials shelved the project. Fortunately, Tommy Flowers, an engineer who had taken part in discussions about Newman's design, decided to ignore Bletchley's skepticism and went ahead with building the machine. Flowers took Newman's blueprint and spent ten months turning it into the Colossus machine, which he delivered to Bletchley Park on December 8, 1943. It consisted of fifteen hundred electronic valves, which were considerably faster than the sluggish electromechanical relay switches used in the bombes. But more important than Colossus' speed was the fact that it was programmable. It was this fact that made Colossus the precursor to the modern digital computer.

Colossus, as with everything else at Bletchley Park, was destroyed after the war, and those who worked on it were forbidden to talk about it. When Tommy Flowers was ordered to dispose of the Colossus blueprints, he obediently took them down to the boiler room and burned them. The plans for the world's first computer were lost forever. In 1945, J. Presper Eckert and John W. Mauchly of the University of Pennsylvania completed ENIAC (Electronic Numerical Integrator and Calculator), consisting of eighteen thousand electronic valves, capable of performing five thousand calculations per second. For decades, ENIAC, not Colossus, was considered the mother of all computers.

Having contributed to the birth of the modern computer, codebreakers continued after the war to develop and employ computer technology in order to break all sorts of ciphers. They could now exploit the speed and flexibility of programmable computers to search through all possible keys until the correct one was found. In due course, the codemakers began to fight back, exploiting the power of computers to create increasingly complex ciphers. In short, the computer played a crucial role in the postwar battle between codemakers and codebreakers.

Using a computer to encipher a message is, to a large extent, very similar to traditional forms of encryption. Indeed, there are only three significant differences between computer encryption and the sort of mechanical encryption that was the basis for ciphers such as Enigma. The first difference is that a mechanical cipher machine is limited by what can be practically built, whereas a computer can mimic a hypothetical cipher machine of immense complexity. For example, a computer could be programmed to mimic the action of a hundred scramblers, some spinning clockwise, some counterclockwise, some vanishing after every tenth letter, others rotating faster and faster as encryption progresses. Such a mechanical machine would be practically impossible to build, but its virtual computerized equivalent would deliver a highly secure cipher.

The second difference is simply a matter of speed. Electronic circuits can operate far more quickly than mechanical scramblers: A computer programmed to mimic the Enigma cipher could encipher a lengthy message in an instant. Alternatively, a computer programmed to perform a vastly more complex form of encryption could still accomplish the task within a reasonable time.

The third, and perhaps most significant, difference is that a computer scrambles numbers rather than letters of the alphabet. Computers deal only in binary numbers—sequences of ones and zeros known as *binary digits*, or *bits* for short. Before encryption, any message must therefore be converted into binary digits. This conversion can be performed according to various protocols, such as the American Standard Code for Information Interchange, known familiarly by the acronym ASCII, pronounced "az-key." ASCII assigns a seven-digit binary number to each letter of the alphabet. For the time being, it is sufficient to think of a binary number as merely a pattern of ones and zeros that uniquely identifies each letter (Table 13), just as Morse code identifies each letter with a unique series of dots and dashes. There are 128 (2^7) ways to arrange a combination of seven binary digits, so ASCII can identify up to 128 distinct characters. This allows plenty of room to define all the lowercase letters (e.g., a = 1100001) and all necessary punctuation (e.g., ! = 0100001) as well as other symbols (e.g., & = 0100110). Once the message has been converted into binary, encryption can begin.

Even though we are dealing with computers and numbers, and not machines and letters, the encryption still proceeds in the traditional way.

For example, imagine that we wish to encrypt the message **HELLO** by employing a simple computer version of a substitution cipher. Before encryption can begin, we must translate the message into ASCII according to Table 13. Each letter of the message is replaced with the appropriate 7-bit ASCII binary number.

As usual, substitution relies on a key that has been agreed between sender and receiver. In this case the key is the word **DAVID** translated into ASCII, and it is used in the following way. Each element of the plaintext is "added" to the corresponding element of the key. Adding binary digits can be thought of in terms of two simple rules. If the elements in the plaintext and the key are the same, the element in the plaintext is substituted for **0** in the ciphertext. But if the elements in the message and key are different, the element in the plaintext is substituted for **1** in the ciphertext:

Message	**HELLO**
Message in ASCII	1001000100010110011001001001111
Key = **DAVID**	10001001000001101011010010011000100
Ciphertext	00011000000100001101000001010001011

The resulting encrypted message is a single string of thirty-five binary digits that can be transmitted to the receiver, who uses the same key to reverse the substitution, thus re-creating the

Table 13 ASCII binary numbers for the capital letters.

A	1 0 0 0 0 0 1	N	1 0 0 1 1 1 0
B	1 0 0 0 0 1 0	O	1 0 0 1 1 1 1
C	1 0 0 0 0 1 1	P	1 0 1 0 0 0 0
D	1 0 0 0 1 0 0	Q	1 0 1 0 0 0 1
E	1 0 0 0 1 0 1	R	1 0 1 0 0 1 0
F	1 0 0 0 1 1 0	S	1 0 1 0 0 1 1
G	1 0 0 0 1 1 1	T	1 0 1 0 1 0 0
H	1 0 0 1 0 0 0	U	1 0 1 0 1 0 1
I	1 0 0 1 0 0 1	V	1 0 1 0 1 1 0
J	1 0 0 1 0 1 0	W	1 0 1 0 1 1 1
K	1 0 0 1 0 1 1	X	1 0 1 1 0 0 0
L	1 0 0 1 1 0 0	Y	1 0 1 1 0 0 1
M	1 0 0 1 1 0 1	Z	1 0 1 1 0 1 0

original string of binary digits. Finally, the receiver reinterprets the binary digits via ASCII to regenerate the message **HELLO**.

Computer encryption was restricted to those who had computers, which in the early days meant the government and the military. However, a series of scientific, technological and engineering breakthroughs made computers, and computer encryption, far more widely available. In 1947, AT&T Bell Laboratories invented the transistor, a cheap alternative to the electronic valve. Commercial computing became a reality in 1951 when companies such as Ferranti began to make computers to order. In 1953 IBM launched its first computer, and four years later it introduced Fortran, a programming language that allowed ordinary people to write computer programs. Then, in 1959, the invention of the integrated circuit heralded a new era of computing.

During the 1960s, computers became more powerful, and at the same time they became much cheaper. Businesses were increasingly able to afford computers, and could use them to encrypt important communications such as money transfers or delicate trade negotiations. However, as more businesses bought computers, and as encryption between businesses spread, cryptographers were confronted with a major problem known as *key distribution*.

Imagine that a bank wants to send some confidential data to a client via a telephone line but is worried that there might be somebody tapping the wire. The bank picks a key (remember that the key defines the exact recipe for scrambling the message) and uses some encryption software to scramble the message. In order to decrypt the message, the client needs not only to have a copy of the encryption software on its computer, but also to know which key was used to encrypt the message. How does the bank inform the client of the key? It cannot send the key via the telephone line, because it suspects that there is an eavesdropper on the line. The only truly secure way to send the key is to hand it over in person, which is clearly a time-consuming task. A less secure but more practical solution is to send the key via a courier. In the 1970s, banks attempted to distribute keys by employing special dispatch riders who had been investigated and who were among the company's most trusted employees. These dispatch riders would race across the world with padlocked briefcases, personally distributing keys to everyone who would receive messages from the bank over the next week. As business networks grew in size, as more messages were sent, and as more keys had to be delivered, the banks found that this distribution process became a horrendous logistical nightmare, and the overhead costs became too high.

The problem of key distribution has plagued cryptographers throughout history. For example, during the Second World War the German high command had to distribute the monthly book of day keys to all its Enigma operators, which was an enormous logistical problem. Also, U-boats, which tended to spend extended periods away from base, had to somehow obtain a regular supply of keys. In earlier times, users of the Vigenère cipher had to find a way of getting the keyword from the sender to the receiver. No matter how secure a cipher is in theory, in practice it can be undermined by the problem of key distribution.

Key distribution might seem a trivial issue, but it became the overriding problem for postwar cryptographers. If two parties wanted to communicate securely, they had to rely on a third party to deliver the key, and this became the weakest link in the chain of security.

Despite claims that the problem of key distribution was unsolvable, a team of mavericks triumphed against the odds and came up with a brilliant solution in the mid-1970s. They devised an encryption system that appeared to defy all logic. Although computers transformed the implementation of ciphers, the greatest revolution in twentieth-century cryptography was the development of techniques to overcome the problem of key distribution. Indeed, this breakthrough is considered to be the greatest cryptographic achievement since the invention of the monoalphabetic cipher, over two thousand years ago.

GOD REWARDS FOOLS

Whitfield Diffie is one of the most enthusiastic cryptographers of his generation. The mere sight of him creates a striking and somewhat contradictory image. His impeccable suit reflects the fact that for most of the 1990s, he has been employed by one of America's giant computer companies—currently his official job title is Distinguished Engineer at Sun Microsystems. However, his shoulder-length hair and long white beard betray the fact that his heart is still stuck in the 1960s. He spends much of his time in front of a computer workstation, but he looks as if he would be equally comfortable in a Bombay ashram. Diffie is aware that his dress and personality can have quite an impact on others, and comments, "People always think that I am taller than I really am, and I'm told it's the Tigger effect—'No matter his weight in pounds, shillings and ounces, he always seems bigger because of the bounces.'"

Diffie was born in 1944 and spent most of his early years in Queens, New York. As a child, he became fascinated by mathematics, reading books ranging from *The Chemical Rubber Company Handbook of Mathematical Tables* to G. H. Hardy's *Course of Pure Mathematics*. He went on to study mathematics at the Massachusetts Institute of Technology, graduating in 1965. He then took a series of jobs related to computer security, and by the early 1970s he had matured into one of the few truly independent security experts, a freethinking cryptographer, not employed by the government or by any of the big corporations. In hindsight, he was the first cypherpunk.

Diffie was particularly interested in the key-distribution problem, and he realized that whoever could find a solution would go down in history as one of the all-time great cryptographers. Diffie was so captivated by the problem of key distribution that it became the most important entry in his special notebook entitled "Problems for an Ambitious Theory of Cryptography." Part of Diffie's motivation came from his vision of a wired world. Back in the 1960s, the U.S. Department of Defense began funding a cutting-edge research organization called the Advanced Research Projects Agency (ARPA), and one of ARPA's frontline projects was to find a way of connecting military computers across vast distances. The ARPANet steadily grew in size, and in 1982 it spawned the Internet. At the end of the 1980s, nonacademic and nongovernmental users were given access to the Internet, and thereafter the number of users exploded. Today, millions of people all over the world use the Internet to exchange all sorts of information, often by sending each other e-mails.

While the ARPANet was still in its infancy, Diffie was farsighted enough to forecast the advent of the information superhighway and the digital revolution. Ordinary people would one day have their own computers, and these computers would be interconnected via phone lines. Diffie believed that if people then used their computers to exchange e-mails, they deserved the right to encrypt their messages in order to guarantee their privacy. However, encryption required the secure exchange of keys. If governments and large corporations were having trouble coping with key distribution, then the public would find it impossible, and would effectively be deprived of the right to privacy.

Diffie imagined two strangers meeting via the Internet, and

wondered how they could send each other an encrypted message. He also considered the scenario of a person wanting to buy something on the Internet. How could that person send an e-mail containing encrypted credit-card details so that only the Internet retailer could decipher them? In both cases, it seemed that the two parties needed to share a key, but how could they exchange keys securely? The number of casual contacts and the amount of spontaneous e-mails among the public would be enormous, and this would mean that key distribution would be impractical. Diffie was fearful that the necessity of key distribution would prevent the public from having access to digital privacy, and he became obsessed with the idea of finding a solution to the problem.

In 1974, Diffie, still an independent cryptographer, paid a visit to IBM's Thomas J. Watson Laboratory, where he had been invited to give a talk. He spoke about various strategies for attacking the key-distribution problem, but all his ideas were very tentative, and his audience was skeptical about the prospects for a solution. The only positive response to Diffie's presentation was from Alan Konheim, one of IBM's senior cryptographic experts, who mentioned that someone else had recently visited the laboratory and given a lecture that addressed the issue of key distribution. That speaker was Martin Hellman, a professor from Stanford University in California. That evening Diffie got in his car and began the three-thousand-mile journey to the West Coast to meet the only person who seemed to share his obsession. The alliance of Diffie and Hellman would become one of the most dynamic partnerships in cryptography.

Martin Hellman was born in 1945 in a Jewish neighborhood in the Bronx, but when he was four his family moved to a predominantly Irish Catholic neighborhood. According to Hellman, this permanently changed his attitude to life: "The other

kids went to church and they learned that the Jews killed Christ, so I got called 'Christ killer.' I also got beat up. To start with, I wanted to be like the other kids, I wanted a Christmas tree and I wanted Christmas presents. But then I realized that I couldn't be like all the other kids, and in self-defense I adopted an attitude of 'Who would want to be like everybody else?' "
Hellman traces his interest in ciphers to this enduring desire to be different. His colleagues had told him he was crazy to do research in cryptography, because he would be competing with the National Security Agency (NSA) and their multibillion-dollar budget. How could he hope to discover something that they did not know already? And if he did discover anything, the NSA would classify it.

In September 1974 he received an unexpected phone call from Whitfield Diffie. Hellman had never heard of Diffie, but grudgingly agreed to a half-hour appointment later that afternoon. By the end of the meeting, Hellman realized that Diffie was the best-informed person he had ever met. The feeling was mutual. Hellman recalls: "I'd promised my wife I'd be home to watch the kids, so he came home with me and we had dinner together. He left at around midnight. Our personalities are very different—he is much more counterculture than I am—but eventually the personality clash was very symbiotic. It was just such a breath of fresh air for me. Working in a vacuum had been really hard."

Since Hellman did not have a great deal of funding, he could not afford to employ his new soul mate as a researcher. Instead, Diffie was enrolled as a graduate student. Together, Hellman and Diffie began to study the key-distribution problem, desperately trying to find an alternative to the tiresome task of physically transporting keys over vast distances. In due course they were joined by Ralph Merkle. Merkle had left another research group where the professor had no sympathy for the impossible dream of solving the key-distribution problem. Says Hellman:

> Ralph, like us, was willing to be a fool. And the way to get to the top of the heap in terms of developing original research is to be a fool, because only fools keep trying. You have idea number 1, you get excited, and it flops. Then you have idea number 2, you get excited, and it flops. Then you have idea number 99, you get excited, and it flops. Only a fool would be excited by the 100th idea, but it might take 100 ideas before one really pays off. Unless you're foolish enough to be continually excited, you won't have the motivation, you won't have the energy to carry it through. God rewards fools.

The whole problem of key distribution is a classic catch-22 situation. If two people want to exchange a secret message over the phone, the sender must encrypt it. To encrypt the secret message the sender must use a key, which is itself a secret, so then there is the problem of transmitting the secret key to the receiver in order to transmit the secret message. In short,

Figure 45 Whitfield Diffie.

Figure 46 Martin Hellman.

before two people can exchange a secret (an encrypted message) they must already share a secret (the key).

When thinking about the problem of key distribution, it is helpful to consider Alice, Bob and Eve, three fictional characters who have become the industry standard for discussions about cryptography. In a typical situation, Alice wants to send a message to Bob, or vice versa, and Eve is trying to eavesdrop. If Alice is sending private messages to Bob, she will encrypt each one before sending it, using a separate key each time. Alice is continually faced with the problem of key distribution because she has to convey the keys to Bob securely, otherwise he cannot decrypt the messages. One way to solve the problem is for Alice and Bob to meet up once a week and exchange enough keys to cover the messages that might be sent during the next seven days. Exchanging keys in person is certainly secure, but it is inconvenient, and if either Alice or Bob is taken ill, the system breaks down. Alternatively, Alice and Bob could hire couriers, which would be less secure and more expensive, but at least they have delegated some of the work. Either way, it seems that the distribution of keys is unavoidable. For two thousand years, this was considered to be an axiom of cryptography—an indisputable truth. However, there is a scenario that seems to defy the axiom.

Imagine that Alice and Bob live in a country where the postal system is completely immoral, and postal employees will read any unprotected correspondence. One day, Alice wants to send an intensely personal message to Bob. She puts it inside an iron box, closes it and secures it with a padlock and key. She puts the padlocked box in the mail and keeps the key. However, when the box reaches Bob, he is unable to open it because he does not have the key. Alice might consider putting the key inside another box, padlocking it and sending it to Bob, but without the key to the second padlock he is unable to open the second box, so he cannot obtain the key that opens the first box. The only way around the problem seems to be for Alice to make a copy of her key and give it to Bob in advance when they meet for coffee. So far, I have just restated the same old problem in a new way. Avoiding key distribution seems logically impossible—surely, if Alice wants to lock something in a box so that only Bob can open it, she must give him a copy of the key. Or, in terms of cryptography, if Alice wants to encipher a message so that only Bob can decipher it, she must give him a copy of the key. Key exchange is an inevitable part of encipherment—or is it?

Now picture the following situation. As before, Alice wants to send an intensely personal message to Bob. Again, she puts her secret message in an iron box, padlocks it and sends it to Bob. When the box arrives, Bob adds his own padlock and sends the box back to Alice. When Alice receives the box, it is now secured by two padlocks. She removes her own padlock, leaving just Bob's padlock to secure the box. Finally she sends the box back to Bob. And here is the crucial difference: Bob can now open the box, because it is secured only with his own padlock, to which he alone has the key.

The implications of this little story are enormous. It demonstrates that a secret message can be securely exchanged between two people without necessarily exchanging a key. For the first time there is some hope that key exchange might not be an inevitable part of cryptography. We can reinterpret the story in terms of encryption. Alice uses her own key to encrypt a message to Bob, who encrypts it again with his own key and returns it. When Alice receives the doubly encrypted message, she removes her own encryption and returns it to Bob, who can then remove his own encryption and read the message.

It seems that the problem of key distribution might have been solved, because the doubly encrypted scheme requires no exchange of keys. However, there are several obstacles to implementing a system in which Alice encrypts, Bob encrypts, Alice decrypts and Bob decrypts. One problem is the order in which the encryptions and decryptions are performed. In general, the order of encryption and decryption is crucial, and should obey the rule "last on, first off." In other words, the last stage of encryption should be the first to be decrypted. In the above scenario, Bob performed the last stage of encryption, so this should have been the first to be decrypted, but it was Alice who removed her encryption first, before Bob removed his. Unfortunately, many encryption systems are far more sensitive than padlocks when it comes to order. The importance of order is most easily grasped by examining something we do every day. In the morning we put on our socks, and then we put on our shoes, and in the evening we remove our shoes before removing our socks—it is impossible to remove the socks before the shoes. The locked box scenario works because padlocks can be added and removed in any order, but for most cipher systems the order of encryption and decryption is critical. The rule "last on, first off" must be obeyed.

Although the doubly padlocked box approach would not work for real-world cryptography, it inspired Diffie and Hellman to search for a practical method of circumventing the key-distribution problem. Then, in 1975, Diffie had a truly brilliant idea. He can still recall how the idea flashed into his mind and then almost vanished: "I walked downstairs to get a Coke, and almost forgot about the idea. I remembered that I'd been thinking about something interesting, but couldn't quite recall what it was. Then it came back in a real adrenaline rush of excitement. I was actually aware for the first time in my work on cryptography of having discovered something really valuable. Everything that I had discovered in the subject up to this point seemed to me to be mere technicalities." It was midafternoon, and he had to wait a couple of hours before his wife, Mary, returned. "Whit was waiting at the door," she recalls. "He said he had something to tell me, and he had a funny look on his face. I walked in and he said, 'Sit down, please, I want to talk to you. I believe that I have made a great discovery—I know I am the first person to have done this.' The world stood still for me at that moment. I felt like I was living in a Hollywood film."

Diffie had concocted a new type of cipher, one that incorporates a so-called *asymmetric key*. So far, all the encryption techniques described in this book have been *symmetric*, which means that the unscrambling process is simply the opposite of scrambling. For example, the Enigma machine uses a certain key setting to encipher a message, and the receiver uses an identical machine in the same key setting to decipher it. Both sender and receiver effectively have equivalent knowledge, and they both use the same key to encrypt and decrypt—their relationship is symmetric. In an asymmetric key system, as the name suggests, the encryption key and the decryption key are not identical. In an asymmetric cipher, if Alice knows the encryption key, she can encrypt a message, but she cannot decrypt a message. In order to decrypt, Alice must have access to the decryption key. This distinction between encryption and decryption keys is what makes an asymmetric cipher special.

Although Diffie had come up with the general concept of an asymmetric cipher, he did not actually have a specific example of one. However, the mere concept of an asymmetric cipher was revolutionary. If cryptographers could find a genuine working asymmetric cipher, a system that fulfilled Diffie's requirements, then the implications for Alice and Bob would be enormous. Alice could create her own pair of keys: an encryption key and a decryption key. If we assume that the asymmetric cipher is a form of computer encryption, then Alice's encryption key is a number, and her decryption key is a different number. Alice keeps the decryption key secret, so it is commonly referred to as Alice's *private key*. However, she publishes the encryption key so that everybody has access to it, which is why it is commonly referred to as Alice's *public key*. If Bob wants to send Alice a message, he simply looks up her public key, which would be listed in something akin to a telephone directory. Bob then uses Alice's public key to encrypt the message. He sends the encrypted message to Alice, and when it arrives Alice can decrypt it using her private decryption key. Similarly, if Charlie or Dawn wants to send Alice an encrypted message, they too can look up Alice's public encryption key, and in each case only Alice has access to the private decryption key required to decrypt the message.

The great advantage of this system is that it overcomes the problem of key distribution. Alice does not have to transport the public encryption key securely to Bob; in fact, she wants to publicize her public encryption key so that anybody can use it to send her encrypted messages. At the same time, even if the whole world knows Alice's public key, nobody, including Eve, can decrypt any messages encrypted with it, because knowledge of the public key is no help in decryption. In fact, once Bob has encrypted a message using Alice's public key, even he cannot decrypt it. Only Alice, who alone possesses her private key, can decrypt the message.

This is the exact opposite of a traditional symmetric cipher, in which Alice has to go to great lengths to transport the encryption key securely to Bob. In a symmetric cipher the encryption key is the same as the decryption key, so Alice and Bob must take the utmost precautions to ensure that the key does not fall into Eve's hands. This is the root of the key-distribution problem.

Returning to padlock analogies, asymmetric cryptography can be thought of in the following way. Anybody can close a padlock simply by clicking it shut, but only the person who has the key can open it. Locking (encryption) is easy, something everybody can do, but unlocking (decryption) can be done only by the owner of the key. The trivial knowledge of knowing how to click the padlock shut does not equip you to unlock it. Taking the analogy further, imagine that Alice designs a padlock and key. She guards the key, but she manufactures thousands of replica padlocks and distributes them to post offices all over the world. If Bob wants to send a message, he puts it in a box, goes to the local post office, asks for an "Alice padlock" and padlocks the box. Now he, along with everyone else, is unable to unlock the box, but when Alice receives it, she can open it with her unique key. The padlock and the process of clicking it shut is equivalent to the public encryption key, because everyone has access to the padlocks, and everyone can use a padlock to seal a message in a box. The padlock's key is equivalent to the private decryption key, because only Alice has it, only she can open the padlock and only she can gain access to the message in the box.

The system seems simple when it is explained in terms of padlocks, but it is far from trivial to find a mathematical function that does the same job, something that can be incorporated into a workable cryptographic system. To turn asymmetric ciphers from a great idea into a practical invention, somebody had to discover an appropriate mathematical *function* to act as a mathematical padlock. A function is any mathematical operation that turns one number into another number. For example, doubling is a type of function because it turns the number 3 into 6, or the number 9 into 18. Furthermore, we can think of all forms of computer encryption as functions because they turn one number (the plaintext) into another number (the ciphertext).

Most mathematical functions are classified as two-way functions because they are easy to do and easy to undo. For example, doubling is a two-way function, because it is easy to double a number to generate a new number and just as easy to undo the function and get from the doubled number back to the original number. If we know that the result of doubling is 26, then it is trivial to reverse the function and deduce that the original number was 13. The easiest way to understand the concept of a two-way function is in terms of an everyday activity. We can think of the act of turning on a light switch as a function, because it turns an ordinary lightbulb into an illuminated one. This function is two-way because if a switch is turned on, it is easy enough to turn it off and return the lightbulb to its original state.

However, Diffie and Hellman were not interested in two-way functions. They focused their attention on *one-way functions*. As the name suggests, a one-way function is easy to do but very difficult to undo. In other words, two-way functions are reversible, but one-way functions are not reversible. Once again, the best way to illustrate a one-way function is in terms of an everyday activity. Mixing yellow and blue paint to make green paint is a one-way function, because it is easy to mix the paint but impossible to unmix it. Another one-way function is the cracking of an egg, because it is easy to crack an egg but impossible then to return the egg to its original condition. For this reason, one-way functions are sometimes called Humpty Dumpty functions.

Padlocks are also real-world examples of a one-way function, because they are easy to lock but very difficult to unlock. Diffie's idea relied on a mathematical padlock, and this is why the Stanford team of Diffie, Hellman and Merkle focused their attention on studying one-way functions.

Modular arithmetic, sometimes called clock arithmetic in schools, is an area of mathematics that is rich in one-way functions. It deals with a finite group of numbers arranged in a loop, rather like the numbers on a clock. For example, Figure 47 shows a clock for modular 7 (or mod 7), which has only the seven numbers from 0 to 6. To work out 2 + 3, we start at 2 and move around three places to reach 5, which is the same answer as in normal arithmetic. To work out 2 + 6, we start at 2 and move around six places, but this time we go around the loop and arrive at 1, which is not the result we would get in normal arithmetic. These results can be expressed as:

$$2 + 3 = 5 \ (\text{mod } 7) \quad \text{and} \quad 2 + 6 = 1 \ (\text{mod } 7)$$

Modular arithmetic is relatively simple, and in fact we do it every day when we talk about time. If it is nine o'clock now, and we have a meeting eight hours from now, we would say that the meeting is at five o'clock, not seventeen o'clock. We have mentally calculated 9 + 8 in mod 12. Imagine a clock face, look at 9, and then move around eight spaces, ending up at 5:

$$9 + 8 = 5 \ (\text{mod } 12)$$

Rather than visualizing clocks, mathematicians often take the shortcut of performing modular calculations according to the following recipe. First, perform the calculation in normal arithmetic. Second, if we want to know the answer in mod x, we divide the normal answer by x and note the remainder. This remainder is the answer in mod x. For example, to find the

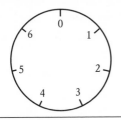

Figure 47 Modular arithmetic is performed on a finite set of numbers, which can be thought of as numbers on a clock face. In this case, we can work out 6 + 5 in modular 7 by starting at 6 and moving around five spaces, which brings us to 4.

answer in modular arithmetic to the question What is 11×9 (mod 13), we do the following:

$$11 \times 9 = 99$$

$$99 \div 13 = 7, \text{remainder } 8$$

$$11 \times 9 = 8 \text{ (mod 13)}$$

Functions performed in the modular arithmetic environment tend to behave erratically, which in turn sometimes makes them one-way functions. This becomes evident when a simple function in normal arithmetic is compared with the same simple function in modular arithmetic. In the former environment the function will be two-way and easy to reverse; in the latter environment it will be one-way and hard to reverse. As an example, let us take the function 3^x. This means take a number x, then multiply 3 by itself x times in order to get the new number. For example, if $x = 2$ and we perform the function, then:

$$3^x = 3^2 = 3 \times 3 = 9$$

In other words, the function turns 2 into 9. In normal arithmetic, as the value of x increases so does the result of the function. So if we were given the result of the function, it would be relatively easy to work backward and deduce the original number. For example, if the result is 81, we can deduce that x is 4, because $3^4 = 81$. If we made a mistake and guessed that x is 5, we could work out that $3^5 = 243$, which tells us that our choice of x is too big. We would then reduce our choice of x to 4, and we would have the right answer. In short, even when we guess wrongly, we can home in on the correct value of x and thereby reverse the function.

However, in modular arithmetic this same function does not

behave so sensibly. Imagine that we are told that 3^x in mod 7 is 1, and we are asked to find the value of x. No value springs to mind, because we are generally unfamiliar with modular arithmetic. We could take a guess that $x = 5$, and we could work out the result of 3^5 (mod 7). The answer turns out to be 5, which is too big, because we are looking for an answer of just 1. We might be tempted to reduce the value of x to 4 and try again. But we would be heading in the wrong direction, because the actual answer is $x = 6$.

In normal arithmetic we can test numbers and can sense whether we are getting warmer or colder. The environment of modular arithmetic gives no helpful clues, and reversing functions is much harder. Often the only way to reverse a function in modular arithmetic is to compile a table by calculating the function for many values of x until the right answer is found. Table 14 shows the result of calculating several values of the function in both normal arithmetic and modular arithmetic. It clearly demonstrates the erratic behavior of the function when calculated in modular arithmetic.

Although drawing up such a table is only a little tedious when we are dealing with relatively small numbers, it would be excruciatingly painful to build a table to deal with a function such as 453^x (mod 21,997). This is a classic example of a one-way function, because I could pick a value for x and

Table 14 Values of the function 3^x calculated in normal arithmetic (row 2) and modular arithmetic (row 3). The function increases continuously in normal arithmetic, but is highly erratic in modular arithmetic.

x	1	2	3	4	5	6
3^x	3	9	27	81	243	729
3^x (mod 7)	3	2	6	4	5	1

calculate the result of the function, but if I gave you a result, say, 5,787, you would have enormous difficulty in reversing the function and deducing the value of x. It would take you hours to draw up the table and thereby work out the correct value of x.

However, this particular one-way function is not adequate to act as a mathematical padlock, because padlocks exhibit a special type of one-way functionality. It is easy to click a padlock and lock it, but it is very difficult to unlock the padlock . . . unless, of course, you have the key! The key is what makes a padlock a special type of one-way function. The true mathematical equivalent of a padlock is a function that is always easy to perform in one direction but generally hard to perform in the opposite direction unless you have some special piece of information, namely, the key.

If such a function existed, then Alice would personalize it, which would give her the special piece of information for reversing the function. She would keep this information secret but distribute the personalized function so that Bob and everyone else can use it to encrypt messages to her. She can decrypt these messages by using the special piece of information. She unlocks the encrypted messages sent to her by using her secret key. Similarly, Bob would personalize the function so that he has his own piece of special secret information. He too distributes his mathematical padlock so that Alice and anybody else can encrypt and send messages to him. Only Bob has the special piece of information required to decrypt the messages sent to him, which have been encrypted using his personalized padlock.

The team of Diffie, Hellman and Merkle had invigorated the world of cryptography. They had persuaded the rest of the world that a solution to the key-distribution problem lay just over the horizon. They had proposed the concept of an asymmetric cipher—a perfect but as yet unworkable system. They continued their research at Stanford University, attempting to find a special one-way function that would make asymmetric ciphers a reality. However, they failed to make the discovery. They were overtaken in the race to find an asymmetric cipher by another trio of researchers, based three thousand miles away on the East Coast of America.

PRIME SUSPECTS

"I walked into Ron Rivest's office," recalls Leonard Adleman, "and Ron had this paper in his hands. He started saying, 'These Stanford guys have this really blah, blah, blah.' And I remember thinking, 'That's nice, Ron, but I have something else I want to talk about.' I was entirely unaware of the history of cryptography, and I was distinctly uninterested in what he was saying." The paper that had made Ron Rivest so excited was by Diffie and Hellman, and it described the concept of asymmetric ciphers. Eventually Rivest persuaded Adleman that there might be some interesting mathematics in the problem, and together they resolved to try to find a one-way function that fit the requirements of an asymmetric cipher. They were joined in the hunt by Adi Shamir. All three men were researchers on the eighth floor of the MIT Laboratory for Computer Science.

Rivest, Shamir and Adleman formed a perfect team. Rivest is a computer scientist with a tremendous ability to absorb new ideas and apply them in unlikely places. He always kept up with the latest scientific papers, which inspired him to come up with a whole series of weird and wonderful candidates for the one-way function at the heart of an asymmetric cipher. However, each candidate was flawed in some way. Shamir, another computer scientist, has a lightning intellect and an ability to see through the debris and focus on the core of a problem. He too regularly generated ideas for formulating an asymmetric cipher, but his ideas were also inevitably flawed. Adleman, a mathematician with enormous stamina, rigor and patience, was largely responsible for spotting the flaws in the ideas of Rivest and Shamir, ensuring that they did not waste time following false leads. Rivest and Shamir spent a year coming up with new ideas, and Adleman spent a year shooting them down. The threesome began to lose hope, but they were unaware that this process of continual failure was a necessary part of their research, gently steering them away from sterile mathematical territory and toward more fertile ground. In due course, their efforts were rewarded.

In April 1977, Rivest, Shamir and Adleman spent Passover at the house of a student, returning to their respective homes sometime around midnight. Rivest, unable to sleep, lay on his couch reading a mathematics textbook. He began mulling over the question that had been puzzling him for weeks: Is it possible to build an asymmetric cipher? Is it possible to find a one-way function that can be reversed only if the receiver has some special information? Suddenly, the mists began to clear and he had a revelation. He spent the rest of that night formalizing his idea, effectively writing a complete scientific paper before day-

Figure 48 Ronald Rivest, Adi Shamir and Leonard Adleman.

break. Rivest had made a breakthrough, but it had grown out of a yearlong collaboration with Shamir and Adleman, and it would not have been possible without them. Rivest finished off the paper by listing the authors alphabetically: Adleman, Rivest, Shamir.

The next morning, Rivest handed the paper to Adleman, who went through his usual process of trying to tear it apart, but this time he could find no faults. His only criticism was with the list of authors. "I told Ron to take my name off the paper," recalls Adleman. "I told him that it was his invention, not mine. But Ron refused, and we got into a discussion about it. We agreed that I would go home and contemplate it for one night, and consider what I wanted to do. I went back the next day and suggested to Ron that I be the third author. I recall thinking that this paper would be the least interesting paper that I will ever be on." Adleman could not have been more wrong. The system, dubbed RSA (Rivest, Shamir, Adleman) as opposed to ARS, went on to become the most influential cipher in modern cryptography.

Before exploring Rivest's idea, here is a quick reminder of what scientists were looking for in order to build an asymmetric cipher:

1. Alice must create a public key, which she would then publish so that Bob (and everybody else) can use it to encrypt messages to her. Because the public key is a one-way function, it must be virtually impossible for anybody to reverse it and decrypt Alice's messages.
2. However, Alice needs to decrypt the messages being sent to her. She must therefore have a private key, some special piece of information, which allows her to reverse the effect of the public key. Therefore, Alice (and Alice alone) has the power to decrypt any messages sent to her.

At the heart of Rivest's asymmetric cipher is a one-way function based on the sort of modular function described earlier in the chapter. Rivest's one-way function can be used to encrypt a message—the message, which is effectively a number, is put into the function, and the result is the ciphertext, another number. I shall not describe Rivest's one-way function in detail here (instead, see Appendix E), but I shall explain one particular aspect of it, known simply as N, because it is N that makes this one-way function reversible under certain circumstances, and therefore ideal for use as an asymmetric cipher.

N is important because it is a flexible component of the one-way function, which means that each person can choose a different value of N and personalize the one-way function. In order to choose her personal value of N, Alice picks two *prime numbers*, p and q, and multiplies them together. A prime number is one that has no divisors except itself and 1. For example, 7 is a prime number because no numbers except 1 and 7 will divide into it without leaving a remainder. Likewise, 13 is a prime number because no numbers except 1 and 13 will divide into it without leaving a remainder. However, 8 is not a prime number, because it can be divided by 2 and 4.

So Alice could choose her prime numbers to be $p = 17{,}159$ and $q = 10{,}247$. Multiplying these two numbers together gives $N = 17{,}159 \times 10{,}247 = 175{,}828{,}273$. Alice's choice of N effectively becomes her public encryption key, and she could print it on her business card, post it on the Internet or publish it in a public-key directory along with everybody else's value of N. If Bob wants to encrypt a message to Alice, he looks up Alice's value of N (175,828,273) and then inserts it into the general form of the one-way function, which would also be public knowledge. Bob now has a one-way function tailored with Alice's public key, so it could be called Alice's one-way function. To encrypt a message to Alice, he takes Alice's one-way function, inserts the message, notes down the result and sends it to Alice.

At this point the encrypted message is secure because nobody can decipher it. The message has been encrypted with a one-way function, so reversing the one-way function and decrypting the message is, by definition, very difficult. However, the question remains—how can Alice decrypt the message? In order to read messages sent to her, Alice must have a way of reversing the one-way function. She needs to have access to some special piece of information that allows her to decrypt the message. Fortunately for Alice, Rivest designed the one-way function so that it is reversible to someone who knows the values of p and q, the two prime numbers that are multiplied together to give N. Although Alice has told the world that her value for N is 175,828,273, she has not revealed her values for p and q, so only she has the special information required to decrypt her own messages.

We can think of N as the public key, the information that is available to everybody, the information required to encrypt messages to Alice, whereas p and q are the private key, the information required to decrypt these messages. This private key is only available to Alice.

The exact details of how p and q can be used to reverse the one-way function are outlined in Appendix E. However, there is one question that must be addressed immediately. If everybody knows N, the public key, then can't people deduce p and q, the private key, and read Alice's messages? After all, N was created from p and q. In fact, it turns out that if N is large enough, it is virtually impossible to deduce p and q from N, and this is perhaps the most beautiful and elegant aspect of the RSA asymmetric cipher.

Alice created N for her one-way function by choosing p and q and then multiplying them together. The fundamental point is that this is in itself a one-way function. To demonstrate the one-way nature of multiplying primes, we can take two prime numbers, such as 9,419 and 1,933, and multiply them together. With a calculator it takes a few seconds to get the answer, 18,206,927. However, if instead we were given 18,206,927 and asked to find the prime factors (the two numbers that were multiplied to give 18,206,927) it would take much longer. If you doubt the difficulty of finding prime factors, then try the following: It took me just seconds to generate the number 1,709,023, but it will take you and a calculator the best part of an afternoon to work out the prime factors.

This system of asymmetric cryptography, known as RSA, is said to be a form of *public-key cryptography*. To find out how secure RSA is, we need to see how difficult it is to factor N, because this is what Eve would have to do to find p and q and thereby work out the private key needed to decipher messages.

For high security, Bob would choose very large values of p and q. For example, he could choose primes that are as big as 10^{65} (this means 1 followed by sixty-five zeros, or one hundred thousand million million million million million million million million million million). This would have resulted in a value for N that would have been roughly $10^{65} \times 10^{65}$, which is 10^{130}. A computer could multiply the two primes and generate N in just a second, but if Eve wanted to reverse the process and work out p and q, it would take inordinately longer. Exactly how long depends on the speed of Eve's computer. Security expert Simson Garfinkel estimated that a 100 MHz Intel Pentium computer with 8 MB of RAM would take roughly fifty years to factor a number as big as 10^{130}. Cryptographers tend to have a paranoid streak and consider worst-case scenarios, such as a worldwide conspiracy to crack their ciphers. So Garfinkel considered what would happen if a hundred million personal computers (the number sold in

1995) ganged up together. The result is that a number as big as 10^{130} could be factored in about fifteen seconds. Consequently, it is now generally accepted that for genuine security it is necessary to use even larger primes. For important banking transactions, N tends to be at least 10^{308}, which is ten million billion times bigger than 10^{130}. The combined efforts of a hundred million personal computers would take more than a thousand years to crack such a cipher. With sufficiently large values of p and q, RSA is impenetrable.

The only caveat for the security of RSA public-key cryptography is that at some time in the future somebody might find a quick way to factor N. It is conceivable that a decade from now, or even tomorrow, somebody will discover a method for rapid factoring, and thereafter RSA will become useless. However, for over two thousand years mathematicians have tried and failed to find a shortcut, and at the moment factoring remains an enormously time-consuming calculation. Most mathematicians believe that factoring is an inherently difficult task and that there is some mathematical law that forbids any shortcut. If we assume they are right, then RSA seems secure for the foreseeable future.

The great advantage of RSA public-key cryptography is that it does away with all the problems associated with traditional ciphers and key exchange. Alice no longer has to worry about securely transporting the key to Bob, or that Eve might intercept the key. In fact, Alice does not care who sees the public key—the more the merrier, because the public key helps only with encryption, not decryption. The only thing that needs to remain secret is the private key used for decryption, and Alice can keep this with her at all times.

RSA was first announced in August 1977, when Martin

Gardner wrote an article entitled "A New Kind of Cipher that Would Take Millions of Years to Break" for his "Mathematical Games" column in *Scientific American*. After explaining how public-key cryptography works, Gardner issued a challenge to his readers. He printed a ciphertext and also provided the public key that had been used to encrypt it:

N = 114,381,625,757,888,867,669,235,779,976,146,612,010, 218,296,721,242,362,562,561,842,935,706,935,245,733,897, 830,597,123,563,958,705,058,989,075,147,599,290,026,879, 543,541

The challenge was to factor N into p and q, and then use these numbers to decrypt the message. The prize was $100. Gardner did not have space to explain the nitty-gritty of RSA, and instead he asked readers to write to MIT's Laboratory for Computer Science, which in turn would send back a technical memorandum that had just been prepared. Rivest, Shamir and Adleman were astonished by the three thousand requests they received. However, they did not respond immediately, because they were concerned that public distribution of their idea might jeopardize their chances of getting a patent. When the patent issues were eventually resolved, the trio held a celebratory party at which professors and students consumed pizza and beer while stuffing envelopes with technical memoranda for the readers of *Scientific American*.

As for Gardner's challenge, it would take seventeen years before the cipher would be broken. On April 26, 1994, a team of six hundred volunteers announced the factors of N:

q = 3,490,529,510,847,650,949,147,849,619,903,898,133,417, 764,638,493,387,843,990,820,577

p = 32,769,132,993,266,709,549,961,988,190,834,461,413,177, 642,967,992,942,539,798,288,533

Using these values as the private key, they were able to decipher the message. The message was a series of numbers, but when converted into letters, it read, "The magic words are squeamish ossifrage." The factoring problem had been split among volunteers, who came from countries as far apart as Australia, Britain, the United States and Venezuela. The volunteers used spare time on their workstations, mainframes and supercomputers, each of them tackling a fraction of the problem. In effect, a network of computers around the world were uniting and working simultaneously in order to meet Gardner's challenge. Even bearing in mind the mammoth parallel effort, some readers may still be surprised that RSA was broken in such a short time, but it should be noted that Gardner's challenge used a relatively small value of N—it was only of the order of 10^{129}. Today, users of RSA would pick a much larger value to secure important information. It is now routine to encrypt a message with a sufficiently large value of N so that all the computers on the planet would need longer than the age of the universe to break the cipher.

THE SECRET HISTORY OF PUBLIC-KEY CRYPTOGRAPHY

Over the past twenty years, Diffie, Hellman and Merkle have become world-famous as the cryptographers who invented the concept of public-key cryptography, while Rivest, Shamir and Adleman have been credited with developing RSA, the most beautiful implementation of public-key cryptography. However, a recent announcement means that the history books have to be rewritten. According to the British government, public-key cryptography was originally invented at the Government Communications Headquarters (GCHQ) in Cheltenham, the top-secret establishment that was formed from the remnants of Bletchley Park after the Second World War. This is a story of remarkable ingenuity, anonymous heroes and a government cover-up that endured for decades.

On April 1, 1965, James Ellis had moved to Cheltenham to join the newly formed Communications-Electronics Security Group (CESG), a special section of GCHQ devoted to ensuring the security of British communications. At the beginning of 1969, the military asked Ellis, by now one of Britain's foremost government cryptographers, to look into ways of coping with the key-distribution problem. Because he was involved in issues of national security, Ellis was sworn to secrecy throughout his career. Although his wife and family knew that he worked at GCHQ, they were unaware of his discoveries and had no idea that he was one of the nation's most distinguished codemakers.

One of Ellis' greatest qualities was his breadth of knowledge. He read any scientific journal he could get his hands on, and never threw anything away. For security reasons, GCHQ employees must clear their desks each evening and place everything

Figure 49 James Ellis.

in locked cabinets, which meant that Ellis' cabinets were stuffed full with the most obscure publications imaginable. He gained a reputation as a cryptoguru, and if other researchers found themselves with impossible problems, they would knock on his door in the hope that his vast knowledge and originality would provide a solution. It was probably because of this reputation that he was asked to examine the key-distribution problem.

Ellis began his attack on the problem by searching through his treasure trove of scientific papers. Many years later, he recorded the moment when he discovered that key distribution was not an inevitable part of cryptography:

> The event which changed this view was the discovery of a wartime Bell Telephone report by an unknown author describing an ingenious idea for secure telephone speech. It proposed that the recipient should mask the sender's speech by adding noise to the line. He could subtract the noise afterwards since he had added it and therefore knew what it was. The obvious practical disadvantages of this system prevented it being actually used, but it has some interesting characteristics. The difference between this and conventional encryption is that in this case the recipient takes part in the encryption process. . . . So the idea was born.

Noise is the technical term for any signal that interferes with a communication. Normally it is generated by natural phenomena, and its most irritating feature is that it is entirely random, which means that removing noise from a message is very difficult. If a radio system is well designed, then the level of noise is low and the message is clearly audible, but if the noise level is high and it swamps the message, there is no way to recover the message. Ellis was suggesting that the receiver, Alice, deliberately create noise, which she could measure before adding it to the communication channel that connects her with Bob. Bob could then send a message to Alice, and if Eve tapped the communications channel, she would be unable to read the message because it would be swamped in noise. The only person who can remove the noise and read the message is Alice, because she is in the unique position of knowing the exact nature of the noise, having put it there in the first place. Ellis realized that security had been achieved without exchanging any key. The key was the noise, and only Alice needed to know the details of the noise.

In a memorandum, Ellis detailed his thought processes: "The next question was the obvious one. Can this be done with ordinary encipherment? Can we produce a secure encrypted message, readable by the authorised recipient without any prior secret exchange of the key? This question actually occurred to me in bed one night, and the proof of the theoretical possibility took only a few minutes. We had an existence theorem. The unthinkable was actually possible." An existence theorem shows that a particular concept is possible but is not concerned with the details of the concept. In other words, until this moment, searching for a solution to the key-distribution problem was like looking for a needle in a haystack, with the possibility that the needle might not even be there. However, thanks to the existence theorem, Ellis now knew that the needle was in there somewhere.

Ellis' ideas were very similar to those of Diffie, Hellman and Merkle, except that he was several years ahead of them. However, nobody knew of Ellis' work because he was an employee of the British government and therefore sworn to secrecy. By the end of 1969, Ellis appears to have reached the same impasse that the Stanford trio would reach in 1975. He had proved to himself that public-key cryptography (or nonsecret encryption, as he called it) was possible, and he had developed the concept of separate public keys and private keys. He also knew that he needed to find a special one-way function, one that could be reversed if the receiver had access to a piece of special information.

Unfortunately, Ellis was not a mathematician. He experimented with a few mathematical functions, but he soon realized that he would be unable to progress any further on his own.

For the next three years, GCHQ's brightest minds struggled to find a one-way function that satisfied Ellis' requirements, but nothing emerged. Then, in September 1973, a new mathematician joined the team. Clifford Cocks had recently graduated from Cambridge University, where he had specialized in number theory, one of the purest forms of mathematics. When he joined GCHQ he knew very little about encryption and the shadowy world of military and diplomatic communication, so he was assigned a mentor, Nick Patterson, who guided him through his first few weeks as a cryptographer.

After about six weeks, Patterson told Cocks about "a really wacky idea." He outlined Ellis' theory for public-key cryptography, and explained that nobody had yet been able to find a mathematical function that fitted the bill. Patterson was telling Cocks because this was the most exciting cryptographic idea around, not because he expected him to try to solve it. However, as Cocks explains, later that day he set to work: "There was nothing particular happening, and so I thought I would think about the idea. Because I had been working in number theory, it was natural to think about one-way functions, something you could do but not undo. Prime numbers and factoring was a natural candidate, and that became my starting point." Cocks was beginning to formulate what would later be known as the RSA asymmetric cipher. Rivest, Shamir and Adleman discovered their formula for public-key cryptography in 1977, but four years earlier the young Cambridge graduate was going through exactly the same thought processes. Cocks recalls: "From start to finish, it took me no more than half an hour. I was quite pleased with myself. I thought, 'Ooh, that's nice. I've been given a problem, and I've solved it.' "

Cocks did not fully appreciate the significance of his discovery. He was unaware of the fact that GCHQ's brightest minds had been struggling with the problem for three years, and he had no idea that he had made one of the most important cryptographic breakthroughs of the century. Cocks' naivete may have been part of the reason for his success, allowing him to attack the problem with confidence, rather than timidly prodding at it. Cocks told his mentor about his discovery, and it was Patterson who then reported it to the management. Cocks was quite diffident and very much still a rookie, whereas Patterson fully appreciated the context of the problem and was more capable of addressing the technical questions that would inevitably arise. Soon complete strangers started approaching Cocks, the wonder kid, and began to congratulate him. One of the strangers was James Ellis, eager to meet the man who had turned his dream into a reality. Because Cocks still did not understand the magnitude of his achievement, the details of this meeting did not make a great impact on him, and so now, three decades later, he has no memory of Ellis' reaction.

Although Cocks' idea was one of GCHQ's most potent secrets, it suffered from the problem of being ahead of its time. Cocks had discovered a mathematical function that permitted public-key cryptography, but there was still the difficulty of implementing the system. Encryption via public-key cryptography requires much more computer power than encryption via a symmetric cipher. In the early 1970s, computers were still relatively primitive and unable to perform the process of public-key encryption within a reasonable amount of time. Hence, GCHQ was not in a position to exploit public-key cryptography. Cocks and Ellis had proved that the apparently impossible was possible, but nobody could find a way of making the possible practical.

At the beginning of the following year, 1974, Cocks explained his work on public-key cryptography to Malcolm Williamson, who had recently joined GCHQ as a cryptographer. The men happened to be old friends. They had both attended Manchester Grammar School, whose school motto is *Sapere aude*, "Dare to be wise." While at school in 1968, the two boys had represented Britain at the Mathematical Olympiad in the Soviet Union. After attending Cambridge University together, they went their separate ways for a couple of years, but now they were reunited at GCHQ. They had been exchanging mathematical ideas since the age of eleven, but Cocks' revelation of public-key cryptography was the most shocking idea that Williamson had ever heard. "Cliff explained his idea to me," recalls Williamson, "and I really didn't believe it. I was very suspicious, because this is a very peculiar thing to be able to do."

Williamson began trying to prove that Cocks had made a mistake and that public-key cryptography did not really exist. He probed the mathematics, searching for an underlying flaw. Public-key cryptography seemed too good to be true, and Williamson was so determined to find a mistake that he took the problem home. GCHQ employees are not supposed to take work home, because everything they do is classified, and the home environment is potentially vulnerable to espionage. However, the problem was stuck in Williamson's brain, so he could not avoid thinking about it. Defying orders, he carried his work back to his house. He spent five hours trying to find a flaw. "Essentially I failed," says Williamson. "Instead I came up with another solution to the problem of key distribution." He had discovered a protocol now known as Diffie-Hellman-Merkle key exchange (because it was discovered independently and in the public realm by the Americans).

By 1975, James Ellis, Clifford Cocks and Malcolm Williamson had discovered all the fundamental aspects of public-key cryptography, yet they all had to remain silent. The three

Britons had to sit back and watch as their discoveries were rediscovered by Diffie, Hellman, Merkle, Rivest, Shamir and Adleman over the next three years.

The scientific press reported the breakthroughs at Stanford and MIT, so the researchers who had been allowed to publish their work in the scientific journals became famous within the community of cryptographers. Cocks' attitude is admirably restrained: "You don't get involved in this business for public recognition." Williamson is equally dispassionate: "My reaction was 'Okay, that's just the way it is.' Basically, I just got on with the rest of my life."

Although GCHQ was the first to discover public-key cryptography, this should not diminish the achievements of the academics who rediscovered it. It was the academics who were the first to realize the potential of public-key encryption, and it was they who drove its implementation. Furthermore, it is quite possible that GCHQ never would have revealed its work, thus blocking the encryption protocol that has enabled what we now call the digital revolution. Finally, the discovery by the

Figure 50 Malcolm Williamson (second from left) and Clifford Cocks (extreme right) arriving for the 1968 Mathematical Olympiad.

American academics was wholly independent of GCHQ's discovery, and on an intellectual par. The academic environment is completely isolated from the top-secret domain of classified research, and academics do not have access to the tools and secret knowledge that may be hidden in the classified world. On the other hand, government researchers always have access to the academic literature. One might think of this flow of information in terms of a one-way function—information flows freely in one direction, but it is forbidden to send information in the opposite direction.

It is difficult to overestimate the level of secrecy maintained by establishments like GCHQ. Even when the academics published RSA, GCHQ remained silent. Even in the late 1980s, when public use of RSA was becoming widespread, GCHQ refused to acknowledge its own invention of public-key cryptography.

Eventually, twenty-eight years after Ellis' initial breakthrough, GCHQ went public. In 1997, Clifford Cocks completed some important work on RSA that was of interest to the wider community and would not be a security risk if it was published. As a result, he planned to present a paper at the Institute of Mathematics and its Applications Conference to be held in Cirencester. The room would be full of cryptography experts. A handful of them, very senior members of the security world, had heard rumors that Cocks, who would be talking about just one aspect of RSA, was actually its unsung inventor. There was a risk that somebody might ask an embarrassing question, such as "Did you invent RSA?" If such a question arose, what was Cocks supposed to do? According to GCHQ policy, he would have to deny his role in the development of RSA, thus forcing him to lie about an issue that was totally harmless. The situation was clearly ridiculous, and

GCHQ decided that it was time to change its policy. Cocks was given permission to begin his talk by presenting a brief history of GCHQ's contribution to public-key cryptography.

On December 18, 1997, Cocks delivered his talk. After almost three decades of secrecy, Ellis, Cocks and Williamson received the acknowledgment they deserved. Sadly, James Ellis had died just one month earlier, on November 25, 1997, at the age of seventy-three. Ellis joined the list of British cipher experts whose contributions would never be recognized during their lifetimes. Charles Babbage's breaking of the Vigenère cipher was never revealed while he was alive, probably because his work was invaluable to British forces in the Crimea. Instead, credit for the work went to Friedrich Kasiski. Similarly, Alan Turing's contribution to the war effort was unparalleled, and yet government secrecy demanded that his work on Enigma not be revealed.

In 1987, GCHQ declassified a document that Ellis had written. It records his contribution to public-key cryptography and includes his thoughts on the secrecy that so often surrounds cryptographic work:

> Cryptography is a most unusual science. Most professional scientists aim to be the first to publish their work, because it is through dissemination that the work realises its value. In contrast, the fullest value of cryptography is realised by minimising the information available to potential adversaries. Thus professional cryptographers normally work in closed communities to provide sufficient professional interaction to ensure quality while maintaining secrecy from outsiders. Revelation of these secrets is normally only sanctioned in the interests of historical accuracy after it has been demonstrated that no further benefit can be obtained from continued secrecy.

1101010101100110100111011001101001110011011
1011011001100101101011001010011000110110
1010111101100101010111001100110101011001011
0111000101100110100011010110010101**6**10001
0111001010110011001101011101100101001
1010101011001101001110110011010010

Pretty Good Privacy

The politics of privacy,
the future of cryptography
and the quest for an
uncrackable code

The exchange of digital information has become an integral part of our society. Already, tens of millions of e-mails are sent each day, the Internet has provided the infrastructure for the digital marketplace, and e-commerce is thriving. Money is flowing through cyberspace, and it is estimated that every day half the world's gross domestic product travels through the Society for Worldwide Interbank Financial Telecommunications (SWIFT) network. Democracies that favor referenda will begin to have online voting, and governments will increasingly use the Internet to help administer their countries, offering facilities such as online tax returns. Without doubt, the Information Age is under way, and we live in a wired world.

Critically, the success of the Information Age depends on the ability to protect information as it flows around the world, and this relies on the power of cryptography. Encryption can be seen as providing the locks and keys of the Information Age. For two thousand years encryption has been of importance only to governments and the military, but today it also has a role to play in facilitating business, and tomorrow ordinary people will rely on cryptography in order to protect their privacy. Fortunately, just as the Information Age is taking off, we have access to extraordinarily strong encryption. The development of public-key cryptography, particularly the RSA cipher, has given today's cryptographers a clear advantage in their continual power struggle against cryptanalysts. If the value of N is large enough, then finding p and q takes Eve an unreasonable amount of time, and RSA encryption is therefore effectively unbreakable. Most important of all, public-key cryptography is not weakened by any key-distribution problems. In short, RSA

Figure 51 Phil Zimmermann.

guarantees almost unbreakable locks for our most precious pieces of information.

However, as with every technology, there is a dark side to encryption. As well as protecting the communications of law-abiding citizens, encryption also protects the communications of criminals and terrorists. Currently, police forces use wiretapping as a way of gathering evidence to counter organized crime and terrorism, but this would be ineffective if criminals used unbreakable ciphers.

In the twenty-first century, the fundamental dilemma for cryptography is to find a way of allowing the public and businesses to use encryption in order to exploit the benefits of the Information Age, without allowing criminals to abuse encryption and evade arrest. There is currently an active and vigorous debate about the best way forward, and much of the discussion has been inspired by the story of Phil Zimmermann, an American cryptographer whose attempts to encourage the widespread use of strong encryption have frightened America's security experts, threatened the effectiveness of the billion-dollar National Security Agency and made him the subject of a major inquiry and a grand-jury investigation.

In the late 1980s Zimmermann, who had long been a political activist, began to focus his attentions on the digital revolution and the necessity for encryption:

> Cryptography used to be an obscure science, of little relevance to everyday life. Historically, it always had a special role in military and diplomatic communications. But in the Information Age, cryptography is about political power, and in particular, about the power relationship between a government and its people. It is about the right to privacy, freedom of speech, freedom of political association, freedom of the press, freedom from unreasonable search and seizure, freedom to be left alone.

According to Zimmermann, there is a fundamental difference between traditional and digital communication, which has important implications for security:

> In the past, if the government wanted to violate the privacy of ordinary citizens, it had to expend a certain amount of effort to intercept and steam open and read paper mail, or listen to and possibly transcribe spoken telephone conversations. This is analogous to catching fish with a hook and a line, one fish at a time. Fortunately for freedom and democracy, this kind of labor-intensive monitoring is not practical on a large scale. Today, electronic mail is gradually replacing conventional paper mail, and is soon to be the norm for everyone, not the novelty it is today. Unlike paper mail, e-mail messages are just too easy to intercept and scan for interesting keywords. This can be done easily, routinely, automatically, and undetectably on a grand scale. This is analogous to driftnet fishing—making a quantitative and qualitative Orwellian difference to the health of democracy.

The difference between ordinary and digital mail can be illustrated by imagining that Alice wants to send out invitations to her birthday party, and that Eve, who has not been invited, wants to know the time and place of the party. If Alice uses the traditional method of posting letters, then it is very difficult for Eve to intercept one of the invitations. To start with, Eve does not know where Alice's invitations entered the postal system, because Alice could use any mailbox in the city. Her only hope for intercepting one of the invitations is to somehow identify the address of one of Alice's friends and infiltrate the local sorting office. She then has to check each and every letter manually. If she does manage to find a letter from Alice, she will have to steam it open in order to get the information she wants, and then return it to its original condition to avoid any suspicion of tampering.

In comparison, Eve's task is made much easier if Alice sends her invitations by e-mail. As the messages leave Alice's computer, they will go to a local server, a main entry point for the Internet; if Eve is clever enough, she can hack into that local server without leaving her home. The invitations will carry Alice's e-mail address, and it would be a trivial matter to set up an electronic filter that looks for e-mails containing Alice's address. Once an invitation has been found, there is no envelope to open, and so no problem in reading it. Furthermore, the invitation can be sent on its way without it showing any sign of having been intercepted. Alice would be oblivious to what was going on. However, there is a way to prevent Eve from reading Alice's e-mails, namely, encryption.

The majority of the e-mails that are sent around the world each day are vulnerable to interception, because most people do not use encryption. According to Zimmermann, cryptographers have a duty to encourage the use of encryption and thereby protect the privacy of the individual:

> A future government could inherit a technology infrastructure that's optimized for surveillance, where they can watch the movements of their political opposition, every financial transaction, every communication, every bit of e-mail, every phone call. Everything could be filtered and scanned and automatically recognized by voice recognition technology and transcribed. It's time for cryptography to step out of the shadows of spies and the military, and step into the sunshine and be embraced by the rest of us.

In theory, when RSA was invented in 1977, it offered an antidote to the Big Brother scenario because individuals were able to create their own public and private keys, and thereafter send and receive perfectly secure messages. However, in practice there was a major problem, because the actual process of RSA encryption required substantial computing resources. Consequently, in the 1980s it was only governments, the military and large businesses that owned computers powerful enough to run the RSA encryption system. Not surprisingly, RSA Data Security, Inc., the company set up to commercialize RSA, developed its encryption products with only these markets in mind.

In contrast, Zimmermann believed that everybody deserved the privacy that was offered by RSA encryption, and he directed his efforts toward developing an RSA encryption product for the masses. He intended to draw upon his background in computer science to design a product with economy and efficiency in mind, thus not overloading the capacity of an ordinary personal computer. He also wanted his version of RSA to have a particularly friendly interface, so that the user did not have to be an expert in cryptography to operate it. He called his project Pretty Good Privacy, or PGP for short. The name was inspired by Ralph's Pretty Good Groceries, a sponsor of Garrison Keillor's *A Prairie Home Companion,* one of Zimmermann's favorite radio shows.

During the late 1980s, working from his home in Boulder, Colorado, Zimmermann gradually pieced together his scrambling software package. His main goal was to speed up RSA encryption. Ordinarily, if Alice wants to use RSA to encrypt a message to Bob, she looks up his public key and then applies RSA's one-way function to the message. Conversely, Bob decrypts the ciphertext by using his private key to reverse RSA's one-way function. Both processes require considerable mathematical manipulation, so encryption and decryption can, if the message is long, take several minutes on a personal computer. If Alice is sending a hundred messages a day, she cannot afford to spend several minutes encrypting each one. To speed up encryption and decryption, Zimmermann employed a neat trick that used asymmetric RSA encryption together with old-fashioned symmetric encryption. Traditional symmetric encryption can be just as secure as asymmetric encryption, and it is much quicker to perform, but symmetric encryption suffers from the problem of having to distribute the key, which has to be securely transported from the sender to the receiver. This is where RSA comes to the rescue, because RSA can be used to encrypt the symmetric key.

Zimmermann pictured the following scenario. If Alice wants to send an encrypted message to Bob, she begins by encrypting it with a symmetric cipher. Zimmermann suggested using a cipher known as IDEA. To encrypt with IDEA, Alice needs to choose a key, but for Bob to decrypt the message Alice somehow has to get the key to Bob. Alice overcomes this problem by looking up Bob's RSA public key and then uses it to encrypt the IDEA key. So Alice ends up sending two things to Bob: the message encrypted with the symmetric IDEA cipher and the IDEA key encrypted with the asymmetric RSA cipher. At the other end, Bob uses his RSA private key to decrypt the IDEA key, and then uses the IDEA key to decrypt the message. This might seem convoluted, but the advantage is that the message, which might contain a large amount of information, is being encrypted with a quick symmetric cipher, and only the symmetric IDEA key, which consists of a relatively small amount of information, is being encrypted with a slow asymmetric cipher. Zimmermann planned to have this complex combination of RSA and IDEA within the PGP product, but the user-friendly interface would mean that the user would not have to get involved in the nuts and bolts of what was going on.

By the summer of 1991, Zimmermann was well on the way to turning PGP into a polished product. Only one problem remained: the U.S. Senate's 1991 omnibus anticrime bill, which contained the following clause: "It is the sense of Congress that providers of electronic communications services and manufacturers of electronic communications service equipment shall ensure that communications systems permit the government to obtain the plain text contents of voice, data, and other communications when appropriately authorized by law." The Senate was concerned that developments in digital technology, such as cellular telephones, might prevent law enforcers from performing effective wiretaps. However, as well as forcing companies to guarantee the possibility of wiretapping, the bill also seemed to threaten all forms of secure encryption.

A concerted effort by RSA Data Security, the communications industry and civil-liberties groups forced the clause to be dropped, but the consensus was that this was only a temporary reprieve. Zimmermann was fearful that sooner or later the government would again try to bring in legislation that would effectively outlaw encryption such as PGP. He had always intended to sell PGP, but now he reconsidered his options. Rather than waiting and risk PGP being banned by the government, he decided that it was more important for it to be available to everybody before it was too late. In June 1991 he took the drastic step of asking a friend to post PGP on a Usenet bulletin board. PGP is just a piece software, and so from the bulletin board it could be downloaded by anyone for free. PGP was now loose on the Internet.

Initially, PGP caused a buzz only among aficionados of cryptography. Later it was downloaded by a wider range of Internet enthusiasts. Next, computer magazines ran brief reports and then full-page articles on the PGP phenomenon. Gradually PGP began to permeate the most remote corners of the digital community. For example, human-rights groups around the world started to use PGP to encrypt their documents, in order to prevent the information from falling into the hands of the regimes that were being accused of human-rights abuses.

Zimmermann began to receive e-mails praising him for his creation. "There are resistance groups in Burma," says Zimmermann, "who are using it in jungle training camps. They've said that it's helped morale there, because before PGP was introduced captured documents would lead to the arrest, torture and execution of entire families." In 1991, on the day that Boris Yeltsin was shelling Moscow's Parliament building, Zimmermann received this e-mail via someone in Latvia: "Phil, I wish you to know: let it never be, but if dictatorship takes over Russia, your PGP is widespread from Baltic to Far East now and will help democratic people if necessary. Thanks."

While Zimmermann was gaining fans around the world, back home in America he was less popular. In February 1993, two government investigators paid Zimmermann a visit on the grounds that the U.S. government included encryption software within its definition of munitions, along with missiles, mortars and machine guns. Therefore PGP could not be exported without a license from the State Department. In other words, Zimmermann was accused of being an arms dealer because he had exported PGP via the Internet. Over the next three years Zimmermann became the subject of a grand-jury investigation and was pursued by government officials.

The investigation into Phil Zimmermann and PGP ignited a debate about the positive and negative effects of encryption in the Information Age. The spread of PGP encouraged cryptographers, politicians, civil libertarians and law enforcers to think about the implications of widespread encryption. There were those, like Zimmermann, who believed that the widespread use of secure encryption would be a boon to society, providing individuals with privacy for their digital communications. Ranged against them were those who believed that encryption was a threat to society, because criminals and terrorists would be able to communicate in secret, safe from police wiretaps.

Law enforcers argue that effective wiretapping is necessary in order to maintain law and order, and that encryption should be restricted so that they can continue with their interceptions. The police have already encountered criminals using strong encryption to protect themselves. A German legal expert said that "hot businesses such as the arms and drug trades are no longer done by phone, but are being settled in encrypted form on the worldwide data networks." A White House official indicated a similarly worrying trend in America, claiming that "organized crime members are some of the most advanced users of computer systems and of strong encryption." For instance, the Cali cartel arranges its drug deals via encrypted communications. Law enforcers fear that the Internet coupled with cryptography will help criminals to communicate and coordinate their efforts.

In addition to encrypting communications, criminals and terrorists are also encrypting their plans and records, hindering the recovery of evidence. The Aum Shinrikyo sect, responsible for the gas attacks on the Tokyo subway in 1995, were found to have encrypted some of their documents using RSA. Ramsey Yousef, one of the terrorists involved in the 1993 World Trade Center bombing, kept plans for future terrorist acts encrypted on his laptop. Besides international terrorist organizations, run-of-the-mill criminals also benefit from encryption. An illegal gambling syndicate in America, for example, encrypted its accounts for four years. A study by Dorothy Denning and William Baugh commissioned in 1997 by the National Strategy Information Center's U.S. Working Group on Organized Crime estimated that there were five hundred criminal cases worldwide involving encryption and predicted that this number would roughly double each year.

In addition to domestic policing, there are also issues of national security. America's National Security Agency is responsible for gathering intelligence on the nation's enemies by deciphering their communications. The NSA operates a worldwide network of listening stations, in cooperation with Britain, Australia, Canada and New Zealand, who all gather and share information. The network includes sites such as the Menwith Hill Signals Intelligence Base in Yorkshire, the world's largest spy station. Part of Menwith Hill's work involves the Echelon system, which is capable of scanning e-mails, faxes, telexes and telephone calls, searching for particular words. Echelon operates according to a dictionary of suspicious words, such as *Hezbollah*, *assassin* and *Pentagon*, and the system is smart enough to recognize these words in real time. Echelon can earmark questionable messages for further examination, enabling it to monitor messages from particular political groups or terrorist organizations. However, Echelon would effectively be useless if all messages were strongly encrypted. Each of the nations participating in Echelon would lose valuable intelligence on political plotting and terrorist attacks.

On the other side of the debate are the civil libertarians, including groups such as the Center for Democracy and Technology and the Electronic Frontier Foundation. The pro-encryption case is based on the belief that privacy is a fundamental human right, as recognized by Article 12 of the Universal Declaration of Human Rights: "No one shall be subjected to arbitrary interference with his privacy, family, home or correspondence, nor to attacks upon his honour and reputation. Everyone has the right to the protection of the law against such interference or attacks."

Civil libertarians argue that the widespread use of encryption is essential for guaranteeing the right to privacy. Otherwise, they fear, the advent of advanced monitoring technology will herald a new era of wiretapping and the abuses that inevitably follow. In the past, governments around the world have frequently used their power in order to conduct wiretaps on innocent citizens.

One of the best-known cases of continuous unjustified wiretapping concerns Martin Luther King Jr., whose telephone conversations were monitored for several years. For example, in 1963 the FBI obtained information on King via a wiretap and fed it to Senator James Eastland in order to help him in debates on a civil-rights bill. More generally, the FBI gathered details about King's personal life, which were used to discredit him. Recordings of King telling bawdy stories were sent to his wife and played in front of President Johnson. Then, following King's receipt of the Nobel prize, embarrassing details about King's life were passed to any organization that was considering conferring an honor upon him.

Possibly the greatest infringement of everybody's privacy is the international Echelon program. Echelon does not have to justify its interceptions, and it does not focus on particular individuals. Instead, it indiscriminately harvests information, using receivers that detect the telecommunications that bounce off satellites. If Alice sends a harmless transatlantic message to Bob, then it will certainly be intercepted by Echelon, and if the message happens to contain a few words that appear in the Echelon dictionary, then it would be earmarked for further examination, alongside messages from extreme political groups and terrorist gangs. Whereas law enforcers argue that encryption should be banned because it would make Echelon ineffective, the civil libertarians argue that encryption is necessary exactly because it would make Echelon ineffective.

Ron Rivest, one of the inventors of RSA, thinks that restricting cryptography would be foolhardy:

> It is poor policy to clamp down indiscriminately on a technology just because some criminals might be able to use it to their

advantage. For example, any U.S. citizen can freely buy a pair of gloves, even though a burglar might use them to ransack a house without leaving fingerprints. Cryptography is a data-protection technology, just as gloves are a hand-protection technology. Cryptography protects data from hackers, corporate spies, and con artists, whereas gloves protect hands from cuts, scrapes, heat, cold, and infection. The former can frustrate FBI wiretapping, and the latter can thwart FBI fingerprint analysis. Cryptography and gloves are both dirt-cheap and widely available. In fact, you can download good cryptographic software from the Internet for less than the price of a good pair of gloves.

Possibly the greatest allies of the civil libertarian cause are the big corporations. Internet commerce is still in its infancy, but sales are growing rapidly, with retailers of books, music CDs and computer software leading the way, and supermarkets, travel companies and other businesses following in their wake. Just a few years from now, Internet commerce could dominate the marketplace, but only if businesses can address the issues of security and trust. A business must be able to guarantee the privacy and security of financial transactions, and the only way to do this is to employ strong encryption.

At the moment, a purchase on the Internet can be secured by public-key cryptography. Alice visits a company's Web site and selects an item. She fills in an order form that asks her for her name, address and credit card details. Alice then uses the company's public key to encrypt the order form. The encrypted order form is transmitted to the company, which is the only entity able to decrypt it, because only it has the private key necessary for decryption. All of this is done automatically by Alice's Web browser (e.g., Netscape or Explorer) in conjunction with the company's computer.

Businesses also desire strong encryption for another reason. Corporations store vast amounts of information on computer databases, including product descriptions, customer details and business accounts. Naturally, corporations want to protect this information from hackers who might infiltrate the computer and steal the information. This protection can be achieved by encrypting stored information, so that even if somebody hacks into the database he cannot read it.

To summarize the situation, it is clear that the debate has been dominated by two camps: Civil libertarians and businesses are in favor of strong encryption, while law enforcers are in favor of severe restrictions. More recently, though, there has been a third option that might offer a compromise. Over the last decade, cryptographers and policy makers have been investigating the pros and cons of a scheme known as *key escrow*. The term *escrow* usually relates to an arrangement in which someone gives a sum of money to a third party, who can then deliver the money to a second party under certain circumstances. For example, a tenant may lodge a deposit with a lawyer, who can then deliver it to a landlord in the event of damage to the property. In terms of cryptography, escrow means that Alice will give a copy of her private key to an escrow agent, an independent, reliable middleman, who is empowered to deliver the private key to the police if ever there is sufficient evidence to suggest that Alice is involved in crime.

The most famous trial of cryptographic key escrow was the American Escrowed Encryption Standard, adopted in 1994. The aim was to encourage the adoption of two encryption systems, called *clipper* and *capstone*, to be used for telephone communication and computer communication, respectively. To use clipper encryption, Alice would buy a phone with a preinstalled chip that would hold her secret private-key information. At the very moment she bought the clipper phone, a copy of the private key in the chip would be split into two halves, and each half would be sent to two separate federal authorities for storage. The U.S. government argued that Alice would have access to secure encryption, and her privacy would be broken only if law enforcers could persuade both federal authorities that there was a case for obtaining her escrowed private key.

The U.S. government employed clipper and capstone for its own communications, and made it obligatory for companies involved in government business to adopt the American Escrowed Encryption Standard. Other businesses and individuals were free to use other forms of encryption, but the government hoped that clipper and capstone would gradually become the nation's favorite form of encryption. However, the policy did not work. The idea of key escrow won few supporters outside government. Civil libertarians did not like the idea of federal authorities having possession of everybody's keys—they made an analogy to real keys and asked how people would feel if the government had the keys to all our houses. Cryptographic experts pointed out that just one crooked employee could undermine the whole system by selling escrowed keys to the highest bidder. And businesses were worried about confidentiality. For example, a European business in the United States might fear that its messages were being intercepted by American trade officials in an attempt to obtain secrets that might give American rivals a competitive edge.

Although the U.S. government has backtracked on its key escrow proposals, many suspect that it will attempt to reintroduce an alternative form of key escrow at some time in the future. Having witnessed the failure of optional escrow, governments might even consider compulsory escrow. Meanwhile, the pro-encryption lobby continues to argue against key escrow. Kenneth Neil Cukier, a technology journalist, has written: "The people involved in the crypto debate are all intelligent, honorable and pro-escrow, but they never possess more than two of these qualities at once."

There are various other options that governments could choose to implement in order to try to balance the concerns of civil libertarians, business and law enforcement. It is far from clear which will be the preferred option, because at present cryptographic policy is in a state of flux. By the time you read this there will have been several more twists and turns in the debate on cryptographic policy.

Nobody can predict with certainty the shape of cryptographic policy ten years from now. Personally, I suspect that in the near future the pro-encryption lobby will initially win the argument, mainly because no country will want to have encryption laws that prohibit e-commerce. If this policy does turn out to be a mistake, then the consequences will not necessarily lead to long-term disaster, because it will always be possible to reverse the laws. If law enforcers could show that wiretaps could prevent terrorist atrocities, then governments would rapidly gain sympathy for a policy of key escrow. All users of strong encryption would be forced to deposit their keys with a key escrow agent, and thereafter anybody who sent an encrypted message with a nonescrowed key would be breaking the law. If the penalty for nonescrowed encryption were sufficiently severe, law enforcers could regain control. Later, if governments were to abuse the trust associated with a system of key escrow, the public would call for a return to cryptographic freedom, and the pendulum would swing back. In short, there is no reason why we cannot change our policy to suit the political, economic and social climate. The deciding factor will be whom the public fears more—criminals or the government.

THE FUTURE OF CRYPTOGRAPHY

In 1996, after three years of investigation, the U.S. attorney general's office dropped its case against Zimmermann. The authorities realized that it was too late—PGP had escaped onto the Internet, and prosecuting Zimmermann would achieve nothing. There was the additional problem that Zimmermann was being supported by major institutions, such as the Massachusetts Institute of Technology Press, which had published PGP in a six-hundred-page book. The book was being distributed around the world, so prosecuting Zimmermann would have meant prosecuting the MIT Press. The authorities were also reluctant to pursue a prosecution because there was a chance that Zimmermann would not be convicted. A trial might achieve nothing more than an embarrassing constitutional debate about the right to privacy, thereby stirring up yet more public sympathy in favor of widespread encryption.

At last, PGP was a legitimate product and Zimmermann was a free man. The investigation had turned him into a cryptographic crusader, and every marketing manager in the world must have envied the notoriety and free publicity that the case gave to PGP. At the end of 1997, Zimmermann sold PGP to Network Associates, and he became one of their senior partners. Although PGP is now sold to businesses, it is still freely available to individuals who do not intend to use it for any commercial purpose. In other words, individuals who merely wish to exercise their right to privacy can still download PGP from the Internet without paying for it.

If you would like to obtain a copy of PGP, there are many sites on the Internet that offer it, and you should find them fairly easily. Probably the most reliable source is at www.pgpi.com/, the International PGP Home Page, from which you can download the American and international versions of PGP. At this point, I would like to absolve myself of any responsibility—if you do choose to install PGP, it is up to you to check that your computer is capable of running it, that the software is not infected with a virus, and so on. Also, you should check that you are in a country that permits the use of strong encryption.

The invention of public-key cryptography and the political debate that surrounds the use of strong cryptography bring us up to the present day, and it is clear that the cryptographers are winning the information war. According to Phil Zimmermann, we live in a golden age of cryptography: "It is now possible to make ciphers in modern cryptography that are really, really out of reach of all known forms of cryptanalysis. And I think it's going to stay that way." Zimmermann's view is supported by William Crowell, deputy director of the NSA: "If all the personal computers in the world—approximately 260 million computers—were to be put to work on a single PGP-encrypted message, it would take on average an estimated twelve million times the age of the universe to break a single message."

Previous experience, however, tells us that every so-called unbreakable cipher has, sooner or later, succumbed to cryptanalysis. The Vigenère cipher was called *le chiffre indéchiffrable,* but Babbage broke it; Enigma was considered invulnerable until the Poles revealed its weaknesses. So, are cryptanalysts on the verge of another breakthrough, or is Zimmermann right? Predicting future developments in any technology is always a precarious task, but with ciphers it is particularly risky. Not only do we have to guess which discoveries lie in the future, but we also have to guess which discoveries lie in the present. The tale of James Ellis and GCHQ warns us that there may already be remarkable breakthroughs hidden behind the veil of government secrecy.

But even if RSA is cracked, there is hope for secure encryption already. In 1984, Charles Bennett, a research fellow at IBM's Thomas J. Watson Laboratories in New York, developed the idea of *quantum cryptography,* an encryption system that is absolutely unbreakable. Quantum cryptography is based on quantum physics, a theory that explains how the universe operates at the most fundamental level. Bennett's idea is based on an aspect of quantum physics known as Heisenberg's uncertainty principle, which states that it is impossible to measure something with perfect accuracy because the act of measurement alters the object being measured.

For example, in order to measure the length of my hand, I must be able to see it, and therefore I must have a source of light, whether it is the sun or a lightbulb. The waves of light stream onto my hand and are then reflected toward my eye, but there are two problems. First, the wavelength of the light limits the accuracy of any length measurement. Additionally, the impact of light waves on my hand will actually change it, just like sea waves lapping against a cliff. As in the case of sea waves, the effect of the light waves is minuscule and is imperceptible at an everyday level. So an engineer trying to measure a bolt to a high degree of precision is limited by the quality of the measuring apparatus long before he runs into the limitations resulting from the uncertainty principle. At the microscopic level, however, the uncertainty principle is a serious problem. At the scale of protons and electrons, inaccuracies in measurement can become comparable to the size of objects being measured. The impact of light can significantly alter the tiny particles being observed.

Bennett came up with the idea of sending messages using fundamental particles, so tiny that if Eve tried to intercept or measure them, then she would mismeasure and alter them. In short, it becomes impossible for Eve to accurately intercept a communication, and even if she attempts to do this, her impact on the communication will become apparent to Alice and Bob, who will know that she is listening and will halt their correspondence.

You might wonder about the following problem: If Alice sends Bob a quantum cyrptographic communication, and Eve cannot read it because of the uncertainty principle, then how can Bob read it? Isn't he also stymied by the uncertainty principle? The solution is that Bob needs to send a cryptic message back to Alice to confirm what he has received. Because Alice knows what she originally sent to Bob, this second message can be used to remove any ambiguity between Alice and Bob, while still leaving Eve in the dark. At the end of this double exchange, Alice and Bob are in a position to enjoy absolutely secure communication.

Figure 52 Charles Bennett.

The whole idea of quantum cryptography sounds preposterous, but in 1988 Bennett successfully demonstrated secure communication between two computers across a distance of twelve inches. Long-distance messages are problematic, because the message is being conveyed by individual particles, which are more likely to be corrupted the farther they have to travel. So, ever since Bennett's experiment, the challenge has been to build a quantum cryptographic system that operates over useful distances. In 1995, researchers at the University of Geneva in Switzerland succeeded in implementing quantum cryptography from Geneva to the town of Nyon, a distance of a little over fourteen miles.

Security experts are now wondering how long it will be before quantum cryptography becomes a practical technology. At the moment there is no advantage in having quantum cryptography, because the RSA cipher already gives us access to effectively unbreakable encryption. However, if a codebreaker found a flaw in RSA, then quantum cryptography would become a necessity. So the race is on. The Swiss experiment has already demonstrated that it would be feasible to build a system that permits secure communication between financial institutions within a single city. Indeed, it is currently possible to build a quantum cryptography link between the White House and the Pentagon. Perhaps there already is one.

Quantum cryptography would mark the end of the battle between codemakers and codebreakers, the codemakers emerging victorious, because quantum cryptography is a truly unbreakable system of encryption. This may seem a rather exaggerated assertion, particularly in the light of previous similar claims. At different times over the last two thousand years cryptographers have believed that the monoalphabetic cipher, the polyalphabetic cipher and machine ciphers such as Enigma were all unbreakable. In each of these cases the cryptographers were eventually proved wrong because their claims were based merely on the fact that the complexity of the ciphers outstripped the ingenuity and technology of cryptanalysts at one point in history. With hindsight, we can see that the cryptanalysts would inevitably figure out a way of breaking each cipher, or developing technology that would break it for them.

However, the claim that quantum cryptography is secure is qualitatively different from all previous claims. Quantum cryptography is not just effectively unbreakable, it is absolutely unbreakable. Quantum theory, the most successful theory in the history of physics, means that it is impossible for Eve to intercept accurately any communication between Alice and Bob. Eve cannot even attempt to intercept anything without Alice and Bob being warned of her eavesdropping. Indeed, if a message protected by quantum cryptography were ever to be deciphered, it would mean that quantum theory is flawed, which would have devastating implications for physicists—they would be forced to reconsider their understanding of how the universe operates at the most fundamental level.

If quantum cryptography systems can be engineered to operate over long distances, the evolution of ciphers will stop. The quest for privacy will have come to an end. The technology will be available to guarantee secure communications for governments, the military, businesses and the public. The only question remaining would be whether or not governments would allow us to use the technology.

THE CODEBREAKER'S CHALLENGE

The Codebreaker's Challenge contains four cryptograms on which you can try out the skills you've learned in the book. Each cryptogram is supposed to be tougher than the previous one, but please move on if you get stuck. Note that the solutions to the encrypted messages are not listed anywhere, so the only way for you to crack the messages is to use your ingenuity and determination. The methods for analyzing each cryptogram are in the book. Good luck and happy cracking!

CRYPTOGRAM 1: CAESAR SHIFT CIPHER (EASY)

L FDQQRW IRUHFDVW WR BRX WKH DFWLRQ RI
UXVVLD LW LV D ULGGOH ZUDSSHG LQ D
PBVWHUB LQVLGH DQ HQLJPD
                        ZLQVWRQ FKXUFKLOO

CRYPTOGRAM 2: CAESAR SHIFT CIPHER (HARDER)

OXGB OBWB OBVB
                        CNEBNL VTXLTK

CRYPTOGRAM 3: MONOALPHABETIC SUBSTITUTION CIPHER

EVA KRC BEOA TRNZEVA CPR BWTFCOWV OB DK
VW UREVB BW AOLLOGFTC EB KWF UONPC DR
TRA CW OUENOVR LZWU CPR LOZBC PEBCK
OVBXRGCOWV WL CPR GPEZEGCRZB CPRBR
GPEZEGCRZB EB EVK WVR UONPC ZREAOTK
NFRBB LWZU E GOXPRZ CPEC OB CW BEK CPRK
GWVHRK E UREVOVN DFC CPRV LZWU IPEC OB
SVWIV WL SOAA O GWFTA VWC BFXXWBR POU
GEXEDTR WL GWVBCZFGCOVN EVK WL CPR
UWZR EDBCZFBR GZKXCWNZEXPB O UEAR FX
UK UOVA EC WVGR CPEC CPOB IEB WL E BOUXTR
BXRGORB BFGP PWIRHRZ EB IWFTA EXXREZ CW
CPR   GZFAR   OVCRTTRGC   WL   CPR   BEOTWZ
EDBWTFCRTK OVBWTFDTR IOCPWFC CPR SRK
LZWU CPR NWTA DFN DK RANEZ ETTEV XWR

CRYPTOGRAM 4: VIGENÈRE CIPHER

CUDRYHSODBODGRZAFDNRFCRQTEL
CTHNVXSOHSGNNBZNSRRQHVROO
CLNTWHRELHHPELNGIOEWHRPOQ
HRAFOZSUGHRUHWNVTUHSBQOSEE
AMAZLNODBODGRDWRDLGKYYRN
QRNODNXHRUHACSLVHDULSTHNV
XSGRMNQYCUOOOEZVHVVIAYEAWIB
QSVQCYXDRWHRVPRHDBPEGHRNQDG
KEPRWPDTPKEE

More cryptograms can be found at
www.simonsingh.com/cryptograms

APPENDIX A

The Opening of *A Void*
by Georges Perec
translated by Gilbert Adair

Today, by radio, and also on giant hoardings, a rabbi, an admiral notorious for his links to masonry, a trio of cardinals, a trio, too, of insignificant politicians (bought and paid for by a rich and corrupt Anglo-Canadian banking corporation), inform us all of how our country now risks dying of starvation. A rumour, that's my initial thought as I switch off my radio, a rumour or possibly a hoax. Propaganda, I murmur anxiously—as though, just by saying so, I might allay my doubts—typical politicians' propaganda. But public opinion gradually absorbs it as a fact. Individuals start strutting around with stout clubs. "Food, glorious food!" is a common cry (occasionally sung to Bart's music), with ordinary hard-working folk harassing officials, both local and national, and cursing capitalists and captains of industry. Cops shrink from going out on night shift. In Mâcon a mob storms a municipal building. In Rocadamour ruffians rob a hangar full of foodstuffs, pillaging tons of tuna fish, milk and cocoa, as also a vast quantity of corn—all of it, alas, totally unfit for human consumption.

1. Begin by counting up the frequencies of all the letters in the ciphertext. About five of the letters should have a frequency of less than 1 percent, and these probably represent **j, k, q, x** and **z**. One of the letters should have a frequency greater than 10 percent, and it probably represents **e**. If the ciphertext does not obey this distribution of frequencies, then consider the possibility that the original message was not written in English. You can identify the language by analyzing the distribution of frequencies in the ciphertext. For example, typically in Italian there are three letters with a frequency greater than 10 percent, and nine letters have frequencies less than 1 percent. In German, the letter **e** has the extraordinarily high frequency of 19 percent, so any ciphertext containing one letter with such a high frequency is quite possibly German. Once you have identified the language you should use the appropriate table of frequencies for that language for your frequency analysis. It is often possible to unscramble ciphertexts in an unfamiliar language, as long as you have the appropriate frequency table.

2. If the correlation is sympathetic with English but the plaintext does not reveal itself immediately, which is often the

case, then focus on pairs of repeated letters. In English the most common repeated letters are **ss, ee, tt, ff, ll, mm** and **oo**. If the ciphertext contains any repeated characters, you can assume that they represent one of these.

3. If the ciphertext contains spaces between words, then try to identify words containing just one, two or three letters. The only one-letter words in English are **a** and **i**. The commonest two-letter words are **of, to, in, it, is, be, as, at, so, we, he, by, or, on, do, if, me, my, up, an, go, no, us, am**. The most common three-letter words are **the** and **and**.

4. If possible, tailor the table of frequencies to the message you are trying to decipher. For example, military messages tend to omit pronouns and articles, and the loss of words such as **I, he, a** and **the** will reduce the frequency of some of the commonest letters. If you know you are tackling a military message, you should use a frequency table generated from other military messages.

5. One of the most useful skills for a cyptanalyst is the ability to identify words, or even entire phrases, based on experience or sheer guesswork. Al-Khalīl, an early Arabian cryptanalyst, demonstrated this talent when he cracked a Greek ciphertext. He guessed that the ciphertext began with the greeting "In the name of God." Having established that these letters corresponded to a specific section of ciphertext, he could use them as a crowbar to pry open the rest of the ciphertext. This is known as a crib.

Appendix C
The So-Called Bible Code

In 1997 *The Bible Code* by Michael Drosnin caused headlines around the world. Drosnin claimed that the Bible contains hidden messages that could be discovered by searching for equidistant letter sequences (EDLSs). An EDLS is found by taking any text, picking a particular starting letter, then jumping forward a set number of letters at a time. So, for example, with this paragraph we could start with the *M* in *Michael* and jump, say, five spaces at a time. If we noted every fifth letter, we would generate the EDLS **mesahirt** . . .

Although this particular EDLS does not contain any sensible words, Drosnin described the discovery of an astonishing number of biblical EDLSs that not only form sensible words, but result in complete sentences. Skeptics are not impressed because the Bible is so large: In a large enough text, it is hardly surprising that phrases can be made to appear by varying both the starting place and the size of the jump.

Brendan McKay at the Australian National University tried to demonstrate the inevitability of Drosnin's approach by searching for EDLSs in *Moby Dick,* and discovered thirteen statements pertaining to assassinations of famous people, including Trotsky, Gandhi and Robert Kennedy.

The monoalphabetic substitution cipher persisted through the centuries in various forms. For example, the pigpen cipher was used by Freemasons in the 1700s to keep their records private. The cipher does not substitute one letter for another; rather, it substitutes each letter for a symbol.

A	B	C
D	E	F
G	H	I

J	K	L
M •	N	• O
P	Q	R

S / T X U / V

W / X • • Y / Z

To encrypt a letter, find its position in one of the grids, then skecth that portion of the grid to represent that letter. Hence:

a = ⌐

b = ⊔

:

:

z = ⌃

If you know the key, then the pigpen cipher is easy to decipher. If not, then it can be broken by:

⌐⌐□⌐<□⊙L< ⌐□⌐L<∨⌐∨

What follows is a straightforward mathematical description of the mechanics of RSA encryption and decryption.

1. Alice picks two giant prime numbers, p and q. The primes should be enormous, but for simplicity we assume that Alice chooses $p = 17$, $q = 11$. She must keep these numbers secret.

2. Alice multiplies them together to get another number, N. In this case $N = 187$. She now picks another number e, and in this case she chooses $e = 7$ (e and $(p - 1) \times (q - 1)$ should be relatively prime, but this is a technicality).

3. Alice can now publish e and N in something akin to a telephone directory. Since these two numbers are necessary for encryption, they must be available to anybody who might want to encrypt a message to Alice. Together these numbers are called the public key. (As well as being part of Alice's public key, e could also be part of everybody else's public key. However, everybody must have a different value of N, which depends on their choice of p and q.)

4. To encrypt a message, the message must first be converted into a number, M. For example, a word is changed into

ASCII binary digits, and the binary digits can be considered as a decimal number. M is then encrypted to give the ciphertext, C, according to the formula $C = M^e \pmod{N}$.

5. Imagine that Bob wants to send Alice a simple kiss: just the letter X. In ASCII this is represented by 1011000, which is equivalent to 88 in decimal. So, $M = 88$.

6. To encrypt this message, Bob looks up Alice's public key, and discovers that $N = 187$ and $e = 7$. This provides him with the encryption formula required to encrypt messages to Alice. With $M = 88$, the formula gives $C = 88^7 \pmod{187}$.

7. Working this out directly on a calculator is tough, because the display cannot cope with such large numbers. However, there is a trick for calculating exponentials in modular arithmetic. We know that since $7 = 4 + 2 + 1$,

$$88^7 \pmod{187} = [88^4 \pmod{187} \times 88^2 \pmod{187} \times 88^1 \pmod{187}] \pmod{187}$$

$$88^1 = 88 = 88 \pmod{187}$$

$$88^2 = 7{,}744 = 77 \pmod{187}$$

$$88^4 = 59{,}969{,}536 = 132 \pmod{187}$$

$$88^7 = 88^1 \times 88^2 \times 88^4 = 88 \times 77 \times 132 = 894{,}432 = 11 \pmod{187}$$

Bob now sends the ciphertext, $C = 11$, to Alice.

8. We know that exponentials in modular arithmetic are one-way functions, so it is very difficult to work backward from $C = 11$ and recover the original message, M. Hence, Eve cannot decipher the message.

9. However, Alice can decipher the message because she has some special information: she knows the values of p and q. She calculates a special number, d, the decryption key,

otherwise known as her private key. The number d is calculated according to the following formula:

$$e \times d = 1 \ (\mathrm{mod} \ (p-1) \times (q-1))$$

$$7 \times d = 1 \ (\mathrm{mod} \ 16 \times 10)$$

$$7 \times d = 1 \ (\mathrm{mod} \ 160)$$

$$d = 23$$

(Deducing the value of d is not straightforward, but a technique known as Euclid's algorithm allows Alice to find d quickly and easily.)

10. To decrypt the message, Alice uses this formula:

$$M = C^d \ (\mathrm{mod} \ 187)$$

$$M = 11^{23} \ (\mathrm{mod} \ 187)$$

$$M = [11^1 \ (\mathrm{mod} \ 187) \times 11^2 \ (\mathrm{mod} \ 187) \times 11^4 \ (\mathrm{mod} \ 187)$$
$$\times 11^{16} \ (\mathrm{mod} \ 187)] \ (\mathrm{mod} \ 187)$$

$$M = 11 \times 121 \times 55 \times 154 \ (\mathrm{mod} \ 187)$$

$$M = 88 = X \ \mathrm{in \ ASCII}$$

Rivest, Shamir and Adleman had created a special one-way function, one that could be reversed only by somebody with access to privileged information, namely, the values of p and q. Each function can be personalized by choosing p and q, which multiply together to give N.

Having described RSA in terms of encrypting a message letter by letter, it is necessary to clarify one particular point. In the previous example, RSA is effectively reduced to monoalphabetic substitution without key distribution. In practice, encryption would proceed according to much larger blocks of binary digits, thus making frequency analysis impossible.

ACKNOWLEDGMENTS

While writing this book I have had the privilege of meeting some of the world's greatest living codemakers and codebreakers, ranging from those who worked at Bletchley Park to those who are developing the ciphers that will enrich the Information Age. I would like to thank Whitfield Diffie and Martin Hellman, who took the time to describe their work to me while I was in sunny California. Similarly, Clifford Cocks, Malcolm Williamson and Richard Walton were enormously helpful during my visit to cloudy Cheltenham. In particular, I am grateful to Fred Piper of the Information Security Group at Royal Holloway College, London, who allowed me to attend the M.Sc. course on information security.

While I was in Virginia, I was fortunate to be given a guided tour of the Beale treasure trail by Peter Viemeister, an expert on the mystery. I am also grateful to the Oxford Centre for Quantum Computation, Charles Bennett and his research group at IBM's Thomas J. Watson Laboratories, Leonard Adleman, Ronald Rivest and Jim Gillogly.

Dr. Mohammed Mrayati and Dr. Ibrahim Kadi have been involved in revealing some of the early breakthroughs in Arab cryptanalysis, and were kind enough to send me relevant documents. The periodical *Cryptologia* also carried articles about Arabian cryptanalysis, as well as many other cryptographic subjects, and I would like to thank Brian Winkel for sending me back issues of the magazines.

I would encourage readers to visit the National Cryptologic Museum near Washington, D.C., and the Cabinet War Rooms in London, and I hope that you will be as fascinated as I was during my visits. Thank you to the curators and librarians of these museums for helping me with my research.

As well as interviewing experts, I have also depended on numerous books and articles. The list of further reading contains some of my sources, but it is neither a complete bibliography nor a definitive reference list. Instead, it merely includes material that may be of interest to the general reader.

Various libraries, institutions and individuals have provided me with photographs. All the sources are listed in the picture credits, but particular thanks go to Sally McClain, for sending me photographs of the Navajo code talkers; and Brenda Ellis, for allowing me to borrow photos of James Ellis. Thanks also go to Hugh Whitemore, who gave me permission to use a quote from his play *Breaking the Code,* based on Andrew Hodges' book *Alan Turing—The Enigma.*

I have had the enormous good fortune to work with some of the best people in publishing. Patrick Walsh is an agent with a love of science, a concern for his authors and a boundless enthusiasm. John Woodruff has done an excellent job in helping to adapt *The Code Book* and has contributed greatly to its overall structure. Last, but certainly not least, my editors, Jennifer Wingertzahn and Beverly Horowitz, helped me to adapt the original version of *The Code Book* into this young readers' edition. Furthermore, it was Beverly's idea to undertake this project. For that I am tremendously grateful.

FURTHER READING

Here are some books you can read if you would like to explore the subject of cryptography in more depth. There is also a great deal of interesting material on the Internet relating to codes and ciphers. In addition to the books, I have therefore listed a few of the Web sites that are worth visiting.

GENERAL

Kahn, David, *The Codebreakers* (New York: Scribner, 1996).
A 1,200-page history of ciphers. The definitive story of cryptography up until the 1950s.

Smith, Lawrence D., *Cryptography* (New York: Dover, 1943).
An excellent elementary introduction to cryptography, with more than 150 problems. Dover publishes many books on the subject of codes and ciphers.

The Code Book on CD-ROM. A fully interactive version of *The Code Book* is now available. It contains encrypting and codebreaking tools, a virtual Enigma machine and video clips. More details on its contents and how to obtain it are available at www.simonsingh.com.

CHAPTER I

Gaines, Helen Fouché, *Cryptanalysis* (New York: Dover, 1956).
A study of ciphers and their solution. An excellent

introduction to cryptanalysis, with many useful frequency tables in the appendix.

Fraser, Lady Antonia, *Mary Queen of Scots* (London: Random House, 1989).

A readable account of the life of Mary Queen of Scots.

CHAPTER 2

Standage, Tom, *The Victorian Internet* (London: Weidenfeld & Nicolson, 1998).

The remarkable story of the development of the telegraph.

Poe, Edgar Allan, *The Complete Tales and Poems of Edgar Allan Poe* (London: Penguin, 1982).

Includes "The Gold Bug."

Viemeister, Peter, *The Beale Treasure: History of a Mystery* (Bedford, VA: Hamilton's, 1997).

An in-depth account of the Beale ciphers written by a respected local historian. It includes the entire text of the Beale pamphlet, and is most easily obtained directly from the publishers: Hamilton's, P.O. Box 932, Bedford, VA 24523.

CHAPTER 3

Tuchman, Barbara W., *The Zimmermann Telegram* (New York: Ballantine, 1994).

An accessible account of the most influential decipherment in the First World War.

Kahn, David, *Seizing the Enigma* (London: Arrow, 1996).

Kahn's history of the Battle of the Atlantic and the importance of cryptography. In particular, he dramatically describes the capture of code material from U-boats that helped the codebreakers at Bletchley Park.

Smith, Michael, *Station X* (London: Channel 4 Books, 1999).

The book based on the British Channel 4 TV series of the same name, containing anecdotes from those who worked at Bletchley Park, otherwise known as Station X.

CHAPTER 4

McClain, S., *The Navajo Weapon* (Boulder, CO: Books Beyond Borders, 1994).

A gripping account that covers the entire story, written by a woman who has spent much time talking to the men who developed and used the Navajo code.

Davies, W. V., *Reading the Past: Egyptian Hieroglyphs* (London: British Museum Press, 1997).

Part of an excellent series of introductory texts published by the British Museum. Other authors in the series have written books on cuneiform, Etruscan, Greek inscriptions, Linear B, Maya glyphs and runes.

CHAPTER 5

Hellman, M. E., "The Mathematics of Public-Key Cryptography," *Scientific American*, vol. 241 (August 1979), pp. 130–39.

An excellent overview of the various forms of public-key cryptography.

Schneier, Bruce, *Applied Cryptography* (New York: John Wiley & Sons, 1996).

An excellent survey of modern cryptography. A definitive and authoritative introduction to the subject (advanced).

CHAPTER 6

Garfinkel, Simson, *PGP: Pretty Good Privacy* (Sebastopol, CA: O'Reilly & Associates, 1995).

An excellent introduction to PGP and the issues surrounding modern cryptography.

Bamford, James, *The Puzzle Palace* (London: Penguin, 1983). Inside the National Security Agency, America's most secret intelligence organization.

Bennett, C. H., Brassard, C., and Ekert, A., "Quantum Cryptography," *Scientific American,* vol. 269 (October 1992), pp. 26–33.
A clear explanation of the evolution of quantum cryptography.

INTERNET SITES

Simon Singh's Web site
www.SimonSingh.com

Bletchley Park
www.bletchleypark.org.uk/
The official Web site, which includes opening times and directions.

Enigma emulators
www.ugrad.cs.jhu.edu/~russell/classes/enigma
An excellent emulator that shows how the Enigma machine works.

Phil Zimmermann and PGP
www.philzimmermann.com

Electronic Frontier Foundation
www.eff.org/
An organization devoted to protecting rights and promoting freedom on the Internet.

Center for Quantum Computation
www.qubit.org/

National Cryptologic Museum
www.nsa.gov:8080/museum/

American Cryptogram Association (ACA)
www.und.nodak.edu/org/crypto/crypto/
An association that specializes in solving cipher puzzles.

RSA's Frequently Asked Questions About Cryptography
www.rsasecurity.com/rsalabs/faq/
Yahoo! Security and Encryption Page
www.yahoo.co.uk/Computers_and_Internet/ Security_
and_Encryption/

PICTURE CREDITS

Line illustrations by Miles Smith-Morris. Hieroglyphs reproduced by kind permission of British Museum Press.

Figure 1 Scottish National Portrait Gallery, Edinburgh; Figure 8 Public Record Office, London; Figure 9 Scottish National Portrait Gallery, Edinburgh; Figure 10 Cliché Bibliothèque Nationale de France, Paris; Figure 11 Science and Society Picture Library, London; Figure 18 *The Beale Treasure—History of a Mystery* by Peter Viemeister; Figure 23 National Archives, Washington, DC; Figure 24 General Research Division, The New York Public Library, Astor, Lenox and Tilden Foundations; Figure 25 Luis Kruh Collection, New York; Figure 31 David Kahn Collection; Figures 32 and 33 Science and Society Picture Library, London; Figures 34 and 35 David Kahn Collection, New York; Figure 36 Imperial War Museum, London; Figure 37 Private collection of Barbara Eachus; Figure 38 Godfrey Argent Agency, London; Figure 39 Imperial War Museum, London; Figures 40 and 41 National Archives, Washington, DC; Figures 42 and 43 British Museum Press, London; Figure 44 Louvre, Paris © Photo RMN; Figure 45 Sun Microsystems; Figure 46 Stanford University; Figure 48 RSA Data Security, Inc.; Figure 49 Private collection of Brenda Ellis; Figure 50 Private collection of Malcolm Williamson; Figure 51 Network Associates, Inc.; Figure 52 Thomas J. Watson Laboratories, IBM.

INDEX

Index

Index

ABOUT THE AUTHOR

SIMON SINGH is an author, journalist and broadcaster who specializes in science and mathematics. His childhood ambition was to be a particle physicist, and eventually he earned his Ph.D. from Cambridge University in England. He went on to work for the British Broadcasting Corporation, and directed the award-winning documentary film on Fermat's Last Theorem that aired on PBS's *Nova* series. He is also the author of the bestselling book *Fermat's Enigma*. The film and the book recount the fascinating quest to solve the greatest math problem of all time. Simon Singh lives in London, where he enjoys games of chance, listening to the Violent Femmes and watching magicians.

You can find him on the Web at www.simonsingh.com.